THE GREAT AMERICAN WEST

A PICTORIAL HISTORY FROM CORONADO TO THE LAST FRONTIER

The Great American West

A PICTORIAL HISTORY
FROM CORONADO TO THE LAST FRONTIER

by James D. Horan

CROWN PUBLISHERS, INC.
NEW YORK

For Brian Boru, Who Is Earning His Spurs

(D)

Contents

Illustrations

> The many hundreds of black-and-white illustrations are integrated with the text and therefore are not listed here.

Color Plates

Introduction

A Decade of Search

MORE than ten years ago I started a project to tell the full story of the American West from the beginning of the Spanish colonization to the great "Run" of settlers into Oklahoma (1889-93) which marked the end of the frontier.

I wanted to present the *whole* story, and I felt that in order to do that I not only would have to tell what happened but also I would have to show how it was, how the land and the people and the things they made appeared at the time. To do the job properly, I would have to fill the book with pictures—documented photographs whenever possible—otherwise contemporary prints and drawings.

I felt there was a need for such a book. There are many fine books about the West, but almost all those intended for the general public cover only segments of the history or sections of the area, like Bernard De Voto's *Across The Wide Missouri* and Walter Prescott Webb's excellent *The Great Plains*. And there is no single history of the West that provides full-scale, comprehensive pictorial coverage that enables the reader to *see* as well as *read* how a fabulous host of Americans built a great empire out of a virgin land.

The pictures were the heart of the matter, and I began hunting for them. My quest for these prints and glass plates spread across many states and parts of Europe.

I soon discovered that unpublished photographs are among the rare items of western history. Outside of state and some government archives and the files of regional historical societies, they are almost nonexistent. You can find them only by persistently following up any and all clues or by accidentally stumbling upon them.

Before I had finished assembling this collection, I was in command of a small army of scouts across the nation and in Europe who were constantly on the alert to write, telegraph or telephone me the moment they spotted a good collection, a rare or exceptionally fine frontier photograph. Among the ranks were friends, scholars, photographers, Americana book dealers, curators and even cowboys.

The first hint I had of what was to prove a prime "find" (the Pitman collection) came a few years ago when some-one mentioned casually that a gentleman in Summit, New Jersey, had some old glass plates in his basement.

The next day I called him and was invited to come out. Pointing to a box which I immediately recognized as a glass-plate holder of the Civil War period, he told me to help myself while he continued packing. He was getting ready to move.

I sensed I had made a find when I picked up one of the cardboard photographic boxes. On the cover was "Carbutt's Keystone Special." Obviously this was the Philadelphia Carbutt who was America's first manufacturer of dry plates and the first American to use a celluloid base for a photographic emulsion. The only time I had seen such a box was in the Library of Congress.

I can recall holding one of the glass plates in my hand for a moment before I raised it to the light, wondering what it held. I soon had my answer: Fort Abraham Lincoln and two troopers of Custer's Seventh in buffalo robes. After a spot-check of the hundreds of plates, I knew I had found a priceless collection of early western camps, armies, forts, Indians. Here was the American West as it really was. The plates were made by General John T. Pitman, a Civil War veteran.

Our business transaction finished, we sat in the warm spring twilight and discussed books, authors, paintings— and of course, photographs. At one point my host seemed rather silent; then almost abruptly he walked to the wall of books and returned with what appeared to me to be three books, all beautifully bound in rich, red leather.

"These should belong to you," he said.

I was well aware of my wife's plea, "Please, no more books, not even if it's Crazy Horse's personally inscribed copy," and so I held up my hand to stop him.

"I can't buy another book," I said.

"Young man, you are too hasty. These are not books," he said, and pulled from one of them a small velvet ribbon that seemed to come out of the book's edge.

It proved to be a handsome photographic container holding about fifty mounted photographs. Staring at me, "all mouth and teeth," as a Dakota doctor was to recall,

[7]

was Teddy Roosevelt as a cowboy. I looked at the cover of the container and saw stamped in gold:

"THEODORE ROOSEVELT—ORIGINAL PHOTOGRAPHS MADE BY HIM AMONG THE BAD LANDS OF NORTH DAKOTA. TITLE OF THE PHOTOGRAPHS ON REVERSE IN HANDWRITING OF ROOSEVELT."

I went through the collection quickly. Here were pictures of Roosevelt as a cowboy, breaking a horse, riding the range, at a roundup. They included three priceless photographs of him aiming a Winchester at three horse thieves whom he had chased 300 miles through the bitter cold of the Dakotas, a journey he later described in an article in the *Century*. In addition to the Roosevelt pictures were some photographs by L. A. Huffman, one of the better frontier photographers.

There were more surprises to be found in this suburban Klondike. The following day not one wooden photographic box but three arrived, all filled with glass plates.

"I found two more boxes," the gentleman from Summit said. "They all belong to you."

Finding this valuable Pitman collection was certainly a stroke of luck. For months I went through the 598 glass plates, virtually a pictorial record of the Dakota Territories and Fort Snelling, Minnesota. One plate may be the only known photograph of the authentic Standing Rock, sacred to the Sioux, after which the famed Standing Rock Indian agency is named.

After the collection had been separated and catalogued, I sought out a veteran photographer who I knew had handled glass plates in his apprenticeship. I selected a few plates each week from which he made prints. It took more than a year of painstaking work, but finally I had a fine pictorial record of one of the last of the West's frontiers.

The Rhode Island Historical Society yielded some facts about Pitman. A member of an old and distinguished Rhode Island family, Pitman volunteered as a private in the First Regiment Rhode Island Detached Militia when the Civil War broke out. He advanced rapidly, and by 1865 was a colonel with an excellent combat record.

After Appomattox he joined the Regular Army, the famous Indian-fighting army that broke the back of the hostile tribes from the Canadian border to the Staked Plains of Texas. He was assigned first to Fort Snelling, later to Fort Abraham Lincoln in Dakota Territory. In the '80s he was appointed General of Ordnance, Dakota Territory. Later he was assigned to the Frankfort arsenal in Philadelphia, where he headed the Army team which developed smokeless powder.

It is possible that Pitman met one of Mathew Brady's photographers during the Civil War and became fascinated by the art of photography. When he joined the Regular Army in 1866 he apparently began making photographs of everything that interested him. These plates were ones he had sent back to his sisters in Summit, New Jersey, where the pictures had been carefully preserved.

Also included in this Pitman collection are some mounted photographs by the Dakota photographer D. F. Barry, nicknamed "Little Shadow Catcher" by the Sioux; one of his notable sitters was the Indian war captain Gall, who had fought Custer at Little Big Horn.

The dust was still on the glass plates made by C. C. Pierce, who made many photographs of Indians of the Southwest, when I received them. His remarkably clear shots of Hopi, Apache and Zuni Indians have a timeless quality.

I was also fortunate in finding rare prints by an English photographer, Charles R. Savage, who was on hand to record the historic ceremony at Promontory Point, Utah, May 10, 1869, celebrating the completion of the first transcontinental railroad.

In my years of research I was constantly on the alert for photographs by such pioneer photographers as William H. Jackson, C. E. Watkins, Robert H. Vance, John Hillers, F. J. Haynes and others.

I was passing by an old print store one day and noticed some beautiful photographs of the Apache country which I was sure were rare pictures taken by Hillers on the John Powell survey. Hillers' prints became famous after they were reproduced by a facsimile method to illustrate Frederick Dellenbau's account of the Powell expedition on the Colorado River. "Are these by Hillers?" I asked the proprietor. The old man peered at me over his spectacles. "How do you know they are Jack Hillers'?" I replied that I was interested in the period. "Maybe they are, mister," he remarked, "but they ain't for sale."

He ignored me to attend to another customer. I dropped by twice, trying my best to adopt a casual air. The old gentleman was cagy. Finally I informed him that I wouldn't accept his photographs on a gold plate. To my surprise a few days later a collection of Hillers' prints arrived, with a bill. Some time later I returned to ask how he came into possession of the stunning photographs. I found the shop empty. I never saw him again.

Mount Hillers in the Henry Mountains of southeast Utah is named after photographer John Hillers, and Mount Haynes in Yellowstone National Park is named after Haynes, who captured the park's primitive beauty.

As a biographer of Mathew Brady, the work of any of his photographers was of interest to me. I found a few Alexander Gardner pictures and some of the prints made by Captain A. J. Russell, who photographed the building of the Union Pacific when it reached Cheyenne in 1869. I knew of the fine catalogued collection of Stanley J. Morrow's works in the archives of the Museum of the University of South Dakota, and I have included a number of his pictures in this book. It is not certain that Morrow was a Brady man, but I believe he was.

The most important Brady alumnus in the West was Tim O'Sullivan. Although not honored by any place name on the map, the work of Tim O'Sullivan, in particular his pictures of the King Expeditions of 1886, 1867 and 1869, is of primary importance. The shy Irish photographer who was with Brady at Gettysburg caught the immensity, the majesty and the terrible loneliness of the great plains. In 1870, O'Sullivan took his camera to the Isthmus of Darien, but in 1871, 1873 and 1874 he returned from the Selfridge Expeditions in the jungles of Panama to the Far West, as official photographer for the Corps of Engineers on the Wheeler Expeditions.

Every book dealer, collector and western historical society knew I wanted badly any existing O'Sullivan photographs of the King Expeditions. I knew O'Sullivan had swum mountain torrents, climbed steep mountains and fought off rattlesnakes to get his pictures from the deserts of California to the Humboldt mountain chain.

One day I received a call from a friend in the New York Corral of the Westerners, whose members are interested in this phase of our national growing up. He told me that "somewhere" he had seen a notice that "someone" on the West Coast wanted to sell some of O'Sullivan's material.

Where? Who? He just couldn't recall. We had only one clue: the West Coast. Now began a search as intense as any for a missing person. Finally the search did turn up a dealer, who sent on a copy of one of the collection of huge mounted prints which he wished to dispose of. It was O'Sullivan at his best. As in the case of the Roosevelt photographs, the story of the origin and ownership of the collection remains a mystery.

Country auctions also produced some photographic finds. At one I found a black box with rare photographs of the building of the Union Pacific made by a Chicago photographer, John Carbutt. The auctioneer was slightly contemptuous because I had turned down an oxen yoke for "some old pictures."

In an antique shop, among old books and rubbish I found the two volumes of F. V. Hayden's rare "sun pictures" which he took of the West in 1872.

Of course there were some disappointments, too. I found no collection of Carvalho prints. S. N. Carvalho was the Baltimore daguerreotypist who had accompanied the Frémont expedition in 1852. When he returned to New York, Carvalho gave Brady his copper plates to copy by wet plate, but his own original plates were lost in a fire which destroyed the Frémont home. One copy of a daguerreotype included in this book may or may not be one of Carvalho's prints taken on this expedition.

And of course there were times when not all the money in the world could pry loose a treasured photograph. Fortunately, I was never refused when I asked permission to make a copy print.

As any frontier historian knows, no book on the West can be complete without a gallery of gunmen and lawmen. This time, however, my discovery did not include photographs, but a large box of rare pen-and-ink sketches of the gunfighters, the marshals, the man-hunters and the other colorful characters who have given the West its aura of romance.

The sketches were by H. O. Rawson, who, despite a prosaic job on an eastern shoe magazine, left behind a highly accurate gallery of the West's most desperate men.

Of course, the resources of those great national repositories of historical material—the National Archives, the Library of Congress, the Bureau of American Ethnology of the Smithsonian Institution—were immeasurably useful and yielded some genuine treasures, including a number that are published for the first time in this book.

While I have emphasized photographers, I have not neglected the great painters of the West like Remington, Russell, Miller, Catlin and Bodmer whose work was based on personal observation and in many instances was made "on the spot."

I have discussed the pictorial research at this great length because, as I said before, pictures are the heart of the matter in this book. But the historical research, less newsworthy because less unusual, was on the same scale, and I was glad to find that though unpublished western historical source material is even scarcer than unpublished photographs, there were still some items to be discovered.

Before the search was finished I had located, among other interesting items, some excellent diaries, first-hand material about the early western windmills, a section of Frémont's survey map of the Oregon Trail, an official Army report on the discovery of gold in the Black Hills laconically filled out by Custer, a detailed journal with beautifully tinted water colors made by an early explorer in 1819, a startling letter written by Custer's comrade-in-arms, Major Marcus Reno, a collection of bitter letters about the O. K. Corral gunfight by a frontier lawyer, which will be edited for an historical quarterly, and many more.

The cooperation and gracious assistance of many persons are necessary to complete a book of this scope. I would like to thank at least some of the friends and total strangers who helped me in this project over the last ten years.

Mrs. Virginia Gilmore, assistant librarian, Montana Historical Society; Mr. A. W. Lund, assistant church historian, The Church of Jesus Christ of Latter-Day Saints; M. T. Jensen, Vice President, Aermotor Company, Chicago, Ill.; Carroll D. Hall, monument supervisor, Sutter's Fort, Sacramento, Calif.; Mr. Frank H. Roberts, Jr., director, Bureau of American Ethnology, Washington, D. C.; Clarkson A. Collins III, librarian, Rhode Island Historical Society; Mrs. Sadie Schmidt, reference librarian, and Eleanor B. Sloan, historical secretary, Arizona Pioneers' Historical Society; Miss Cheryle Hughes, assistant, Iconographic Collections, State Historical Society of Wisconsin; Miss Virginia Daiker, Miss Alice Parker, and the staff of the Department of Prints and Photographs, Library of Congress; Miss Marjorie M. Pyle, cataloguer, Hispanic Society of America; W. G. Burden, director of public relations, Union Pacific Railroad; Mrs. Drucilla Denny, secretary, and Dr. David Gebhard, director, Roswell Museum and Art Center, Roswell, N.M.; Mr. Robert Zimmerman, administrative assistant, New Mexico State

Tourist Bureau, Santa Fe, N. M.; Miss Josephine Cobb, Still Pictures Branch, National Archives; Mr. David R. Watkins, chief research librarian, Yale University Library; Mr. Archibald Hanna, Coe Collection, Yale University; Mr. Harry Brown, public relations department, United States Steel Corporation; Mrs. Margaret Fuller, librarian, American Iron and Steel Institute; Mr. Stewart H. Holbrook; Mr. Joseph J. Fucelli; Miss Virginia Walton, librarian, Montana Historical Society; Mrs. Paul M. Rhymer, curator of prints, Chicago Historical Society; Mr. R. G. Vail, director, the New-York Historical Society; Miss Sarah Guitar, reference librarian, Missouri State Historical Society; Mr. Leo A. McCoy, Red Bluff, Calif.; Mr. Don Baxter, managing editor, *Westward;* Mr. George D. Wolfe, Knoxville, Tenn.; Mr. Preston McMann; Miss Mari Sandoz; Mr. Clifton Waller Barrett; Mr. H. J. Swinney, director, Idaho Historical Society; Mr. George Oslin, Western Union; Mrs. C. E. Cook, curator of the Museum, Oklahoma Historical Society; Mr. Kenneth W. Duckett, librarian, and Mr. Thomas Vaughan, curator, Oregon Historical Society; Mr. Eugene D. Becker, curator of pictures, Minnesota Historical Society; D. W. Thompson, secretary, the Hamilton Library and Historical Association of Cumberland County, Pa.; Mrs. Alys Freeze, head, Western History Department, Denver Public Library; Mrs. Katherine Schmeltekopf, library assistant, Barker Texas History Center, University of Texas; Mr. Robert W. Hill, keeper of manuscripts, and Mr. Paul Rugen, his assistant, Manuscript Room, the New York Public Library; Mr. David S. Foote, assistant director, Springfield Museum of Fine Arts, Springfield, Mass.; Mr. Pat McDonough, bowling editor of the New York *World-Telegram;* Mrs. Margaret Shepherd, curator of photographs, Utah Historical Society; Mr. Beaumont Newhall, director, George Eastman House, Rochester, N. Y.; Mr. Paul Vanderbilt, Wisconsin State Historical Society; Mr. Francis W. Cunningham, curator, Oneida Historical Society; Mr. Roscoe P. Conkling, Inglewood, California; Mr. Wesley R. Hurt, director of the Museum, G. Johnson; Miss Ruth Bergman, librarian, State University of South Dakota, Vermillion, S. D.; Mr. Maurice E. Peabody and Mr. Nick Eggenhofer.

I would be remiss in my appreciation if I did not point out the long and faithful research done for me by Helen and Donald R. Foyer of Alexandria, Va., who on their trips to Carlisle, Pa., made sure to seek out the splendid pictorial record of the young warriors who attended and graduated from the famous Indian school.

Others to whom I owe special thanks are Mr. Glen Dawson of Dawson's well-known book shop in Los Angeles; Mr. Peter Decker, who is not only a well-known dealer in Western Americana but an author as well; Mr. Cedric L. Robinson, of Windsor, Conn., who went to great pains to make sure we had the Watkins series of photographs of the Columbia River; Mr. J. E. Reynolds, Van Nuys, Calif., who was never too busy in his busy shop to make sure we knew at once of his latest arrivals in western photographs; Jo and Fred Mazzulla of Denver, whose enthusiasm and assistance in seeking out rare prints will always be appreciated; Dr. A. Carlson, curator of prints, New-York Historical Society, who spent many hours exploring his archives for suitable material; Florence, Jim and Maureen, who watched the hearth; and Mrs. Clark Kellett of the Brown County (Minn.) Historical Society, who searched so diligently for the reminiscences of men and women who had taken part in the New Ulm massacre.

As always, we must reserve a special niche for Mr. Sylvester Vigilante, whose name has appeared in so many books on the American West. It was through his efforts that the McLaury letters relevant to the famous Battle of the O.K. Corral have been published here for the first time.

I was most fortunate in meeting Mr. Montagu Hankin of Summit, N. J., who turned over to me both the Pitman glass-plate collection and the Theodore Roosevelt cowboy photographs. I will always recall with a great deal of pleasure the leisurely hours we spent in his wonderful library.

Mr. Melvin J. Nichols, also of Summit, N. J., is another western enthusiast who provided expert advice along with photographs, drawings and manuscripts from his superb Martin Garretson collection for this book. Mr. Vincent Mercaldo, head of Mercaldo Archives, gave us, not only rare prints from his famous collection but also enthusiastic encouragement down through the years. Probably the one closest to this project was Mr. William Kelleher, whom I like to call the dean of the western Americana dealers, but who insists he is not that old. More than a decade ago, Bill found the first picture for this book; ironically, he also provided one of the last. I always looked forward to his "I think I've found something . . ." It usually turned out to be an Alexander Gardner photograph of Spotted Tail or a rare Tim O'Sullivan photograph.

These notes of acknowledgment must include Mr. J. Leonard Jennewein, Mitchell, S. D. and his friends in the North Dakota and South Dakota Historical Societies who gave so much of their time to help to establish dates and to identify individuals and places shown in the Pitman plates. Mr. Jennewein also graciously contributed the rare photographs taken of Sitting Bull at Fort Randall after his return from Canada. Thanks to Miss Helen Staeuble for her editorial skill and devotion to this book, to Miss Judy Weiermiller for her careful corraling of our pictures, and to Mr. C. Leo Henrichs, one of New Jersey's finest photographers, who spent so many hours carefully developing prints from the fragile Pitman glass plates.

There is ancient authority that the last shall be first. What man can write a book without the assistance, seen and unseen, of his wife? I least of all. Thus to Gertrude, the biggest thanks of all.

Horan's Boondocks
October, 1959

The First White Men in the West

THE area of the West, as the term will be used in this book, is all of that vast land bounded on the north by the Canadian border, on the south by the Mexican border, on the west by the Pacific Ocean, and on the east by the western edge of the Mississippi River Valley, including also western Wisconsin, as well as Minnesota, Iowa, Missouri, Arkansas, and western Louisiana.

The first white men to set foot in this land were the Spanish. The overture to their entrance took place in March, 1536, when a man almost naked, with a thick beard and tangled hair, stumbled toward a party of soldiers on the plain some 80 miles north of Culiacan, Mexico. He was accompanied by eleven Indians and a Negro. Tears rolling down his cheeks, he told them they were the first white men he had seen in eight years. He gave his name as Alvar Nuñez Cabeza de Vaca, and he called the Negro with him Estevanico, better known to history as Estevan, or "an Arab Negro from Azamor." Two other Spaniards, he told the soldiers, Alonzo del Castillo Maldonado and Andres Dorantes, were a day's journey in the rear, with a number of Indians who had followed them from the north. When the soldiers had recovered from their surprise, they brought the ragged man back to Diego de Alcaraz, commander of an outpost, who sent out a party to bring the other Spaniards back.

According to his own account, translated into English in 1905 by Fanny Bandelier, de Vaca told his story—and told it well—in Mexico City. Never before in this city of nobles and adventurers had such a tale been heard. He and his companions had been in the expedition of Panfilo de Narvaez, which eight years before had set sail to conquer Florida for His Catholic Majesty. After landing on the Florida coast they moved inland. They hacked and pushed their way through the tangled jungle, fought off Indians, and finally, on the verge of starvation, killed their horses for food.

After fantastic adventures they made their way to the west coast of Florida. There the ingenious blacksmith of

The title page and an extract from de Casteñada's account of Coronado's expedition.

the expedition made a forge and horsehide bellows, then hammered their swords into saws and nails for the purpose of building several small boats. These indomitable men made several boat frames, covered them with horsehide, fashioned ropes from manes and tails, and set sail.

A storm and heavy seas defeated them. Some of the boats capsized and their occupants drowned, others were blown out to sea, never to be seen again. Only de Vaca and a small number survived. Somehow in the wild gale they were blown up on the shore of what is now Galveston, Texas. Friendly Indians found them and helped them. When they recovered their strength they made their way westward, moving from tribe to tribe. De Vaca became a medicine man and, as he recalled in his memoirs, the tribes accepted him "without asking to see my diploma."

It was appropriate that de Vaca's strange tale should be told in the square of Mexico City. It was only eight years since Hernando Cortez had entered the ancient Aztec city to begin the conquest of Mexico. In the crowd listening to de Vaca were men who had marched with Cortez; there were also many nobles and knights who had sailed for New Spain, eager for adventure, conquest and gold. But after Mexico it seemed that there were no new worlds to conquer. . . .

Now de Vaca was telling them not only about shining Cities of Gold, but of the "copper hawk's-bell, thick and large, figured with face" which an Indian had given him, along with a tale of how it had come from the earth. Other Indians, de Vaca told the crowd, had informed him that in the place from which it came were many plates of the same metal.

Actually, there was little fact to the whole tale; the only real evidence was the bell. But the imagination of the people was unleashed. The towns that the Indians had described to de Vaca were now lined with gold; silversmith shops and the doors of houses were inlaid with turquoise. Precious gems and gold were commonplace. The strange copper bell figured with a face now had a name—the Gilded Man.

At last de Vaca was summoned by Don Antonio de Mendoza himself. Undoubtedly the Viceroy was now convinced that perhaps there might be another Peru or Mexico with new lands to conquer, new riches for His Catholic Majesty, the Emperor Charles V. And, more importantly, now that Spain had made herself the champion of Rome, more souls to bring to Holy Mother Church.

Mendoza, however, was cautious; he decided that first he would send his own men north to see what there was to this story. In the meanwhile he dispatched de Vaca to Spain to regale the king with his wondrous tales.

There was a delay of a few years, but finally, in 1539, Friar Marcos de Niza of the Franciscan order, who had gained experience in the jungles of conquered Peru, was selected to go north. With the Negro Estevan and some other native Indians he set out to find what everyone was calling the Seven Cities of Gold. But Estevan, the former slave, was beginning to believe his own lies and impor-

Friar Marcos de Niza.

tance. He wore gaudy robes to which were sewed many tiny bells so that he walked across the wild land to a strange symphony of tinkling bells and the rattling of the red-painted "magic gourd" which he carried.

Women and his unbearable arrogance led to his murder by the Zuñis. Friar Marcos, however, pushed on and finally reached Cibola, which he saw only from a distance. He returned to Mexico City repeating the tales of the Indians—that Cibola was larger than Mexico City and "has some large houses ten stories high . . . they say that the portals and fronts of the chief houses are of turquoise. . . ."

The restless nobles and adventurers unconsciously polished the friar's story, which actually was only gossip he had heard.

King Charles was besieged by petitions from nobles, among them Hernando Cortez, to lead an expedition to conquer the golden cities. But the king decided that Mendoza should select the leader, and thus the Viceroy summoned his close friend, Francisco Vasquez de Coronado, a thirty-year-old Salamanca aristocrat who had come to the New World with Mendoza to seek his fortune only a year before the ragged de Vaca had walked into the plaza of New Mexico. He was a dashing, handsome man, liked by both men and women.

Now there was a kind of madness in the land. Men of every station in life, from nobleman to tutor, begged to be allowed to join Coronado. Nobles sold their land and belongings and rode to New Galicia, the desert province where Coronado was stationed. Large sums were collected and sent to New Galicia. Galleons from Madrid delivered artillery from the royal armory—although later the bronze cannons would fail to penetrate a mud wall—as well as food, pack horses, the best of soldiers. Nothing was too good for the mightiest expedition Spain was to launch in the New World.

But it was the horses, some sent by Mendoza himself from his best stock farms, that were most important, not only to the success of this expedition, but to the history of the American West. In fact they would produce a revolution among the American aborigines comparable only to the introduction of the gasoline engine to the civilized world.

The Spanish horses that Coronado used were tough and durable. They were horses of the Moors, of the desert, animals that could live on grass and forage and not entirely on grain. The Spanish mustang, the Indian pony, would someday be the cow horse of the cattle kingdom.

With their mail and mounted on horses, the Spaniards were invincible. They were mobile against a race that was on foot. They could now move across a land at will, with its occupants barely able to impede their advance.

When the horses, the arms and provisions had been gathered, Mendoza announced that in addition to the overland march he intended to dispatch three ships under Hernando de Alarcon with the army's extra baggage and supplies. The *San Pedro, Santa Catarina* and *Santa Gabriel* were to move up along the coastline with orders to contact Coronado whenever possible.

In February, 1540, Coronado announced that the expedition was ready to start.

As Pedro de Castañeda, a chronicler of the expedition, described the scene, Coronado was resplendent in armor and plumed helmet. Some of his troops were dressed in buckskin or nondescript dress of the period. In addition to the professional *conquistadores* there were some 800 Mexican helpers, grooms, sheep-herders, Negro servants. There were also three women, all wives of members of the party. Mother Church was represented by four friars, led by Friar Marcos, who had been elevated to the post of Father Provincial for his report on Cibola.

The army moved out on a March morning, and from de Castañeda's manuscript—he was a superb reporter—one can see the bright sunshine glinting on the huge two-handed swords and cannons, the colorful banners flapping in the morning breeze, the clouds of dust rising from under the hoofs of the horses. That morning there were brave speeches, gay music and high hopes as the first army of white men moved into the great vastness of the American West.

What Coronado Found

Coronado's expedition lasted about two years; he returned to Mexico in midsummer, 1542. He, or elements

Coronado. No contemporary portrait of Coronado is known to exist, but the upper picture, from the permanent collection of the Roswell Museum and Art Center (Roswell, New Mexico) appears to have some documentary support.

Routes of Coronado, de Soto and Moscoso.

of his expedition, traversed Lower California, Arizona, New Mexico, Texas, Oklahoma, and probably southern Kansas. They camped and explored along the Rio Grande, Colorado and Canadian Rivers (and others), crossed the Yuma Desert and the Painted Desert, "discovered" the Grand Canyon and the Rock of Acoma and wintered in the Rio Grande Valley near what is now Albuquerque. In the second year they reached as far northeast as the fabled site of Quivira (generally believed to be near Wichita, Kansas). What Coronado and his men found in all this territory and did not find determined the future history of the West, and of the world.

They did not find gold or other treasure. They found Indians—Zuñis, Hopis, Apaches and others living in pueblo settlements—who were friendly at first but then went on the warpath when the Spaniards plundered their towns and massacred the inhabitants. Word of the brutal massacre at Tiguex on the Rio Grande, where the army wintered, spread among the tribes.

South of Cibola, the Zuñis, who had never seen white men or heard sounds of guns or had seen horses, attacked the army, touching off the first large-scale engagements between red men and white men. The veteran fighters sent the Indians flying back to the walls of Cibola. Coronado then sent one of his captains to the pueblo with an interpreter to ask peace, but he was greeted by a flight of arrows.

The commander gave the order for attack. Crying "Santiago," the traditional Spanish war cry, the army stormed the pueblo, with Coronado in his glittering armor and plumed helmet leading the attack.

Showers of boulders thundered down from the walls. Arrows hissed through the narrow streets, which echoed with the roar of the big muzzle-loaders. Coronado himself was badly hurt by a boulder and removed from the battle. His enraged troops, even though weakened by the long march and attendant hardships, brought the battle to the enemy until the Zuñis fled.

Cibola

The following description is an example of the thoroughness of Pedro de Casta-ñeda's report of the expedition:

The seven Cities are seven little villages, all within a radius of four leagues (15 to 20 miles). . . . The largest is called Mazaque. . . . The largest may have 200 houses, and two others about 200, and the others somewhere between 30 and 60. . . . There might be in all 500 hearths. . . . Hawikuh has 200 houses all surrounded by a wall. . . . The walls are of stone and mud. . . . The houses, as a rule, are three and four stories high, but at Mazaque there are houses four and seven stories high. . . .

The natives here are very intelligent. . . . They cover the privy and immodest parts of their bodies with cloths resembling table napkins, with fringes and a tassel at each corner, tying them around the hips. . . . They wear cloaks made with feathers and rabbit hair, and cotton blankets. . . . They wear shoes of deerskin. . . . The women wear blankets wrapped tightly around their bodies and fastened or tied over the left shoulder, drawing the right arm over them; they also wear well-fashioned cloaks of dressed skins. . . . They gather their hair over their ears in two wheels that look like coif puffs. . . . An Indian woman will carry a jar of water up a ladder without touching it with her hands.

These Indians cultivate maize, which does not grow tall, but each stalk bears three and four large and heavy ears with 800 grains each. . . . They have very good salt in crystals. . . . They make the best tortillas that I have ever seen anywhere. . . . There are in this province large numbers of bears, mountain lions, wildcats, porcupines, deer, wild goats and otters. . . . They have no knowledge of fish. . . . There are very fine turquoises although not in the quantity claimed. . . . The natives gather and store pine nuts for the year. . . . A man has only one wife. . . .

There are *estufas (kivas)* in the pueblos, in which they gather to take counsel. . . . They have no rulers, but are governed by the counsel of their oldest men. . . . They have their priests, whom they call papas. These priests mount the high terrace of the pueblo in the morning as the sun rises, and from there, like public criers, preach to the people, who all listen in silence, seated along the corridors. The priests tell the people how they should live. I believe that they give them some commandments to observe, because there is no drunkenness among them, nor do they eat human flesh, or steal. . . . They hold their rituals and sacrifices before some idols. . . . What they worship most is water. . . . They make the cross as a sign of peace.

The shaggy-coated buffalo of the American plains appeared in Gomara's *Historia de las Indias Saragossa*, c. 1554. When Cortez's forces reached Montezuma's capital they reported having seen "a rare Mexican bull, with crooked shoulders, a hump on its back like a camel and with hair like a lion." Both Cabeza de Vaca and Coronado saw the "crooked-back oxen" on its native range.

The copper-skinned Indians Cortez brought back from the New World to the Spanish court excited lively interest, for they were exotic beings "from a land two thousand miles away, where gold is found in the water." A German artist and silversmith, Christoph Weiditz, made watercolors of them about 1529 and commented on their colorful regalia. It was believed that these savages wore precious stones in their faces and breasts.

Although these photographs were taken by Tim O'Sullivan in the course of Wheeler's geographical surveys (1871-73), they might have been recorded, had cameras been available to Coronado's men, as early as 1540. Coronado and his men saw and described such sights as the Zuñi and Hopi Pueblos, Acoma, the "Sky City," herds of buffalo, great canyons and rivers, including the Grand Canyon and the Colorado River.

Explorers Column, Canyon de Chelly, Arizona.

Grotto Spring, Grand Canyon of the Colorado River.

Zuñi Indian girl, with water olla.

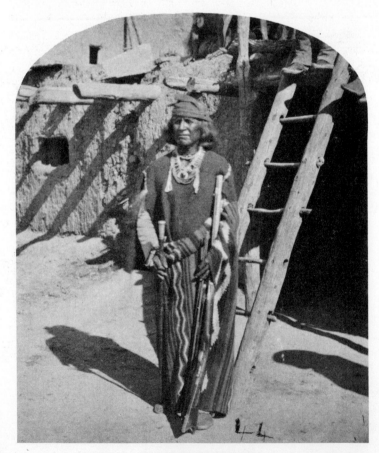

A Zuñi war chief.

When Coronado found Cibola to be far from the fabled golden city he sent Friar Marcos back in disgrace but kept on, always hopeful that the next tale would be true, the next pueblo would offer the golden temples and doorways studded with precious gems.

But they found only heat, dust, endless distances, high, keening winds and numbing cold. The land was forbidding—either desert-dry or rocky and wild, unfit for cultivation.

The remnants of the expedition—about one-third of the force that had started out with such high hopes in 1540—returned to Mexico in 1542.

Coronado's troubles were many in the years to come. He was removed from office and brought to Mexico City to face charges of the misconduct of the expedition. But he was found to have fulfilled his duties faithfully and was exonerated in full.

The trial did not end the accusations. His enemies continued to denounce him and blame him for what they called a dismal failure. Few would realize in their own lifetime that Coronado had discovered far greater things than gold-sheathed walls or doors studded with turquoise. . . .

He had discovered a new and mighty land in which he had left a heritage of hatred—and several mustangs.

De Soto and the Mississippi

Spain's other elaborate expedition to explore the interior of North America was that of Hernando de Soto's, who, like Coronado, failed to find golden cities but did discover the mightiest river in America.

The report of the expedition made by an anonymous Portuguese of Elvas fails to cite dates. Ranjel, De Soto's secretary, kept a day-by-day journal, but unfortunately his diary breaks off before the death of De Soto, leaving no account of the westward march when the command was under Moscoso. Like Coronado's, De Soto's expedition was disappointing to the royal court because he failed to find treasure.

De Soto's expedition was the last of the full-scale attempts by the Spanish to move into the West. Santa Fe was occupied by 1599, but between that place and St. Augustine, Florida, there was a great sag where Spain had failed to move northward.

Spanish Colonization

While Spain hesitated, the great revolution of the plains was beginning. It was some time in the seventeenth century or possibly earlier that somewhere on the western plains an Indian buck carefully approached one of the lost horses of the Spaniards, put out a trembling hand to touch the velvet coat. When he found it was not a courier of the strange white man's gods he threw a leg over and mounted the steed. One can only guess at the wild triumph which filled the heart of this copper-skinned man as he found himself soaring across the sea of grass.

After that initial adventure he and his tribe must have figured out the technique of riding. Once they learned to stay on, they discovered the horse could not only be used for fast travel but also for hunting. Now he could race along the flanks of the thundering herds of buffalo, now he could lean over and drive home his lance, again and again, leaving the shaggy beasts behind for the women to skin and carve.

Now also he was a fearsome man of war. He could strike a blow and vanish speedily. He could move whole

Indian pueblo of Zuñi, New Mexico. View from the interior.

A Zuñi woman with her hair over her ears in two wheels, as described by de Casteñada. *Photo by C. C. Pierce.*

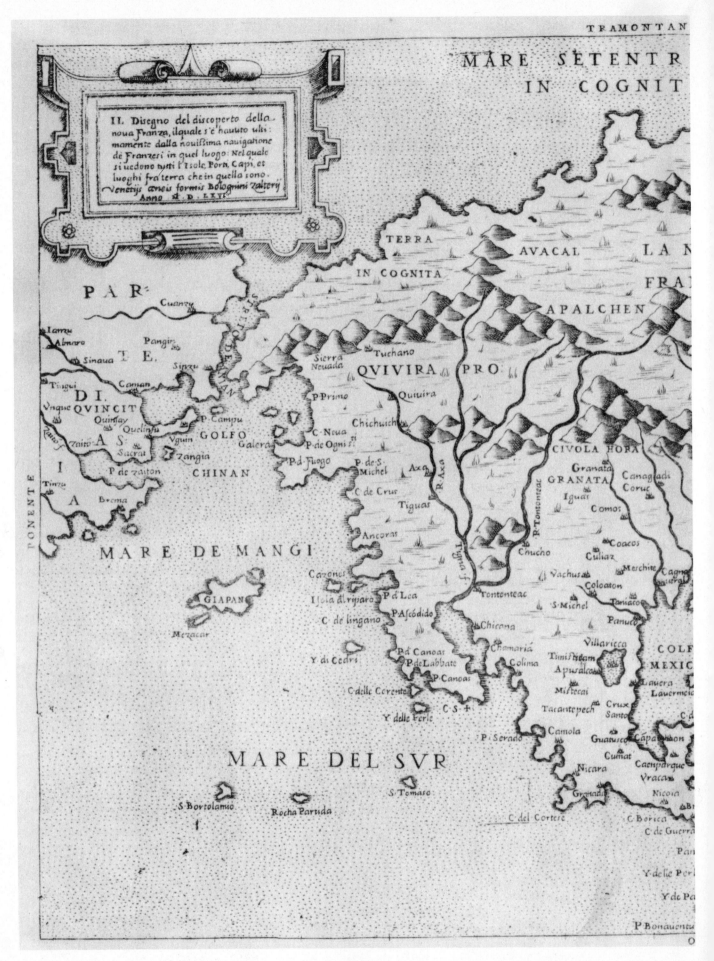

Map of North America made in Bologna, Italy, dated 1566.

[18]

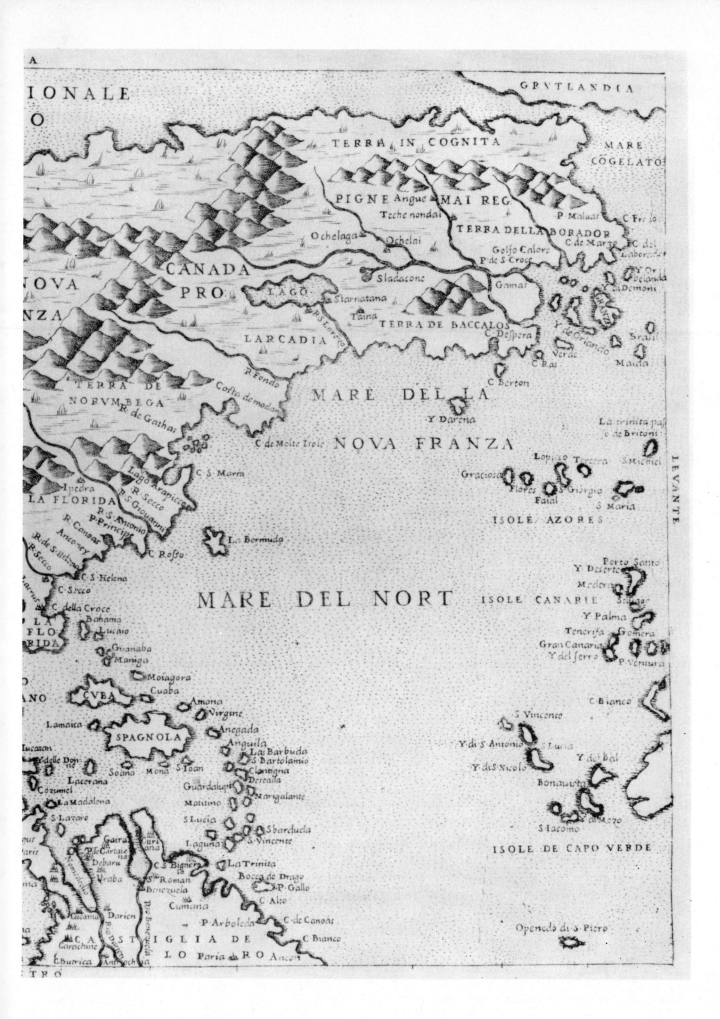

towns in one-fifth the time he had been accustomed to. Before, as the Spaniards had noted with amazement, the travois, the Indian vehicle, had been attached to the dog; now it could be attached to the horse and piled high with skins, poles, utensils and weapons.

By the beginning of the eighteenth century, when Spain started to establish missions from California to Florida, the Indians on horseback were a strong foe. If it hadn't been for the friendly Pimas it is doubtful if any of the early settlements would have survived.

In 1757 the red men demonstrated how effective they were as a mounted foe. A large band of Comanches, now the undisputed cavalrymen of the plains, swept in to massacre all but four persons in the mission of the San Saba River near the present town of Menard, Texas.

The aroused Spaniards were determined to avenge the martyred San Saba dead. An army of 600 or more Spaniards, Mexicans and a large band of Apaches raided a Comanche village on the Red River near Ringgold. But the villagers had been warned of the approach of the Spanish expedition and were waiting. In the ensuing battle the Comanches, equipped by the French, defeated the Spaniards and sent them fleeing back to San Antonio.

More than a decade later Charles III of Spain had a more serious problem to consider than the defeat of a frontier expedition. The Spanish court was now shaken by the far-off rumbling of the cannons of General Wolfe, who had smashed the French army under Montcalm on the Plains of Abraham. The significance of that defeat was quite obvious to the royal statesmen in the quiet of the Escorial, where King Charles was deciding the future policies of Spain in the New World.

When news of the battle reached him Charles was rightly disturbed. A look at the map of New Spain could easily show him how the situation was altering: Spain's colony of New Spain—Mexico—now had on its borders the aggressive English colonists. Not even the close family ties of the kings of France and Spain had been able to stop the English. Even when her armies were not on the march her daring seamen like Drake were striking the Pacific coast.

Spain's weakest points were in the northern borders of New Spain. Here the line consisted only of a rag-tag line of missions, ranches and presidios, which extended from the French border of Louisiana across Texas and as far north as Pimeria Alta, the southern part of Arizona. The northwest province of Sonora, the outpost of Spanish colonization, was constantly under attack from the fierce Apaches, while lower California was under the firm rule of the Jesuits, who had virtually carved out of the wilderness a series of missions.

The English colonists were not the only threat to the empire; there were the Russians gradually edging down the Pacific Coast from Siberia. In 1723 Vitus Bering sailed into the strait that bears his name, opening the way for his countrymen, who began moving down the coast in their feverish search for the skin of the sea-otter.

Father Junipero Serra.

All explorations of the California frontier in the seventeenth century had been done by missionaries, usually Jesuits, working from their base in Mexico. After the English victory in Canada, Spain decided to abolish the Jesuits from Alta California and replace them with an order easier to govern.

In their place were substituted the Franciscans as the colonizers of Alta California. The supervision of the missionary efforts was given to Father Junipero Serra, who already had a reputation not only as a learned man but as a missionary and explorer.

Serra, born on the Island of Mallorca in 1713, abandoned a life that had offered scholastic and religious honor and chose to go to the frontiers of New Spain. In February, 1768, Serra and 16 brother Franciscans boarded the packet boat *Concepcion*, which had brought back the Jesuit missionaries, and set sail for Alta California. On Easter Sunday he took up his duties as father-president of the missions in lower California.

In the years Serra was in California, he extended the missions north to the bay of San Francisco. In time they became known as "Serra beads." The missions established by Serra and his successors extended in a ragged line from San Diego y Alcala to San Francisco del Solano de Sonoma in the north, a distance of more than 600 miles. All but three were founded prior to 1800. They were spaced a day's journey apart and were connected by a trail called El Camino Real—the King's Highway.

The missions contained a unique collection of artisans, farmers, priests and educators. They occupied millions of acres of the richest pastureland in the West, on which were raised thousands of head of cattle, horses and livestock. Confined within the mission walls were bakers, cooks, shoemakers, soap-makers, musicians, carpenters, tile-makers, plasterers, shepherds, cart-makers, weavers, vine-yardists, hunters, blacksmiths, silversmiths, tallow-renderers and of course, the *vaqueros*—cowboys whose dress would become an integral part of the costume of the cow-punchers of the plains.

All of the missions were built by native labor. The massive walls were usually at least four feet thick and composed of sun-dried clay bricks (adobe). Across the tops of the walls were laid hand-hewn timbers which were fastened with rawhide. On these was placed a layer of reeds, then the traditional red tile. Mission life was active, with the first monk up at five and the chapel filled soon after with kneeling Indians. The sun was peering over the hills when they trooped into the fields, the vineyards, the mill, the shop, while the shepherds and their dogs moved out with their flocks to the grassy slopes.

Father Serra, the missions' founder, was a tireless, devoted humble man who was adored by the Indians, the soldiers, and his religious colleagues alike. At his death his faithful friend and brother priest, Fray Palou, wrote the simple words in the burial register of Carmel Mission —words which can still be read today—"On the twenty-ninth of August, 1784, in this Church of San Carlos, in the sanctuary before the altar of Our Lady of Dolores, the office of the dead having been recited, and a Requiem Mass having been sung, I gave ecclesiastical burial to the

San Diego del Alcala Mission (1769), the first of Father Serra's missions, as it appeared in the 1890's.

The Carmel Mission, established in 1770 as San Carlos Borromeo at Monterey, was moved in 1771 to Carmel. *Photo by C. E. Watkins.*

San Juan Capistrano Mission before the earthquake of 1812.

San Gabriel Mission.

Buffalo cow and calf.

Antelope.

Prairie dogs.

Deer, buck and doe.

Jackrabbit.

Elk.

Black bear.

Coyote.

Wildcat.

Rattlesnake.

Mountain lion.

Sage hen.

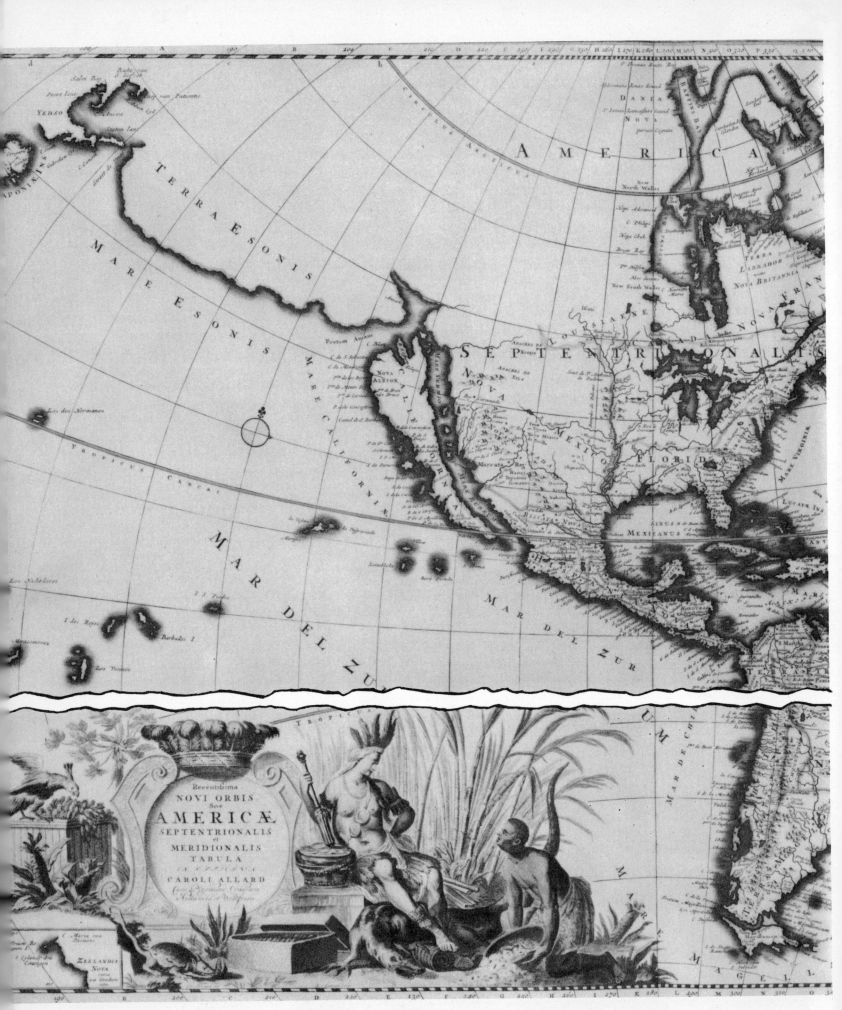

Part of a map of North America, made in Amsterdam, Holland, about 1700. Even
as late as this, California was believed to be an island.

body of Father Lecturer, Fray Junipero Serra, President and Founder of the Missions." Palou's further service to his beloved friend was to write a biography of Serra, one of the most valuable source-books of early western history including descriptions of the Indian tribes and the wild life of the area.

Besides the ecclesiastical reorganization, additional steps were taken to insure the safety of Spain's American frontier. In 1766 the Marqués de Rubí was appointed to make a tour for the purpose of a possible military and administrative reorganization. His party journeyed from Louisiana to California and made a report on conditions, with recommendations for a radical change in policy. The king accepted Rubí's proposal and in 1772 issued a royal order for the establishment of 15 presidios in southern Texas to ensure a firm frontier, leaving everything to the north "to nature and the Indians," as Rubí had put it.

The presidios were to stretch from Bahia del Espiritu Santo to the Gulf of California. Santa Fe and San Antonio, far to the north of the line, would remain as outposts. The royal order also included some of Rubí's recommendations for solution of the Indian problem. They were simple: wipe out the Apaches, who were making trouble with the Comanches. Thus with the Apaches out of the way, the Comanches would calm down and let the settlements alone.

It took the Spaniards five years to try to carry out the king's proposal to wipe out the Apaches. In 1777 El Caballero de Croix arrived in Chihuahua and immediately set the wheels in motion for a mighty Indian campaign. In the end, it was decided to join forces with the Comanches.

The plan called for three large forces to converge on the Apaches from three different directions and force them into an ambush on the Rio Grande. There the Apaches were to be exterminated to the man or else forced into reservations. De Croix proposed that after the Indians were wiped out the Spanish frontier could be advanced further northward and made into a line of demarcation: all those above it were to be considered enemies, all those below it friends, of New Spain.

But the grand plan which certainly would have changed the history of the West was never carried out. Spain suddenly found herself embroiled in European affairs and had no time to think about savages on an endless frontier.

But the Franciscans were still arriving to make Father Serra's dream come true. The last of "Father Serra's beads," San Francisco Solano de Sonoma, was established in 1823. The later missions, many of which can be seen today, were much more successful and effective than the earlier ones and exerted a notable influence on American life not only in California but throughout the Southwest.

In 1821 Mexico rebelled against Spain, won its independence and took over sovereignty of Spanish North America. In 1832 the Mexican government seized church property, and the missions were virtually abandoned (until years later when the property was returned and in some degree restored). By 1848, Mexico itself had lost all its sovereignty over the southwest part of what is now the United States, and the active, direct influence of the Spanish and the Mexicans on American life ceased. What remained was the Spanish heritage.

What did the Spanish leave for the Anglo-Americans who were coming from the East? As we have seen, they implanted a hatred for white men in the hearts of red men. They had also given the Plains Indians horses. To their credit they had cemented an unbreakable friendship with many Indian tribes, especially in California. They introduced longhorn cattle, a colorful fibre in the tapestry of western history; they introduced into the American West the cultivation of orange and lemon trees, as well as orchards and vineyards all of which had a strong effect on the economy and the life of the West. They left behind another kind of seed and fruit—Spanish culture, which is still visible in language, dress and tradition.

The Presidio of San Francisco, 1822.

Pioneers from the East

IT was after the American Revolution that the colonists on the Atlantic Seaboard looked to the West. Within a few years after Yorktown they began their trek, headed for a new and different world. For generations they had glimpsed this unploughed sea of grass through the leaves and boughs of their eastern forests with mingled fears and dreams. Now they were ready to mold the dream to reality.

But the West and its great future were nothing new to the planners of our infant republic. Even during the Revolution, George Washington had his mind on the West. In 1779, although his Continentals and the Redcoats were deadlocked on the Hudson, he was engaged in a vast strategy that would affect the history of the American West.

By this time Washington was sure that the end of the war was in sight. He saw that when the terms of settlement were drawn, if the young nation got nothing but a strip of land along the East Coast there would be no room for expansion westward. A study of Washington's papers of this period shows that he was carrying on a heavy correspondence with rangers, scouts, travelers, trappers, soldiers and missionaries seeking information about trails, routes, waterways, traders' posts, settlements and the temper of the western tribes. While George Rogers Clark's rifles were storming Vincennes, secret American agents were moving among the western tribes trying to persuade the great Sioux Chief Wabasha to remain neutral, despite the offers made by British agents from Detroit.

Before Yorktown, General Schuyler in his Albany mansion was already moving a pointer across a map of the western frontier and telling his officers that America's destiny lay westward.

After the Revolution many of the men who had fought from Valley Forge to Yorktown moved west to claim their bounty lands. Many Americans, independently of their infant government, rode westward across the Mississippi to seek adventure, to trade with the Indians, to trap and bring back furs, to survey the land. But there were also many organized expeditions and explorations, arranged and financed by companies of merchants as well as by the government.

Captain Gray and the Columbia River

One of the first of these was the expedition of the Boston Marine Association. Its ship, the *Columbia*, with

Captain Robert Gray.

Captain Robert Gray in command, set sail in 1790 for the Pacific Northwest. After making several attempts to penetrate the breakers of the body of water known as Deception Bay, in the spring of 1792 Captain Gray finally succeeded, naming the river he discovered the Columbia in honor of the ship. This discovery gave the United States clear claim to the Oregon country—Oregon, Washington and Idaho—which Great Britain recognized in the Oregon Treaty of 1846. And the reports of the discovery and the nature of the land in the Columbia valley did much to stimulate interest in and emigration to Oregon.

Lewis and Clark

It was Thomas Jefferson who conceived, sponsored and organized the Lewis and Clark expedition, authorized by Congress in 1803. He knew it was important for the young nation to make a survey of the unexplored western lands. Jefferson's secretary, Meriwether Lewis, was in charge, William Clark was selected as associate commander.

The year 1803 is probably best known to most Americans for the Louisiana Purchase, and this great event had a curious impact on the Lewis and Clark expedition. It was the popular opinion that the purpose of the expedition was to map out the new territory, rather than to survey the West to the Pacific. As a result of the Purchase, national interest was stimulated in the expedition and all news of it was eagerly awaited, repeated and discussed

Meriwether Lewis.

William Clark.

Zebulon Pike in the uniform of an officer of the War of 1812.

throughout the country. This accounts, in part, for the great fame of the Lewis and Clark expedition, which was and is probably greater than it deserves, for it did not really accomplish the satisfactory survey which was its purpose. In comparison to the records kept by chroniclers of Coronado's expedition, the journals and reports kept by its members are vague and lack scientific detail.

The expedition assembled near St. Louis and on March 14, 1804, started up the Missouri River. When it neared the Columbia River it made portages over the intervening land, went down the Columbia to the Pacific and was back in St. Louis on September 23, 1806. Their return sparked nation-wide excitement and spurred the organization of many emigrant parties to the West. In this clarion "call to the West" lies its real significance.

The Louisiana Purchase and the Influence of the French on the West

The Louisiana Purchase from France for about $15,000,-000 in 1803 more than doubled the size of the United States. Included in this vast territory west of the Mississippi was the land incorporating the states of Arkansas, Missouri, Iowa, most of Minnesota, North Dakota, South Dakota, Nebraska, most of Kansas, Oklahoma, parts of Montana, Wyoming and Colorado and almost all of Louisiana, including New Orleans.

France had owned this territory until 1762, when she ceded it to Spain. Then, in 1800, Spain ceded it back again to the French. In 1803 Napoleon, needing the money, sold it to the United States. The importance of the addition of this great area to the territory of the United States cannot be overestimated. But at the time, except in southernmost Louisiana, there was very little white settlement.

The French influence on the American West was rather

negligible. Apart from the area near New Orleans, where the French culture put down enduring roots, there is little in the rest of the Louisiana Territory to show the French had ever been there, except for place names, of which there are many.

The Zebulon M. Pike Expedition

While the Lewis and Clark expedition was moving across the West, Zebulon M. Pike set out from St. Louis on a July day in 1806. He had 23 white men and 51 Indians and a plan to cross the plains to the Rocky Mountains. He went up the Arkansas River to its source, then moved southward to the Rio Grande country, where he was captured and brought before the governor of (Spanish) New Mexico at Santa Fe. Eventually he was taken across Texas and brought to the Louisiana border. Pike left behind careful journals of his expedition, especially of Texas and the plains country.

Summit of Pike's Peak. *Photo by W. H. Jackson.*

To the Senate & House of Representatives of the United States

In pursuance of a measure proposed to Congress by a message of Jan. 18. 1803 and sanctioned by their appropriation for carrying it into execution, Capt Meriwether Lewis of the 1st regiment of in-

copies of his map of the river, from it's mouth to the Hot-springs, make part of the present communications. the ex-amination of the Red river itself. is but now commencing.

Th: Jefferson

Feb. 19. 1806.

Portion of Jefferson's letter to Congress, February 19, 1806, reporting on the Lewis and Clark expedition.

A map of the Pike's Peak region, 1806, from Pike's journal.

The Yellowstone or Stephen H. Long Expedition

In 1819 the United States launched one of its most important western explorations. Not only soldiers and adventurers but also men of science accompanied Major Stephen A. Long's small army, which was ordered to seek sites for posts which would offset the British strength which had been spreading and growing in the north. The party spent the winter of 1819-20 at Engineer Cantonment, near Council Bluffs. Congress changed its plans and, following its instructions, in the spring the party went up the River Platte, sighted the Rocky Mountains and encamped at what is now Denver. At the Arkansas River the party split; one division came down the Arkansas; the other, under Long, set out for the Red River, but by mistake struck the Canadian. The reports of Long's expedition by Edwin James, a physician, which were full of botanical, geological and other scientific data, proved to have great value and importance.

Trappers, Fur Traders, Mountain Men

Besides these three major expeditions there were a number of other explorations during this period and shortly after it. More important perhaps were the commercial activities of trading and fur companies, which helped to blaze trails and prepare the way for emigrants. Outstanding among these were the companies founded by John Jacob Astor, Manuel Lisa and General William H. Ashley.

In 1811 Astor established an important post on the Columbia River and later set up outposts on the Willamette, Spokane and Kanogan Rivers in the Northwest.

Beginning about 1800, Manuel Lisa and his Missouri Fur Company operated all over the Southwest, the Missouri and Arkansas country and the Rocky Mountain area. He set up many trading posts and settlements, made friends of the Indians, loaned them traps, taught them much more about agriculture and medicine and helped them in many other ways.

In the War of 1812 Lisa defeated the attempts of the British to unite the Sioux. More than a year before the war he had warned General Clark that secret agents of the British were attempting to bribe the Sioux to take up arms against the Americans. Had they done so it would have been impossible to estimate the damage done to the posts on the Missouri.

When the war was over the chagrined British agents discovered that more than 40 chiefs whom they had counted as supporters "had intelligence from Lisa" and

Manuel Lisa.

"Jim Bridger Crossing a River." *Sketch by Alfred Jacob Miller.*

Antoine Clement, mountain man, scout and hunter.

Bill Burrows, a Rocky Mountain trapper.

were preparing a campaign of several thousand warriors against the tribes of the Upper Missouri. Only then was is learned that Lisa had quietly sent his own agents among the tribes during the war, inciting them to make war against one another and thus "keeping them too busy with their own affairs to permit them to interfere with the war between England and the United States."

General Ashley and the men he led on his fur-trading ventures in the 1820's were notable for the trails they blazed in the northern Rocky Mountain country. Among Ashley's "mountain men" were a number who became famous and established their places in Western history as scouts, fur-traders, keelboatmen, Indian fighters—Jedediah Smith, the five Sublette brothers, Jim Bridger, Mike Fink, Robert Campbell, Jim Beckwourth and others.

Smith and Bill Sublette "discovered" the South Pass across the Rocky Mountains. At least they were the first to report about this passage, which became a crucial factor in the Oregon Trail migration in the years to come. They also found and gave full details about the Cimarron cut-off and other shortcuts on the way west.

Not only did these mountain men provide much valuable information about the previously unknown mountain country but also they cleared and eased the way—by marking trails, establishing landmarks and posts—for the great wagon-trains of emigrants, a number of which they guided.

Britain's Hudson's Bay Company was quite active in the Northwest country at the time and made many trespasses into the United States' Oregon territory. The mountain men helped to defend the territory against the British company. (Their resistance was an important factor in the celebrated "54-40 or fight" controversy with the British, which was resolved by the Oregon Treaty in 1846, which defined the Oregon border at 49° North Latitude.)

Forts and Cavalry Posts

As the trappers and traders moved into the West they established at strategic points supply and trading posts, fortified against attacks by Indians. The Army also set up military posts as the need for them became apparent (Fort Leavenworth was established in 1827), but there was no organized program of frontier defense until 1845, when Congress voted to establish a series of military posts along the trail to Oregon, and to organize a regiment of expert "Mounted Riflemen" to garrison the forts.

The route of the Mounted Riflemen, May-October, 1849.

Fort Leavenworth, 1849.

The Mexican War broke out before the regiment of mounted riflemen could start on their western orders. But in 1849, after distinguished service at Cerro Gordo, Chapultepec and elsewhere in Mexico, they started on their route from Council Bluffs along the Oregon Trail to Oregon City. The posts they established became the nucleus of the War Department's network of forts and garrisons to protect and police the western lands, all exclusively under federal jurisdiction until the establishment of state governments. The "cavalry" had taken its stand.

The explorations and ventures of the traders and trappers and many others like them were opening up the West. Though Lewis and Clark chose to travel on the rivers, later expeditions and venturers into the West found it better and easier to travel overland. By about 1840 there were two fairly well established Trails across the West— the Santa Fe Trail and the Oregon Trail.

Fort Laramie, 1849.

Landing at Weston, May, 1849.

Fort Hall, 1849.

Texas: Province, Republic, State

Stephen Austin.

Sam Houston. *Photo by Mathew Brady.*

IT was in 1821 that Stephen F. Austin led a group of Americans into the Mexican province of Texas and founded a colony along the Brazos and Colorado Rivers. It was highly successful; word of it spread to the East, and the colony of Americans flourished and expanded.

Austin was astute in his dealings with the Indians, but the colony was not without trouble with some of the tribes, especially when it spread beyond the original borders. In 1826 Austin called a conference at which it was arranged to have 20 to 30 mounted guards constantly ranging the borders of the colony. These rangers were the forerunners of the famed Texas Rangers.

The Texan colonists had trouble not only with the Indians but also with the Mexican government, and this eventually, in 1835, erupted into revolution. Sam Houston was made commander-in-chief of the Texas army and the bitter struggle with the Mexicans, led by Santa Anna, began. The climax of the war was the famous battle of the Alamo, which lasted from February 23 to March 6, 1836.

One hundred and eighty Texans, commanded by Colonel W. B. Travis and including Davy Crockett, James Bowie and other well-known heroes were surrounded by a Mexican army of 1,600 and besieged in a fort that was formerly a mission known as the Alamo. The Texans fought until the last defender was killed. Their heroic

fight and the rallying cry "Remember the Alamo" inspired the Texans and undoubtedly was a factor in speeding victory for the revolutionists. In the battle of San Jacinto months later Sam Houston defeated Santa Anna, independence was won and the Lone Star Republic of Texas was established with Sam Houston as its president.

During the Revolution the Texas Rangers had been given official status as a law-enforcement agency. The new Republic was not recognized by Mexico, and besides the chaos of the war there was constant harassment by both the Mexicans and Indians. In time the Rangers became a guardian force of the young nation.

By 1840 the Rangers had become a permanent fixture on the frontier, with headquarters at San Antonio under Colonel John Coffee Hays. Their weapons were those of the frontier: cap-and-ball rifle, which took a minute to load—a minute which could be fatal—the horse pistol, single-action revolver or the smaller derringer. The hard-riding Texans were desperate for a better weapon when Sam Colt appeared on the scene. The former sailor whittled a model of the famous six-shooter when he was serving aboard a clipper enroute to Calcutta from Boston. He took out his first patent in 1836, the year Texas established its independence.

In 1838 Colt began manufacturing revolvers in Paterson, New Jersey. He could not get the U. S. Army or

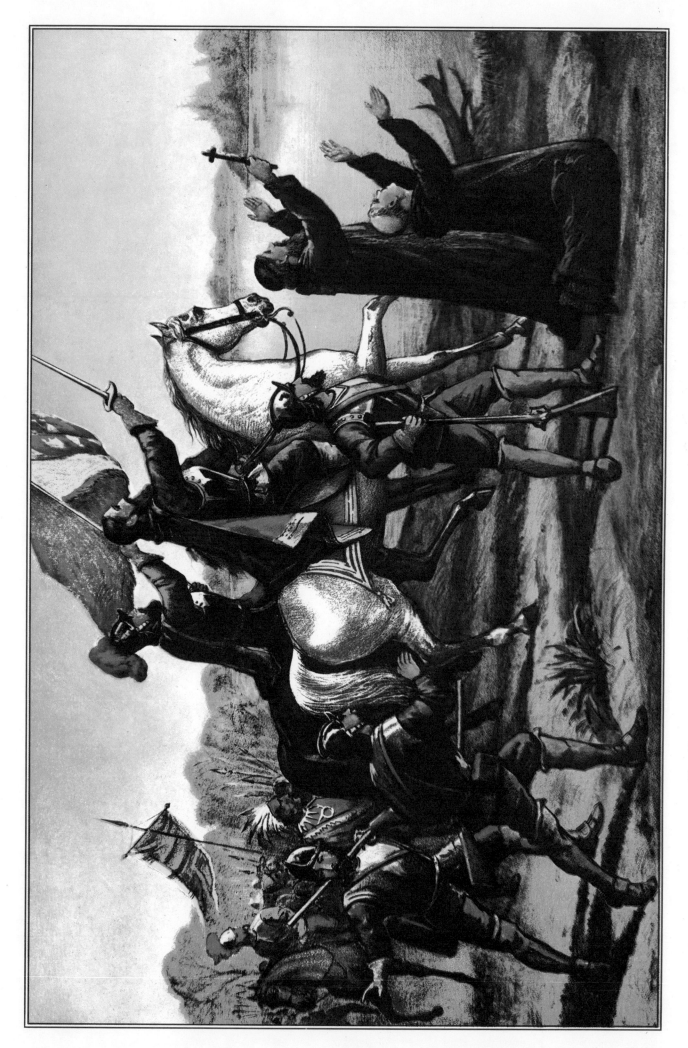

THE DISCOVERY OF THE MISSISSIPPI. From a Currier & Ives print first published in 1876. The artist's sources for details of costumes, appearances, etc. are not known, and probably many of the elements are figments of the artist's imagination. But Currier & Ives endeavored, whenever possible, to make their prints accurate.

View of the two principal channels of the rapids on the Fox River called the Grand Kakhalin taken from the point marked × looking to the S.E.

→ North

Map of the Grand Kakhlin.

1. Where the boats unloaded
2. Portage about 1000 yards
3. Place where the boats reloaded
4. Smooth water
5. Course of the boats up the rapids.

Scale 3 miles to the inch

A PAGE FROM THE DIARY OF CAPTAIN HENRY WHITING. He led the Wisconsin Expedition from Green Bay to Prairie du Chien, June 7 to June 30, 1819. This expedition, like many others of the period, was designed to increase knowledge of remote regions and to strengthen federal authority over the frontier.

A View of the Entrance into Lake Winebago

View of the Ouisconsin from the St. Camp near at the Portage.

View of the Landscape on the portage, taken from a small hill. NE view of the Fox river.

A View of the Entrance into the Highlands of the Ouisconsin.

View of the Village of Le Butte de Mort.

View of the Sugar loaf hill in the Highlands of the Ouisconsin.

FROM THE DIARY OF CAPTAIN HENRY WHITING.

THE BULL DANCE OF THE MANDANS. This was a ritual dance by means of which the Indians hoped to insure success in their buffalo-hunting. *Painted by George Catlin, 1832.*

A SHAWNEE CHIEF. *Drawn on stone by L. Lima.* This portrait and those on the next two pages are from McKenney and Hall's famous work, *Indian Tribes of North America*, which Bernard De Voto called "a monument of American culture, solely because of the portraits." The plates were lithographed, and the work

(see next page)

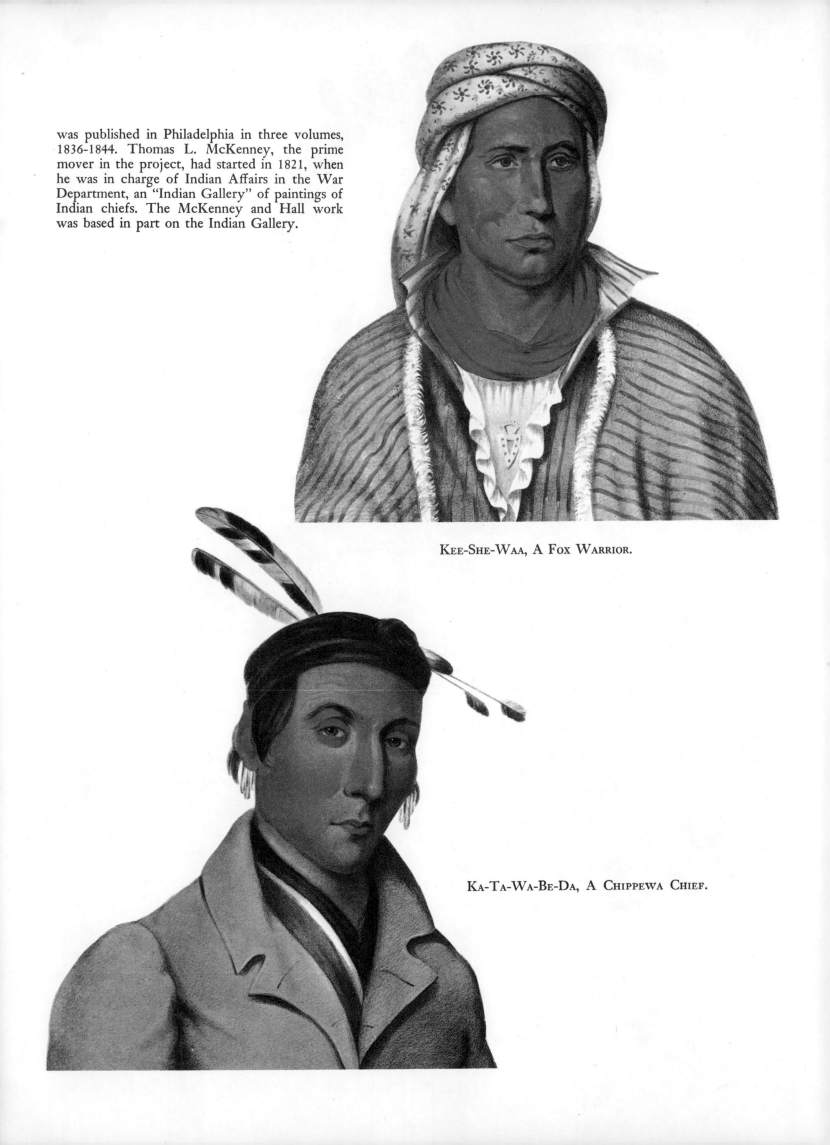

was published in Philadelphia in three volumes, 1836-1844. Thomas L. McKenney, the prime mover in the project, had started in 1821, when he was in charge of Indian Affairs in the War Department, an "Indian Gallery" of paintings of Indian chiefs. The McKenney and Hall work was based in part on the Indian Gallery.

KEE-SHE-WAA, A FOX WARRIOR.

KA-TA-WA-BE-DA, A CHIPPEWA CHIEF.

WA-BISH-KEE-PE-NAS (THE WHITE PIGEON), A CHIPPEWA.

PEAH MUS-KA, A MUSKOGEE CHIEF.

Fort Union: The Assiniboins Breaking Up Their Camp, 1833. *Painted by Charles Bodmer.*

The last message of Colonel Travis, "We have 100 men and are determined to defend the Alamo to the last. Give us assistance—"

Colonel Jack Hays.

From a daguerreotype of Captain Samuel H. Walker.

Sam Houston's famous letter of March, 1836.

DAILY BULLETIN---EXTRA.

GAZETTE OFFICE, JANUARY 18, 1842.

FROM SANTA FE.

Capture of the Texian Expedition confirmed—Indignity to the American Consul, and the Resident Americans in Santa Fé!!¡

Under the above caption we find in the Missouri Republican of the 24th, three letters, received from Independence the evening previous, announcing painful intelligence from Santa Fé, and confirming the news of the capture of the Texian Expedition. The recital of the treatment shown the American citizens (the Republican thinks) will rouse the blood of every one, and calls for revenge. "The treatment of our Consul, Senor Alvarez, and the destruction of the property of

Howland, with two more, was sent in advance as spies, to ascertain the disposition of the Mexicans towards them.

Not understanding the nature of their embassy sufficiently, and from their contradictory statements concerning the place from whence they hailed, they were stripped and ordered not to leave the bounds. In the meantime they made their escape—but after travelling five days and only progressing fifty miles, they were taken by some shepherds, brought in and shot. Seven more from the company were again sent in—among them was Kendall, the editor of the Picayune, a son of Leslie _____ of _____ and a Mr. Lewis—they had in

A newspaper report of the Santa Fe massacre.

28th Congress. Second Session. Begun and held at the city of Washington, in the District of Columbia, on Monday the second day of December, eighteen hundred and forty-four.

Joint Resolution for annexing Texas to the United States.

Resolved by the Senate and House of Representatives of the United States of America...

...nt the sum of one hundred thousand dollars be, and the same is hereby, appropriated to defray the expenses of missions and negotiations, to agree upon the terms of said admission and cession, either by treaty to be submitted to the Senate, or by articles to be submitted to the two Houses of Congress, as the President may direct.

JW Jones Speaker of the House of Representatives.

Willie P. Mangum President, pro tempore, of the Senate.

Approved March 1. 1845

John Tyler

Resolution of Congress for the annexation of Texas.

Navy to buy his revolvers; but orders began to come in from Texas and the six-shooter got to be known as the "Texas." In the forties Ranger captain Sam H. Walker came to New York to buy revolvers and met the inventor.

Walker made several suggestions and a new and improved weapon, which Colt called the "Walker Pistol," was made. This new six-shooter made its great reputation in the battle of Pedernales, in which Colonel Hays and 14 rangers were engaged by 70 Comanches. Before the battle ended, 30 redskins were killed. It was a major victory, and the success was clearly due to the newly designed six-shooter that a mounted man could use easily. It gave the Ranger, or any mounted man who had it, the edge to outfight and outgun the Indians. It helped to establish the Colt as a major weapon, a firearm of crucial importance in the history of the West for the next 50 years. But national and world fame did not come until war with Mexico broke out and the Rangers offered their services to General Zachary Taylor. Under pressure from the Rangers, Taylor ordered a thousand Colts at a price of $28,000.

Every soldier in the war marveled at the Rangers' finely balanced six-shooter. With widespread recognition and enthusiasm for his revolver, Colt soon became a millionaire. Now no one went west without a Colt on his hip.

The Mexican War

The United States' war with Mexico started in 1846, primarily because the Republic of Texas, which in 1836 asked to be admitted to the Union, was finally annexed as the twenty-eighth state, in December, 1845. Mexico still regarded Texas as Mexican territory. There were other frictions and pressures in addition to claims of aggression by Mexico, which could not be resolved by negotiation. The was began in May, 1846. In rather rapid succession, Santa Fe was captured; California came under U. S. control and Santa Anna and his army were defeated, but not at all routed, at Buena Vista (February, 1847). In March, 1847, Winfield Scott, with Navy help, took Vera Cruz. The war virtually ended when Mexico City was occupied September 14, 1847.

The peace treaty was ratified in March, 1848. Mexico ceded about half its territory—its provinces of New Mexico and California—out of which also parts of the states of Nevada, Utah, Colorado and Wyoming were carved. The Texas-Mexico border was fixed at the Rio Grande.

A portion of northwestern Texas was ceded to the United States for $10,000,000, by the Compromise Act of 1850. This land eventually became part of the States of New Mexico, Colorado, Wyoming, Kansas and Oklahoma.

In 1853, through the Gadsden Purchase, the United States acquired from Mexico another 45,000 square miles —for the most part south of the Gila River—now the tip of southwest New Mexico and the southern extreme of Arizona. This fixed the southwest boundary of the United States as it is today.

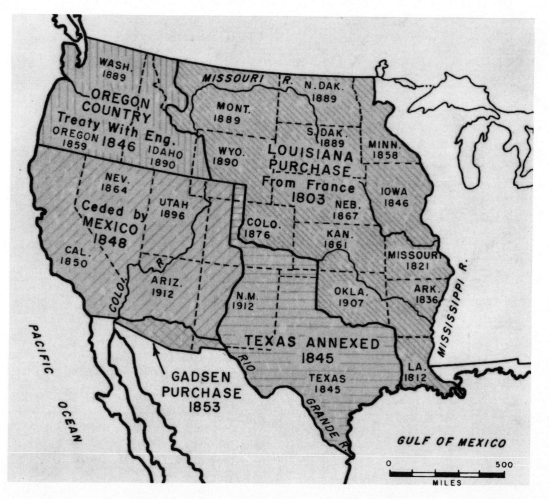

The acquisition and annexation of the western territory, with dates of admission of the states. Though the United States' claim to the Oregon territory dated back to 1792, the British disputed it and the area was under joint jurisdiction from 1816 to 1846. Wisconsin and eastern Minnesota were part of the Northwest Territory organized in 1787. British claims to the area were abandoned in 1814 (Treaty of Ghent). The area shown as part of the 1845 Texas annexation that is not now Texas was ceded to the United States for $10,000,000 by the Compromise of 1850.

Trails West

IN 1834 Congress passed the Indian Intercourse Act designed to resolve relations with the tribes. Among other things, this act provided that an area be set aside for the resettlement in the West of eastern and southern Indians including the Five Civilized Tribes—Cherokees, Creeks, Seminoles, Choctaws and Chickasaws. The territory set aside was part of what is now northeast Oklahoma, and it came to be known as Indian Territory. The program of forcible removal of the Indians actually started following the War of 1812, when some property of the Creek nation was confiscated because some of their

John Ross, the Scots-Indian chief of the Cherokees.

warriors had followed their great chief Tecumseh to the side of the British. This war loot was sold to white settlers four decades later for $11,250,000. In 1817 a delegation of Cherokee chiefs journeyed to Washington. They left with their X's drying on the parchment, suffering monstrous hangovers and with most of their land gone. The liquor bill for getting the chiefs so drunk they didn't know what they were signing was $1,298.50.

The shattering blow fell after Andrew Jackson became President. With the discovery of gold in northern Georgia, whites began to encroach on the treaty lands of the Cherokee—with the connivance of the backwoods President, no friend of the Indians. The tribes struck back with

the white man's weapon: an appeal to the courts. They, finally, under the leadership of John Ross, the Scots-Indian chief of the Cherokees, fought the case up to the Supreme Court, where Chief Justice John Marshall said they were right but the court couldn't help them. Under relentless pressure, the Indians were forced off their ancestral lands.

At last the Five Civilized Tribes were rooted up and transferred to lands in the present state of Oklahoma. For many of the refugees, the trip which the red men knew as the "Trail of Tears" was a death march. Many of the old, the infirm, the sick and the children died on the way. Of 1,000 Choctaw emigrants, Captain Jacob Brown wrote in 1830, "only 88 survived."

For some 40 years they would live in relative peace until once again the white man could covet the lands of the Five Civilized Tribes, dreaming of his plow biting deep into the sweet green grass that bent under the prairie wind.

The Oregon Trail

The mass emigration from the East to the Promised Land of Oregon's beautiful Willamette Valley has no precedent in American history, perhaps none in the world. The Promise started with Captain Gray and his reports on the discovery of the Columbia River. It was renewed by Lewis and Clark and reinforced by the accounts of such fur traders and trading companies as John Jacob Astor, the Northwest Company, the Hudson's Bay Company, Frémont and others.

In the 1830's, when some of the older employees of the Hudson's Bay Company, especially the French trappers and bateauxmen, began to talk of retirement, the company urged them to settle in the Willamette Valley.

A tall, young minister, Reverend Jason Lee, who had established a small mission in this valley, helped touch off the great emigration. In an attempt to raise funds for the mission, he had embarked on a lecture tour in the East. Lee's magnetic descriptions of the valley excited audiences wherever he went. It seemed all America was repeating the stories told by the Reverend.

There were many others, like the pioneer Jesse Applegate, who helped to spur on the great emigration. At first, small groups started out, but the real movement came with the development of the "emigrant train," a large, organized self-sufficient party of many families, perhaps hundreds, each skilled at a trade or profession. Almost all went by wagon, oxen-drawn, starting from Missouri. The jumping-off places were chiefly Independence and Kansas

City (then Westport Landing), and sometimes Omaha.

As many noted in their diaries and memoirs, Independence teemed with life. On the dusty streets the emigrants stared at the swarthy-faced Spanish traders with large black hats, or the mountain men, whose fringed buckskin jackets rustled softly as they walked toe in. There were also impeccably dressed gamblers, drunken bucks and snarling Indian dogs. One thing they all recalled: above the noise of the creaking wagons, the whooping and shouting and the cracking of the whips was the steady, constant clanging of hammers on anvils from the numerous blacksmith shops where the wagons were being readied or repaired.

When the trappers or the company men brought in word that the plains were again green, the wagon-master, always a man of much experience with the tribes and the trails, gathered his captains and gave the word to pull out.

The next day at sun-up the wagon-master would stand in his stirrups, wave his hat and point west. The long line of canvas-covered prairie-schooners would begin covering the first 50 miles to the Platte, then along that boiling river to the North Platte and the Sweetwater, across the Rocky Mountains at South Pass to the Bear and Snake, then through the Blue Mountains to the Columbia and down that river to the valley and the Pacific.

At the Raft River some trains headed south on the California trail, but most kept on the Snake to the Oregon border 300 miles away. In this journey that spanned half a continent the average wagon traveled two miles an hour, 12 miles a day.

When they reached the Platte the emigrants were in buffalo and hostile Indian country. There they found also that firewood was buffalo dung—"buffalo chips" or "prairie coal." One woman proudly noted in her journal that her son could fill a basket in one minute. Once on the Great Plains the pioneers saw herds of buffalo and were

Wagon trains at Independence Rock. The Sweetwater River is seen at the left.
From a painting by W. H. Jackson.

awed. Armies of the big shaggy-haired beasts seemed to come out of the ground, making the earth tremble as they moved across the land, the pall of dust rising to the empty sky. One man who had waited for hours for a herd to pass wrote in wonderment: "They are still here."

Oxen were chosen by the first pioneers for three reasons: they were more durable; they could be used for plowing in Oregon, and they tasted better than horseflesh. A team usually cost fifty dollars. An average wagonload consisted of 150 pounds of flour, 15 of coffee, 25 of sugar and baking soda. Matches were kept in a corked bottle. Then there were pots, pans and the inevitable gutta-percha bucket for water. Percha was a paintlike waterproofing substance. The head of the house also carefully selected spare wagon parts, along with a Colt, rifle and ammunition.

It was in 1842 that the first emigrant train (led by Elijah White) reached Oregon, but in 1841 an earlier train did reach California. Thereafter, for many years the "trains" rolled in constantly.

The many journals, diaries and letters left by these "men of destiny" paint a vivid picture of the almost unbelievable human tenacity, ingenuity and raw courage that enabled the thousands of men, women and children to cross 2,000 miles of an alien, hostile land. They stopped only for birth and death. They battled sandstorms, snow, sleet, freezing cold and boiling heat; cholera left a trail of graves from Missouri to Oregon. So did the arrows of the Sioux. But the emigrants did not turn back. They were pointed West and nothing could turn their heads.

The Santa Fe Trail

There was another old route west, starting from Missouri at Independence or Westport Landing. That was the Santa Fe trail, used since the 1820's, but almost exclusively by traders. It ended, more or less, at Santa Fe.

In addition to the overland routes there was a waterway which the more wealthy used. Clipper ships sailed from New York around South America to Hawaii, then to

Francis Parkman. *Photo by Benjamin Kimball.*

The trails west.

Crossing the Platte.

[46]

San Francisco and on to Fort Vancouver. Fare: $500. During the gold strike of '49 miners sailed from New York to the Isthmus of Panama, crossed the mountains with a pack horse or mules and sailed on up the Pacific Coast to San Francisco. The time of the grueling trip was about six weeks.

The Pathfinder—John Charles Frémont

In the 1840's the foremost individual stimulator of "Oregon fever" was the popular idol John Charles Frémont, who came to be known as "The Pathfinder." In 1842 he explored the Trail as far as South Pass, Wyoming. He also ascended the summit of the second peak of the Wind River Mountains, today known as Frémont's Peak. In 1843 he was sent to complete the survey of the trail to the mouth of the Columbia River. His guide on this trip

General John C. Frémont. *Photo by Mathew Brady.*

was Kit Carson, one of the West's greatest scouts. They traveled south and east by way of Klamath Lake to Northwestern Nevada, continuing to the Truckee and Carson Rivers. The reports Frémont sent back captured the imagination of the country and stirred the wanderlust to fever pitch. Emigration boomed.

In the spring of 1845 Frémont led his third expedition to the Great Basin and Pacific Coast. But this time he carried secret orders. He and a party of 62 men traversed the Great Basin down to the valley of the Humboldt. In January, 1846, he reached California.

When news of the outbreak of the Mexican War reached California, Frémont carried out his secret orders and all of the northern region of California fell into American hands. In January, 1847, Frémont and Commodore Stockton had completed the conquest of California, but the young Pathfinder found himself between two opposing army factions and resigned after a bitter court-martial.

Following his resignation, Frémont set out on a fourth expedition to find passes for the Pacific Railroad. This time, instead of the reliable Carson, he had the erratic Bill Williams as a guide. The party was caught in a blizzard and 11 men died. Frémont's party finally wound up in California, to be greeted by the news of the great gold strike at Sutter's Mill.

On to Zion

In between the first great emigration to Oregon and the mad rush to the gold fields of California there was another notable movement of Americans across the wilderness of the West. This time it wasn't the yellow metal or the yearning for new lands that lured them on. It was the more important desire for religious freedom.

The men, women and children who would take part in the march to a new Zion were Mormons, members of Joseph Smith's Church of Jesus Christ of Latter Day Saints. The movement west actually grew out of the fron-

This photograph of an Indian village may possibly be one taken by S. N. Carvalho. The plate which was found in the Mathew Brady daguerreotype collection, Library of Congress, may have been copied by wet-plate by Brady.

October 5 Hot Springs The morning was calm and clear and at sunrise the thermometer was at 32. The road to-day was occasionally extremely rocky with hard volcanic fragments, and our travelling very slow. In about nine miles the road brought us to a group of smoking hot springs with a temperature of 164. There were a few helianthi in bloom with some other low plants and the place was green round about, the ground warm and the air pleasant with a summer atmosphere that was very grateful in a day of high and cold searching wind. The rocks were covered with a white and red incrustation and the water has on the tongue the same unpleasant effect as that of the Basin spring on Bear river. They form several branches and bubble up with force enough to raise the small pebbles several inches.

Fremont's Report

October 1 Fishing Falls Our encampment was about one mile below the Fishing Falls, a series of cataracts with very inclined planes which are probably so named because they form a barrier to the ascent of the salmon and the great fisheries from which the inhabitants of this barren region almost entirely derive a subsistence commence at this place. These appeared to be unusually gay savages, fond of loud laughter and in their apparent good nature and merry character struck me as being entirely different from the Indians we had been accustomed to see. From several who visited our camp in the evening we purchased in exchange for goods dried salmon. At this season they are not very fat, but we were easily pleased. The Indians made us comprehend that when the salmon came up the river in the spring they are so abundant that they merely throw in their spears at random, certain of transpiercing out a fish.

Fremont's Report

1. The figures on the road indicate the distance in miles from Westport Landing
2. This is the most trying section for the traveller on the whole route. Water, though good and plenty is difficult to reach, as the river is hemmed in by high and vertical rocks and many of the by streams are without water in the dry season. Grass is only to be found at the marked camping places and barely sufficient to keep strong animals from starvation. Game there is none. The road is very rough by volcanic rocks, detrimental to wagons and carts. In sage bushes consists the only Fuel. Lucky, that by all these hardships the traveller is not harassed by the Indians, who are peaceable thieves.
3. West of the Fishing Falls salmon, fresh and dried, can be obtained from the Indians

Section six of a seven-section topographical map based on the field notes and journal kept by Frémont, compiled by Charles Preuss, 1846. The notes for October 1—Fishing Falls—and for October 5—Hot Springs—have been enlarged.

TOPOGRAPHICAL MAP
OF THE
OAD FROM MISSOURI TO OREGON

NG AT THE MOUTH OF THE KANSAS IN THE MISSOURI RIVER
AT THE MOUTH OF THE WALLAH WALLAH IN THE COLUMBIA

In VII Sections

SECTION VI

From the field notes and journal of Capt. J. C. Fremont

d from sketches and notes made on the ground by his assistant Charles Preuss

Compiled by Charles Preuss. 1846

By order of the Senate of the United States

SCALE 10 MILES TO THE INCH

Three Buttes

Latitude 43°   Longitude 113°

FORT HALL

American Falls

LEWIS FORK OF THE COLUMBIA

Sept. 24 American Falls. The river here enters between low mural banks, which consists of a fine vesicular trap rock, the intermediate portions being compact and crystalline. Gradually becoming higher in its downward course, these banks of scoriated volcanic rock form with occasional interruptions, its characteristic feature along the whole line to the Dalles of the Lower Columbia, resembling a chasm which had been rent through the country and which the river had afterwards taken for its bed. The immediate valley of the river is a high plain, covered with black rocks and artemisia. In the south is a bordering range of mountains which, although not very high, are broken and covered with snow, and at a great distance to the north is seen the high snowy line of the Salmon river mountains in front of which stand out prominently in the plain the three isolated rugged looking little mountains commonly known as the Three Buttes. Between the river and the distant Salmon river range, the plain is represented by Mr Fitzpatrick as so entirely broken up and rent into chasms as to be impracticable for a man even on foot. In the sketch annexed the point of view is low but it conveys very well some idea of the open character of the country, with the buttes rising out above the general line. By measurement the river above is 870 feet wide immediately contracted at the fall in the form of a lock by jutting piles of scoriaceous basalt over which the foaming river must present a grand appearance at the time of high water.

Fremont's Report

Sept. 30. Subterranean River. Immediately opposite to us a subterranean river bursts out directly from the face of the comparison, and falls in white foam to the river below. In the views annexed you will find with a sketch of this remarkable fall, a representation of the natural precipices which enclose the main river, and which form its characteristic feature along a great portion of its course. A melancholy and strange looking country, one of fracture and violence and fire.

Fremont's Report

October 6. Change in the river of the country. The morning warm, the thermometer 48° at sunrise, the sky entirely clouded. After travelling about three miles over an extremely rocky road, the volcanic fragments began to disappear, and entering among the hills at the point of the mountain we found ourselves suddenly in a granite country. Here the character of the vegetation was very much changed, the artemisia disappeared almost entirely, showing only at intervals towards the close of the day and was replaced by Purshia tridentata with flowering shrubs, and small fields of dieteria divaricata which gave bloom and gayety to the hills. These were every where covered with a fresh and green, short grass like that of the early spring. This is the fall or second growth, the dried grass having been burnt off in the the Indians, and wherever the fire has passed, the bright green color is universal. The soil among the hills is altogether different from that of the river plain, being in many places black, in others sandy and gravelly but of a firm and good character appearing to result from the decomposition of the granite rocks which is proceeding rapidly.

Fremont's Report

EOROLOGICAL OBSERVATIONS

Thermometer	Altitude	Remarks
31 Fahr.	4779 Feet	Wind S begins to rain
42		do do partly clear partly rainy clouds
32		calm snow falling thick
45		nearly calm clear over head
35		calm overcast
55		breeze from S clear
56		gale from S clear
55		almost overcast
40		Wind SW rain last night
44	4232 Feet	sharp wind NW clouds and clear
40		light breeze to S rainy clouds
48		gale to SW thunder in E clear and clouds
45		slight breeze to S rain clouds
35		cold wind to NE
36		wind SW
50		wind SW
28		air to SE light clouds
65		wind squalls to N clear
55	3473 Feet	wind N clear
74		calm and clear
48		calm and clear
70		do do
42		air from SE clear and light clouds
60		do do
57		calm and clear
52		gale to NW cloudy
47		calm and clear
46		wind NW overcast
51	3226 Feet	do do do rainy appearance
45		do do clear
57		do do do
58		calm and clear
62		do cloudy horizon
56		calm and clear
68		do scattered clouds
55		calm and clear
62	1392 Feet	do do

Elevation above the Gulf of Mexico

Joseph Smith.

Brigham Young.

tier's antagonism toward the Mormons, which finally exploded when a mob of 200 men with blackened faces stormed the jailhouse at Carthage, Illinois, to murder Smith and his brother. Brigham Young, who inherited the Prophet's mantle, decided that he and his people must find a new Zion.

In March, 1846, Brigham Young and a band of Mormons, after spending a terrifying winter at Nauvoo, Illinois, began moving toward they "knew not what." Food was scarce and the roads were almost impassable. Despite great hardships, the Mormons displayed a powerful sense of organization. Teams were formed to build and repair wagons, and to make chairs, stools, beds, tubs and barrels for sale on the road. Others split logs, and still others roamed the countryside to "invite" rich Gentiles to contribute to the needs of the Saints. Because of the wet weather which delayed them for weeks a main camp was set up in a day at a point called Mount Pisgah. When the weather broke, the train set out with the Saints "coming in all directions from hills and dales and groves and prairies with their wagons, flocks and herds by the thousands. It looked like the movement of a nation."

When they reached the banks of the Missouri, near the present city of Council Bluffs, they erected a ferry and began moving their people across. So great was the number that the task was not completed until late fall, when a winter camp was established across the river.

In the meantime other groups were preparing a more sturdy winter camp about six miles north of Omaha, Nebraska. Called "Winter Quarters," it spread across some 800 acres. Within a short time there were 558 log cabins and 83 sod buildings.

A Mormon emigrant train.

In addition to the homes and workshops, a grist mill and a large tabernacle were erected. Not only men but women worked from dawn to dusk. However, the regular diet of salt pork, corn bread and no vegetables brought on scurvy and finally death. By mid-year one in ten was seriously ill. But death, suffering and hardship were no strangers to the Mormons and could not break their spirit.

Finally spring came and Young and a select corps of men moved out to explore the land for their new Zion. This body, known officially as the Pioneers, gathered on the Elkhorn River and left on April 14, 1847. An advance group went ahead to scout out the land. Every ten miles guideboards were erected. Sometimes messages were put inside or on a buffalo skull, stuck in a split board or a buckskin pouch.

The train was again delayed when mountain fever laid low most of the Pioneers. Brigham Young ordered those who were still physically able to move on while he remained with the sick. The advance scouts found the valley now known as Salt Lake City Valley and on July 24, Brigham Young arrived. After silently gazing over the valley, he said, "This is the place." A week later houses were springing up and 50 acres were under the plow.

In August word was sent back to Winter Quarters, or "Misery Bottom," as the veterans called it, and a second party, 1,500 Saints in 560 wagons, left the following June.

For the next 20 years emigrants left from some point or other on the Mississippi or Missouri to cross the plains to Salt Lake City Valley.

In the year 1849 a plan was put into effect which brought many Mormons to America and across the plains to Salt Lake. The tide of emigration was so strong that Young introduced hand carts, the strangest method of transportation in the history of the West.

The carts were two-wheeled vehicles about the width of a wagon with a four-foot-long box balanced on the axle with a handle and long cross-bar to pull and balance the cart. The carts could hold a load of 500 pounds, although the only iron part was the wheel rim. During four

Main Street, Salt Lake City, probably in the 1850's.

years more than 3,000 Saints pulled these carts across the 1,031-mile journey.

In 1856 the largest hand-cart expedition, known as the Hand Cart Brigade, started out. Unfortunately, the lack of vehicles had delayed the departure until late in the season.

For many, the trip was a grim one. One man recalled how his infant sister died and a tiny grave was dug. Services were quickly over and the weary, heartsick mother stepped back into her position at the cross-bar. In South Pass more than 15 Saints died. In another company starvation and the bitter cold claimed one-sixth of its numbers.

Yet, on the whole not all the hand-cart expeditions were disasters. Those that started in a sensible time of the year walked and dragged their carts the 1,400 miles from Iowa City in nine weeks and had fewer deaths than the wagon trains. Some days they made as much as 30 miles, twice the mileage of the oxen teams.

Mormon hand-cart train.

[51]

Gold Strike

ON the morning of January 24, 1848, as James W. Marshall set to work to widen the mill race of the mill he and John Sutter had built on the south fork of the American River in California, he saw a glittering stone in the water, reached down and picked it out. For more than ten years he had heard the Mexicans talk of finding gold in the waterways.

Now as he examined the stone he felt mounting excitement. He hurried back to the camp and put the nugget into boiling lye. Late that afternoon when he retrieved it, the dull gold look had not been tarnished. Almost surely his stone was a nugget of gold.

That night he brought the nugget to Sutter and they made further tests. It was undeniably gold.

Before they parted both men had agreed to keep the news secret. Sutter had good reason; he knew what would happen to the pleasant frontier barony he had established on a 43,000-acre land grant from Mexico's Governor Alvarado. He had built a mill, factory, blacksmith shop and even a distillery. He had Hawaiians and Indians tilling the fertile soil; he even had schooners moving up and down the Sacramento River. There were few trappers or travelers who didn't know of New Helvetia, as he called his empire. Lately Americans from the States had leased some of his land. It was not only profitable but homey. But if word of the gold strike got out, Sutter knew, a human avalanche would pour into his peaceful domain.

The news did leak out. In June, 1848, it was being discussed freely in New York and in Honolulu. One of the biggest gold rushes of world history was on.

Down in drowsy Monterey, the capital, Walter Colton, the *alcade*, or town magistrate, wrote in wonderment: "The blacksmith dropped his hammer, the carpenter his plane, the mason his trowel, the baker his loaf ... some came on crutches ... one man was carried in a litter ...!"

The editor of the New York *Herald* remarked, "Even the bachelors are departing their comforts ..."

Commodore Jones, commanding the U. S. Naval Squadron in Monterey harbor, reported that shiploads of men had deserted for the gold fields, "even men who are owed nine months' pay."

In the year 1852 the fields actually produced $200,000,-

William T. Sherman's map of the gold regions, 1848.

000 in gold. That same month John Sutter was writing this sad entry in his diary: "Hosts are arriving by water and land for the mountains." These same "hosts" would swarm over his peaceful land like a horde of locusts, finally driving him into bankruptcy.

How many people were lured to the fields is anybody's estimate. But the census figures show that in 1848, prior to the strike, there were 20,000 residents in California. By 1852 this had grown to 225,000. However, the population was so transient it is almost impossible to arrive at an exact figure.

The miners traveled the same trail—up to a point—that the settlers took to the Oregon Trail. They also could use the water route to San Francisco or the overland trail or Sante Fe Trail via the Isthmus of Darien (Panama) which could be crossed in six weeks by mule train.

Countless thousands died on the way; almost as many graves marked the southern arm of the Oregon Trail as marked the one which led to the Willamette Valley. At sea many clippers sank off the Horn. The terrible jungle heat of Darien also claimed many lives.

And when the gold-seeker did reach the fields he found that the tales he had heard were exaggerated; one did not just reach in a stream and pick up nuggets as big as a hen's egg. To get gold a man sometimes had to stand eight hours a day in waist-high icy water and pan perhaps only enough gold to keep him alive. And if he made a modest pile he would probably have to spend it all on food; $6 for half a dozen eggs, $100 for a small barrel of flour. . . .

A few weeks after Marshall's discovery, the joint Army and Navy commanders at Monterey agreed that Washington should be notified immediately of the great strike. It was decided that two picked men should leave—one

Gold mining in California. *A daguerreotype made about 1854 by R. H. Vance.*

was to take an overland route, the other, a water one.

The Army selected a Lieutenant Loeser; the Navy, Lieutenant Edward Fitzgerald Beale, one of the unsung heroes of the American West. Beale was summoned, given a canvas bag with some nuggets and dust, and told to start for Washington and not to come back if he arrived and found his Army counterpart waiting for him.

Oddly enough, Lieutenant Loeser was ordered to travel by water; Beale, the sailor, was to ride across the continent on horseback. Beale was the first to arrive in Washington, after completing a virtually impossible trip across Mexico to Vera Cruz, thence to Mobile, and from Mobile to Washington by stage. He had encountered every kind of hazard, peril and attack from outlaws, storms, floods. News of his journey had preceded him and he was given "ovations" wherever he stopped. In Washington he was introduced to the members of the Senate, who gave him a rousing reception.

While Beale gave the Senate the golden word, thousands of "companies" were being organized across the nation. For example, the New York *Tribune* ran a column of advertisements under "California."

> "Via Panama. A company of a hundred men is now forming to proceed to the Gold Regions and will forthwith dispatch an agent to charter a vessel to the Pacific side to convey the company to San Francisco. The Company will leave New York by the 10th of February. For particulars inquire at 121 Water Street, upstairs."

The New Year turned and Senator Jefferson Davis publicly endorsed the southwestern route starting from Fort Smith, Arkansas, as the best one to the gold fields. Posters soon appeared—all put out by the enterprising merchants of Fort Smith—guaranteeing that a company could reach Monterey 60 days after leaving Fort Smith.

Lieutenant Edward Fitzgerald Beale, disguised as a Mexican, carrying the dispatches to Washington which reported the California gold strike.

The Sardine claim. *Photo by R. H. Vance.*

Certificate of John S. Ellis, 1850.

The wagons soon creaked into Fort Smith, loaded up with supplies, then moved out along the road leading to the Choctaw and Shawnee villages and down the South Canadian. It was just beyond Shady Creek and the abandoned Comanche camp that they encountered El Llano Estacado—the great "Staked Plains." From then on the journey was monotonous until the wagons reached La Cuesta Valley. Here the old Santa Fe Trail, coming down from Bent's Fort, crossed the Arkansas route. It wasn't long before they saw the spires of Santa Fe and the first (820-mile) leg of the trip was over. There was still a great distance to go before they reached the gold fields.

At Guadaloupe Pass, the gold-seekers found that, like the emigrants far to the north, they had to lower their wagons by ropes. Then water had to be hoarded for the dry trip to the valley of Santa Cruz. Tucson was the first sign of civilization and the breathing-place before the companies set out for the Gila Valley. From there some of the foolhardy tried to take a short cut known as the "Jornada de las Estrellas," only to die in the frightful heat which shrank the wooden wagon parts and forced the men and women to make the trip on foot. Few made it.

For those trapped in the desert there was little hope. The few wells were soon fouled by the many wagons and dead cattle. The temperature was usually 110° and the air was stagnant and foul with the stench of decaying animal flesh.

But despite the hardships and the tales of terrible suffering that were sent back to New York, the gold fever continued to mount. When new strikes were reported the companies increased in size. Now there was another great factor to make the country face west, an even stronger and more compelling lure than the Promised Land of Oregon had been. Now almost all the West, not only the Northwest, was opening up.

Those who reached San Francisco found it a bedlam of shacks, tents, a few buildings, rotting ships and signs in Chinese, French, English, Spanish and German. Dust swirled along the unpaved streets. Violence and death were commonplace. The gold-seekers of 1849 and 1850 found the town was bossed by a tough band of thieves and killers from New York's Bowery known as the "Hounds." They hid out in the dingy saloons and clapboard houses along Pacific Street called "Sydney Town." With the gold dust rolling in, the gambling centers boomed day and night.

By 1850 great changes were taking place in the fields. Wooden flumes which carry water from mountain streams to the sluices were being constructed. River-bed mining, in which whole streams were diverted from their natural course so the bed could be examined for gold, was being introduced. The changes were costly, and much capital was needed for the operations. Now it was the day of gold companies, and the individual with the pan and shovel was rapidly disappearing.

There were still the wild alarums and excursions. It got so that anybody could start a rumor that would result in whole camps, towns or even cities being completely evacuated. Many were the wildest of tales, but the gold-hungry miners never bothered to evaluate them.

In addition to hoaxes, fire and flood added to the hardships of the prospectors. In March, 1852, Sacramento was flooded, and on November 2 and 3 of that same year the city was also gutted by a fire which resulted in the loss of $10,000,000.

San Francisco was almost wiped out in a similar holocaust. When rumors blamed the gangs in Sydney Town, the *Alta Californian* urged the formation of a Vigilante Committee. A small army of the city's leading merchants and professional men agreed that the newspaper was right and at a meeting formed a large group. Under the direction of editor Edward Gilbert, companies of armed men patrolled the streets, staged raids and cleaned up the city.

By 1855, however, much of the lawlessness and wild living had vanished, although there were still bear fights and dog fights and the gambling houses still operated in San Francisco. There were now dozens of churches and schools. There were even wooden sidewalks and Sarony, Archer and Company were distributing lithographs in full color to advertise their fine dressing cases, canes and gents' hats.

Sacramento Street, 1856.

Fort Vigilance, 1856.

Montgomery Block, 1856.

Battery Street, 1856.

Communications

Uncle Sam's Camels

IN the 1850's a unique attempt to provide for. transportation needs in the plains country was made by the Camel Brigade, one of the most fascinating episodes in western frontier history.

In 1853, when Jefferson Davis became President Pierce's Secretary of War, one of his first acts was to draw up plans for a United States Army Camel Corps. He pointed out that the "dromedary" would be excellent for "transportation with troops moving rapidly across the country . . . for military expresses . . . for reconnaissance . . ." The camel had many obvious advantages: the ability to thrive in arid lands, great strength—200 camels could do the work of 1,000 horses and a camel could carry a 1,000-pound load—superior durability under all conditions.

Congress failed to act, but the idea of such a corps caught the public imagination. In 1855 Congress made an appropriation for the purchase of camels for military service. Edward Fitzgerald Beale, who had brought Congress the news of the California gold strike, was chosen as the commander of the Camel Corps. Naval Lieutenant —later Admiral—David Dixon Porter and Major Wayne, an early champion of the Camel Corps, were in charge of the Purchasing Commission. Porter was given command of the transport ship, the *Supply,* Wayne the business end of the expedition.

In July the pair sailed to Tunis, where they bought a camel for experimental purposes. When the Bey of Tunis heard of their mission he presented them with two more. The three were loaded on the *Supply,* with Wayne refusing to split hairs on what is a camel and what is a dromedary. (Actually the two-hump animal is a camel, the one-hump kind a dromedary.)

"I shall distinguish them from each other by the qualification of the countries from which they are said to have originally come—Bactria and Arabia. I shall call the two-humped camel the Bactrian Camel and the one-humped camel the Arabian Camel," wrote Wayne.

The expedition continued via Malta, Smyrna, Salonika and Constantinople to Balaklava, then the focal point in the Crimean War, to find out how the British liked their camel corps. Along the front they found that a corps of camels could make as much as 70 miles in 12 hours. In addition, the animals could be made to kneel in a square, "forming, as it were, a base of operation from which others operated as infantry. . . ."

More than a thousand men crouching behind this wall

A rare daguerreotype of a camel at Drum Barracks, 1865.

of animals could effectively hold off an attacking force, Wayne stated. The next stop for the *Supply* was Alexandria, which they reached in December, 1855.

Granted a special permit, the officers bought nine animals. In January, 1856, they sailed for Smyrna, where they purchased another shipment.

On the morning of February 15, 1855, with a fresh breeze filling her sails, the *Supply* set sail for America with its strange cargo of 39 camels.

After a terrible journey of three months the *Supply* limped into Indianola, Texas, a small port 120 miles south of Galveston, on May 14, 1856. Wayne and Porter had done their job well—only one camel had died, while two had been born.

While Wayne proceeded to San Antonio, Porter was ordered by Washington to return at once to Asia Minor for a second load of camels. Wayne's brief trip, at least in part, supported the theory that the camel could be used successfully on the arid frontier. After a journey of two weeks in steaming heat the camels were as fresh as when they had started.

A permanent camp called Camp Verde was established at Green Valley, sixty miles northwest of San Antonio, but before the Camel Corps really could be absorbed into the service, the administration changed. President Buchanan's Secretary of War, John B. Floyd, ordered a military reconnaissance made of a wagon road from Fort Defiance to the Thirty-Fifth Parallel on the Colorado River. The purpose of the expedition, Floyd announced, was not only to find a new road to California, but also to test the fitness of the camel as a beast of burden in the southwestern plains.

Beale set out upon the 4,000-mile round-trip journey in May, 1857, leading a strange and unusual caravan, which included 25 camels. During the journey, lasting some nine months, the camels were subjected to every kind of test and experience. They survived nobly and the expedition was a success. After receiving Beale's report, Secretary Floyd announced in 1858: "The entire adaptation of camels to military operations on the plains may now be taken as demonstrated."

Floyd tried to get Congress to buy more camels but failed. The Civil War then administered a death-blow to this unique experiment. After various attempts to use the camels—to transfer freight and for other purposes—the Army finally disposed of them at public auction.

Stages, the Pony Express and the Singing Wire

Speedy communication came to the western plains, suddenly and dramatically. On September 15, 1858, John Butterfield, who had made such a success with his stage-coach line in Utica, New York, established his famous Butterfield Overland Stagecoach line, and a letter could now be delivered across 2,800 miles of wilderness and through hostile country for a dollar.

In his initial trip he used 100 coaches, 2,000 horses, 500 mules and 750 men, including 150 drivers. Before he was finished in 1861, when the government withdrew the line because of the outbreak of the Civil War, Butterfield had buried 111 Americans and 56 Mexicans, to deliver that mail.

Not only did the Apaches plunder and raid the stations strewn across the plains and deserts, but road agents—refugees from the California Vigilante Committee—held up the coaches and near Tucson "did a thriving business." Yet it is remarkable to consider that despite the enemies,

red and white, and the swollen rivers, sandstorms, blizzards and other torments of nature, it is on record that the stage was late only three times.

In Tucson, when the high, clear notes of the driver's horn and then the thunder of the galloping hoofs of the teams were heard, "we always consulted our watches; a man could set his timepiece by the Butterfield Line..."

In 1860 the Pony Express cut the traveling time to nine days, and before this romantic chapter in our West had ended, plans were being made to extend a telegraph line across the vast plains and mountains. In 1860 Congress passed a law extending the "electric telegraph," to link the Atlantic coast with the Pacific. Bids were taken with the proviso that the line had to be linked by July 31, 1862. Another stipulation was that a ten-word message between Brownsville, Nebraska, and San Francisco should not cost more than three dollars.

Hiram Sibley of New York, president of Western Union, won the bid and dispatched his general manager, J. H. Wade, to California by steamer via the Isthmus of Darien. He also sent Edward Creighton to survey a route to California.

On November 18, 1860, Creighton left Omaha by stage and soon arrived in Salt Lake City, where he interested Brigham Young in the project. He then rode a mule to California, making the route as he went along. Meanwhile, Wade had forced the smaller California telegraph companies to consolidate with the California State Telegraph Company to establish the one company, the Overland Telegraph Company.

Creighton was now handed the task of building the line. When he started, the western line had already been extended to within 400 miles of Salt Lake City. He set his first pole in July at Julesburg, Colorado. Creighton did not spare expense in equipping his company. He had 75 strong

John Butterfield.

From the New York *Herald's* account of the Overland Mail route, November 19, 1858.

Hiram Sibley.

wagons, a small tent city, cooking stoves and the best cooks. A large herd of milk cows was driven ahead of each day's route. And the food, as Creighton boasted, "was the best that could be conveyed across the plains and the mountains." Hundreds of oxen and mules were used to bring the materials up the line. Scores of wagons carried up to 4,500 pounds of wire. One of Creighton's obstacles was the vast stretch of treeless plains. Sometimes poles had to be carried 240 miles.

At first the Indians did not bother the lines. There are numerous legends as to why, but Henry M. Porter, who was part of Creighton's team, told in his autobiography that once the Sioux burned down some poles 12 miles west of Fort Kearney. A telegrapher from an "outer" station sent out word to the fort, and the cavalry rode up before the Indians left the spot. From that incident— and other similar ones—the Plains tribes came to believe there was something supernatural about the "Singing Wire."

During the Civil War, ranchmen were hired to keep testing the wires which were cut by Confederate agents trying to stir up the tribes. The line was of extreme importance when the Civil War broke out and during the Indian Wars. There is no doubt that without the telegraph, conquering the West would have taken many more years.

A Pony Express rider exchanges greetings with a crew putting up telegraph poles while Indian warriors watch. *From a painting by W. H. Jackson.*

Slavery and the Civil War in the West

THE great political contest between the free-state and slave-state forces had its impact on the developing West, and was a delaying factor in the formal organization of territories and states. Texas applied for admission to the Union in 1836 but did not gain acceptance until December, 1845, chiefly because of the slavery issue and the threatened disturbance of the delicate balance between free and slave states. Most notable was the case of "Bleeding Kansas."

The Kansas-Nebraska Act in 1854 established the territories of Kansas and Nebraska and provided that the popular vote of the citizens of each territory would decide whether it should be "free" or "slave." The sentiment in Nebraska was clearly "free," but Kansas became the scene of a bloody contest between pro-slavery and anti-slavery fighters. It was a time of bitterness and terror, demonstrating that the enmity and hatred had gone too far and that only the force of arms—actual war—could resolve the issue. Kansas was established as a free state early in 1861, not many weeks before the Civil War broke out.

The white man's Civil War was a godsend to the Plains tribes. The Army posts were stripped or abandoned or else became stepchildren of the War Department, places for the convalescent, the old and the low-grade, raw recruit from the East. These green troops were easily terrified and made to retreat by the sight of a thousand howling, painted Indians beating drums, whirling rattles or screeching their wild cries. In the end the situation became so bad that Rebel prisoners—"galvanized Yankees," as their fellows contemptuously called them—were induced to join the Union Army to fight the Indians.

The newspapers of the period gave a vivid picture of conditions along the frontier after Lincoln called his countrymen to arms. On August 10, 1861, the *Arizonian* reported that a large band of Apaches, possibly more than a hundred bucks, attacked the town of Tubac, riding boldly into the streets to drive off the town's stock and killing anyone they could find on the streets.

The writer for the *Arizonian* then went on: "We are hemmed in on all sides by the unrelenting Apache... since the withdrawal of the Overland Mail and the garrison troops the chances against life have reached the maximum height. Within but six months nine-tenths of the whole male population have been killed off, and every ranch, farm and mine in the country have been abandoned in consequence...."

But if the Apaches were raiding it was not without cause. Mangas Colorados, the great Apache chief, had been murdered "while escaping arrest." Cochise, straight and strong as an arrow shaft, took his place. He was savage in his retaliation.

In 1861 he was accused of kidnapping a small white boy, Mickey Free, who would play a minor role in the later Apache war. When he came into council with Lieutenant George Bascom of the Seventh Cavalry at the soldiers' camp near Apache Pass, the soldiers tried to arrest him. Cochise cut his way free, but his three companions were arrested.

Cochise captured several white settlers as hostages but the exchange never came off. The Apaches killed the helpless men. Within a few hours after their butchered bodies were found the three Apaches were stiffening in the evening wind.

Cochise was relentless. He seemed to specialize in the most hideous tortures. Prisoners were planted in sand

Left, Cochise's wife. *Photo probably by Camillus Fly. Right,* Little Crow. *Photo probably by Martin's Gallery.*

Left, Little Crow's son. *Photo by Upton. Right,* Standing Buffalo, Sioux chief in the New Ulm massacre.

Refugees from the New Ulm massacre pause for dinner on the prairie. *Photo taken by one of the party.*

hills and wild honey poured on their heads. The Apaches squatted on their haunches to watch the men die. Others were tied to wagon-wheels and burned. Some were sliced into pieces and still others dragged to death at the end of rope.

In 1862, in peaceful New Ulm County, Minnesota, the Indians struck unexpectedly. It is ironical that in 1861, just the year before, the *Pioneer*, Minnesota's only newspaper, printed in German in New Ulm, pointed out that it was far safer to live on the prairie than under "the guns of the police in the largest city . . . let us enjoy our land." The massacre began on August 18. Before the sun was high in the heavens the population was scattering. Horsemen were quickly spreading the word for all to hurry to Fort Ridgely, a few miles from New Ulm, because "the Indians are killing everyone." Many were killed on the way to the fort, but those who did reach that haven defended the besieged post against Little Crow and his warriors for nine frightful days. The odds were all against the defenders, but help came on the 27th.

A First-hand Report of the New Ulm Massacre

BY MINNIE BOLSCH

My parents, Mr. and Mrs. Werner Bolsch, were among the early settlers of Renville County, living three miles from Fort Ridgely on the main road to the Lower Sioux agency nine miles away. We were accustomed to seeing the Indians daily, and no one seemed afraid of them. They were friendly and not a bit backward about coming into our home. Often they gave us game or fish as appreciation for the food and clothing that Mother gave them.

During the months of June and July, 1862, great uneasiness was noticed among the Indian men. Sometimes they were seen in war paint and minus clothing, performing war dances . . . people wondered what it meant. Rumors were that they were dissatisfied with the treatment of the agents, that their annuities were being held back and they were in great need. Moreover their food allotments had been most unsatisfactory; they had been given moldy flour, wormy food and tainted meat.

The Indians spent a great deal of time at the fort watching the soldiers make preparations to leave for the Civil War; they noticed too the 'old men' who were not going. By the middle of August all the regular soldiers had left the fort. On the 16th the Renville Rangers (mostly half-breeds under the Indian agent, Gailbraith) had also gone. On the 17th the departure of Lt. Sheehan and fifty men left the fort virtually unprotected.

Early in the morning of Monday, August 18th, a friend stopped at our home to tell us that we must leave immediately, as the Indians were killing the settlers and burning the houses at the agency. Father left on horseback to inform the neighbors, Mother gathered some clothes for us and, throwing a large feather-bed into the wagon, put us on it and we started for the fort at breakneck speed.

The Sutler's Report

BY MAJOR B. H. RANDALL

All told, there were not more than forty muskets at the fort, the Sharps rifle of J. W. De Camp, two Sharps belonging to the guards for the Indian annuity payment money, a double barrel of Reverend Sweet and two of my double barrels. None of the refugees had a gun.

At dusk on the 18th came the news that twenty-eight of the men who had gone to the agency had been killed. This greatly increased our fears. Refugees were constantly streaming in all day, many wounded and crazed with grief; some had been without food and water.

When evening came, guards were stationed at all the doors with either axe, shovel, club or anything else that could be used as a weapon. The women worked all night making cartridges out of slugs cut by the men for the small number of guns they had been able to give the sentinels.

Twenty old-style Dragoon carbines were found in the magazine and put into condition by Patrick Hefron, who had been for fifteen years a sergeant in the Second Infantry. The women made cartridges for these by cutting up iron rods into slugs. That night Jones sent up rockets as evidence that the fort was still there; they were seen at New Ulm eighteen miles distant.

There was a great fear of fire, for everything was very dry. Buckets of water were placed at one of the four scuttles that led to the barracks roof. It rained the next morning.

On Friday near noon came an attack from three sides. By opening up the hall of the commanding officer's quarters that protected Jones' position on the south, he was able to fire the stable by sending a shell through the hall. Little Crow's charges and orders were distinctly heard but frustrated by the grape and cannister. On the 27th assistance arrived, the first opportunity for real rest since news of the outbreak had been received on the 18th.

General H. H. Sibley. *Photo by J. W. Campbell.*

enclosure. The battle was not long in starting and the air was filled with bullets and arrows as the howling braves rode at breakneck speed in a circle around the wagons.

At the end of the day only one of Captain March's 96 horses was alive. The weary men dragged the carcasses and propped them up against the wagon wheels. The second night a half-breed volunteered to ride to Ridgely on the only surviving animal and try for reinforcements. But he had got only a few yards from the wagon when the horse was riddled with bullets and he ran back. The second day reinforcements under Sibley came up and after a fierce skirmish drove off the Indians. They arrived to find a hundred men dead, scores of wounded and the dead horses. Following Birch Coolie, Sibley was denounced for not coming up sooner, but Governor Ramsey upheld him.

A second major Indian fight took place later that year at Wood Lake, where Sibley, with 1,600 irregulars and a company of the First Minnesota, engaged 2,600 Sioux warriors, the cream of the nation. Here another fierce battle took place before the Indians were defeated. Now winter set in and the tribes withdrew to their winter camps with their hundreds of captives.

Left, Medicine Bottle, who participated in the New Ulm massacre. *Photo by Whitney at Fort Snelling. Right,* Old Bets, a Sioux Squaw who helped the Minnesota captives.

Left, Red Iron, a Sioux chief who remained friendly to the white settlers during the New Ulm massacre. *Right,* Ta-O-Pi (Wounded Man), a friendly Sioux. *Photo by Martin's Gallery.*

That summer Brevet Major General H. H. Sibley took command and drilled his civilian soldiers unmercifully. By mid-August the fort heard that Little Crow had the support of two powerful Sioux chiefs, Red Iron and Standing Buffalo, and that they were joining ranks for an all-out assault on the frontier.

On September 2, 1862, Sibley sent out a burial party from the fort under the command of a young officer, Captain March. He had 20 wagons and 135 men. At Birch Coolie the small detachment met Little Crow's army and began one of the bitterest Indian engagements of the war.

When March's outriders caught sight of Little Crow's warriors he ordered his men to form their wagons in a circle, and the horses and mules were driven into the

For a time it appeared that Little Crow might bring about the torture and death of the hundreds of captives, but Red Iron, at a large war council, said he would kill the first warrior who touched a woman or child. It was apparent to Red Iron that the end was near and perhaps they would have to make terms with Sibley. It could hardly be expected that victorious frontiersmen would have much mercy at the sight of their slaughtered women and children.

During that winter Sibley caught the camp by surprise, freeing all the captives and capturing the leading chiefs and war captains of the Sioux Confederacy. The camp was later named "Camp Release" in honor of the captives.

The Indian prisoners were charged with murder and the trial was held in a large barnlike place. It attracted little notice; the nation's attention was taken up by larger engagements thousands of miles away.

Eighty-five war chiefs were found guilty of murder and sentenced to hang. But Lincoln granted amnesty to all but 35 of them. In a moving scene these chiefs mounted the platform of the gallows, clasping hands and singing their war chants. None, not even an old man, faltered. "White men, we will show you how to die," one called out as the white caps dropped over their faces. Some even helped adjust the noose. A place of honor among the spectators was accorded those white people who had suffered the most losses in the raid. The man who cut the rope releasing the traps was a settler whose wife, sister and three children had been killed and scalped.

That year Little Crow, who had escaped, was killed, but Cut Nose and other war chiefs took up his campaign against the whites. In the spring a large army of Sioux was defeated by Sibley at Little Mound, Dakota. Realizing they had reached the point of no return, the united Sioux engaged Sibley again at Dead Buffalo Lake. This battle lasted all day, and at one point some of the Sioux braves almost succeeded in driving off the little army's horses.

Nature, too, seemed on the side of the Indians. The Army's animals were badly jaded because of the severe drought which had burned up the grass and the troops were burning up with thirst; the water they had found was discovered to be alkaline. Each company, in addition to fighting off the reckless Indian charges, had to dig a well; 60 wells were dug under intense fire in one afternoon.

A few days later at Stony Lake, Dakota, the Sioux made their stand. Sibley this time adopted the British hollow square tactics as the Indians circled the camp. While one kneeling soldier fired, another fired over his head. Reserves forces were kept in the center of the squad.

When the Sioux withdrew, Sibley followed. A running battle took place. The soldiers chased the Sioux across the Mississippi, but animals and men were so exhausted that Sibley called it a day.

In the summer of 1864 the Sioux gathered on the Knife a large army of 1,600 tepees and 12,000 men, women and children. The First Minnesota charged the village. Until late afternoon the Sioux fought off the cavalry charges. But finally they began to withdraw into the Badlands— "Hell with the fires out," as Sibley called it.

On August 4, 1864, an estimated 8,000 Sioux fought a bloody battle in the Badlands against the small makeshift white command. When more than 500 braves and chiefs had been killed by sunset, the war chiefs broke up their bands into separate units. These slipped away under the cover of darkness.

The Sand Creek Massacre

In Colorado Territory, Denver and the smaller settlements had been under Indian attack almost since the first shell had exploded at Fort Sumter. By 1862 more than 50 men, women and children had been killed by the Indians. It was almost suicide to move beyond the city limits. Most of the families were placed in a stout blockade on Blake Street with a few men on guard.

One of Colorado's most noted soldiers in the period was John Milton Chivington, whose military genius and fearlessness had destroyed the Confederate supply base

Execution of the 35 Sioux.

Colonel Samuel H. Tappan.

Black Kettle, (*front row, second from left*) and Cheyenne sub-chiefs.

in the battle of Santa Fe on March 27, 1862, many times called "The Gettysburg of the Southwest."

The base was located four miles west of the summit of Glorieta Pass. In order to reach the camp Chivington had his men make leather ropes, 125 feet long, with which they made the descent along the eastern ridge of Apache Canyon. A hazardous enough feat in daylight, in the darkness it was hair-raising. After the command had reached safety, Chivington led his men in a complete surprise attack. Haystacks, ammunition dumps, food and corn cribs along with more than a hundred mules were destroyed.

As Oriskany was the turning-point for the Battle of Saratoga, this was the pivot on which swung the Confederate defeat. Had the Confederates been successful in securing the gold fields of Colorado, Arizona, California and Nevada it is doubtful if the war would have ended at Appomattox. But bickering marred the Union victory. Colonel Slough, commander of the expedition, resigned and Chivington took his place. He was passed over Lieutenant Colonel Sam Tappan, who would prove to be his bitterest enemy.

In November, 1862, Chivington was successful in getting his command converted into cavalry. With his men now in the saddle, Chivington was constantly fighting the raiding Cheyennes, Arapahos, Kiowas and Sioux.

By 1864 nearly every rancher had been burned out or killed along the South Platte. One valley of hay was completely burned. Freighters refused to make the hazardous trips and Denver was cut off from provisions. In 1863 flour was so scarce it sold for $45 a sack. Conditions became so bad the mail was stopped.

Then in 1864 the emotions of the territory rose to a boiling hatred for the red men when the Hungate family, who lived 30 miles east of Denver, was horribly massacred. Eighty bullet holes were found in the mutilated body of Hungate. His wife and tortured children were found tied together in the well. Governor Evans telegraphed a plea

to Washington for help, but as in every war the frontier was told to look to itself. One or more murdered families could not be counted when whole armies were locked in decisive battles.

With Denver practically helpless, the Indians stepped up their raids. Even large settlements were placed under heavy attack. Finally, in desperation, Evans issued a general order that any citizen of the territory could hunt down the hostiles and kill them. He also received belated permission from the War Department to raise a volunteer battalion for an enlistment period of a hundred days.

The newly recruited command was stationed at Fort Weld under Chivington. In the summer of 1864 Black Kettle, chief of the Cheyennes, proposed an exchange of prisoners at Fort Lyons, Colorado Territory. The council was held at Fort Weld rather than Fort Lyons in the fall of that year. Black Kettle, Bull Bear, Chief of the Dog Soldiers, and Neva, another field chief, attended. The council was a failure and the chiefs left in a sullen mood. However, Black Kettle insisted he wanted peace and led his people to a camp on the Big South Bend of Sand Creek, some 30 miles northeast of Fort Lyons. To prove he was peaceful he raised an American flag over it.

While the meeting was going on, the Plains tribes were launching attacks of such strength against the western Army garrisons that General Curtis at Leavenworth sent an urgent message to Chivington suggesting counter-offensives..."I want no peace till the Indians suffer more," he wrote.

Chivington was placed in command of an expedition to Sand Creek which was supposed to open up communications cut off by the redskins' war. At Fort Lyons his men were joined by the First Colorado Cavalry under Major Scott Anthony. The next day they set out for the Indian camp.

On November 29 they halted a mile from the camp, and a detachment was sent on ahead to cut off the pony herd from the camp's warriors. The official order was not to fire unless fired upon. It was a ridiculous order; what Indian is going to stay calm while a white man cuts loose his pony herd?

The inevitable happened. An Indian saw the soldiers at the herd and fired, knocking the bluecoat out of his saddle. The entire command was soon firing. Two howitzers were brought into action and the camp, with an American flag flying, was put under bombardment. Between 600 and 700 Indians, including women and children, were killed before the uneven battle ended. The fight was promptly called a "massacre." Chivington was put on trial and resigned his commission in 1865 to go into the freighting business. He died in 1894.

The "Sand Creek Massacre" is as controversial in western history as Little Big Horn. To read the report of the *Congressional Investigation of the Chivington Massacre*, published in 1867, is to lose oneself in a maze of charges and counter-charges. In the end the reader who has finished the 700 pages of fine print comes to only one conclusion: Black Kettle and his people were killed at the hands of Chivington's soldiers.

Chivington, a stiff, proud man, had made many enemies who were ready to use the "massacre" to disgrace him. Among them was Samuel F. Tappan, who never forgave Chivington for being promoted over his head. Tappan, a former Washington newspaper correspondent, fed the eastern press with some wild tales, all of which painted Chivington as the blackest of villains.

Although Chivington may have been wrong in trying to neutralize a camp of savages by cutting loose their horses and not expecting them to retaliate, one must consider the temper of the times. Every man in his command had suffered in some way at the hands of the marauding tribes. When they rode into Black Kettle's camp, the Hungate massacre must have loomed large in their minds.

And although Black Kettle was under the protection of the American flag, he was not exactly a "peaceful" Indian. This was underscored by the fresh scalps of men, women and children found on the bodies of his warriors. Certainly the sight of saddle blankets fringed with women's hair as found in Black Kettle's camp didn't make Chivington's troopers look with mercy on the Indians they were slaughtering.

On the other hand, there were the ugly rumors that the volunteers were all gold-field prospectors who feared they were about to be called East to fight in the war and had deliberately touched off the battle to start an Indian war.

Other reports have Chivington ordering the massacre out of pure hatred for the Indians he had been fighting against so hard and for so long.

In 1864, about the time of the Sand Creek massacre, the Confederacy ordered that a high council of the western tribes be held. In one of the most dramatic and little-known episodes of the Civil War in the West, a young Creek warrior, Tuk-a-Ba-Tche-Miko, was sent as an emissary by the tribes still at peace to as many tribes in the Southwest as possible to induce them to attend a grand council. For weeks on horseback and on foot, he journeyed north to the country of the Osages and the Pawnees, then southwest to the Iowas, Kickapoos and Pottawatomies, then on to the Wichitas, Kiowas, Comanches and Apaches, then north to the Southern Cheyennes and Arapahoes. He crossed the Panhandle of Texas to meet the Navajos, Mescalero Apaches, Northern Cheyennes and Unkpapas, the Teton and Yankton Sioux. After each meeting he would send back a group of small notched sticks which represented the bands and their numbers. On May 1, 1865, the council was finally held on the Washita River. Captain T. M. Scott, Assistant Adjutant General, C. S. A., reported that 20,000 Indians, one of the largest councils ever to be held in the Southwest, answered the Confederates' call. They did not know of Appomattox.

The council agreed to stop raiding and to maintain peace on the frontier. In the main, there was peace in the Southwest for many years, with only occasional raids and atrocities stirring up the old hatred and bitterness.

The Sand Creek massacre. The American flag hoisted by Black Kettle can be seen (*right center*).

Transportation:
From the Horse to the Iron Horse

THE horse was, of course, the principal means of transportation in the West until the advent of "The Iron Horse"—the railroad. But other animals were used to a considerable extent—mules, burros, oxen, dogs—and, on water, clipper ships and river packets.

There was a wide variety of vehicles of which the stagecoach and the covered wagon were the most publicized. Indians, scouts, trappers, emigrants and settlers made their vehicles to meet their needs and to fit in with the nature of the country. As a result, a number of distinctive types were developed, designed specifically to achieve a particular purpose or to overcome a difficult condition—rough roads, weather hazards, heavy loads.

"Trains" were common, notably for emigrant travel but also for freighting. They were more economical—fewer guides and guards were needed to escort 50 wagons moving together than for the same number traveling separately or in small groups. They were more convenient and more likely to be self-sufficient. In a large train almost every possible item of equipment, almost every possibly useful article could be carried, whereas an individual wagon or small group would have to cut down its load to the barest necessities. Trains were safer—not only because a large group was less vulnerable to attack from Indians but also because in a large group of people almost every kind of medical and mechanical help and skill was available. And finally it was pleasanter and more sociable to travel in a large company than in a small one.

Because so many of the pictures in other sections of this book show means and methods of transportation only a selection is presented here.

A bull-boat made of buffalo hide. *Photo by S. J. Morrow.*

Dog and horse travois. *Photos by General John T. Pitman and J. Anderson.*

The essential beast of burden. *Photo by Alexander Martin.*

A Mormon wagon-train.

Freighters meet on the plains. *Photo by Dan Dutro*.

Red River carts. These were made without metal parts. *Photo by Whitney*.

The last large bull train to the Black Hills. *Photo by Grabill*.

A river packet in the 1870's.

Poster advertising the Oregon Line of stagecoaches and railroad, dated July 19, 1866.

Halliday's Express at Smoky Hill River, 1855.

Heavy freight was transported by freight teams, by river packet or around the Horn by clippers or other vessels. Light or valuable freight, including gold, was sent by "express," privately owned fast transportation. The express companies, such as Wells Fargo, occupied an important role in the resistance to and the fight against outlaws and hostile Indians. They had to protect their valuable shipments and therefore maintained an effective guard and security system and also employed detective agencies, Pinkerton's and others, to track down bandits.

Mail, usually carried by a contractor, went the best and fastest way, which might be by pony, stagecoach, wagon or ship.

The Railroads

While the Civil War fostered the activity of hostile Indians, it also stimulated and speeded railroad-building in the West.

For years efforts had been made to arouse Congress to the need of a transcontinental railroad. Some short railroads had been built in the West before the Civil War, notably the Sacramento Valley line in 1855. But a transcontinental railroad was obviously an enormous project that required not only the government's license and authority but also government financing and privileges.

The great leader of the movement for the Pacific Railroad, the man who organized the committees, raised the money and planned the campaign for the legislation was Theodore Dehone Judah, a visionary sometimes called Crazy Judah, a true hero of the West who is almost unknown now. Almost singlehanded, he pushed the Pacific Railroad Act through Congress. He had failed to win the legislation at several sessions of Congress, but when the War broke out his task was easier and on July 1, 1862, President Lincoln signed the Pacific Railroad Act.

This act provided for the building and operating of a railway between the Missouri River and Sacramento, California. Two companies were given the contracts, the grants and the financing for its construction: the Central Pacific and the Union Pacific. Judah had organized the Central Pacific with four merchants, later to be known

Theodore D. Judah.

as the Big Four, as investors: Leland Stanford, Charles Crocker, Mark Hopkins, Collis P. Huntington. The Central Pacific actually was organized only to build a railroad from Sacramento across the Rockies through the Donner Pass to the silver cities of Nevada. Judah planned that eventually the Central Pacific would build the transcontinental railroad, but he did not tell the merchants that. Just the same they have been given credit for the great vision that was really Judah's. But Judah died in 1863, after having split with his associates, and he was rather promptly forgotten. The Big Four and the fortunes they made from the Central Pacific (now part of the Southern Pacific) had a major influence in the next fifty years of western history.

The other company, named the Union Pacific, was incorporated by the Pacific Railroad Act. The two companies were to build simultaneously, Central starting from the West, Union from the East. For each mile built the railroad would get a loan of $16,000 to $48,000, depending on the difficulty of construction in the specific area, and a grant of ten alternate sections of land on both sides of the railroad.

With such rich rewards, and with the further incentive of extra loans and extra lands for every extra mile it built, each railroad set about energetically and efficiently to outbuild the other. To augment the labor supply the Union Pacific brought west many Irishmen from New

Charles Crocker.

Mark Hopkins.

Leland Stanford.

Collis P. Huntington.

Omaha, N. T., from Capitol Hill. *This and the other photographs on this page were taken by John Carbutt in 1866.*

T. Durant and Union Pacific department heads.

The Platte River opposite Platte City.

Pawnee warriors in front of Union Pacific palace cars.

Carmichael's graders' camp at North Bitter Creek Valley.

A Union Pacific construction train, 1868.

Representatives of the press at the Union Pacific excursion to the 100th Meridian, 1866. *Photo by John Carbutt.*

#1, General Sherman. This wood-burner, first locomotive on the Union Pacific, was brought to Omaha by steamboat in 1865.

York and from Ireland. The Central found it very advantageous to use Chinese laborers, bringing them to the work camps from San Francisco and even from China.

The competition was keen and ruthless—and wasteful. Since no meeting-point of the two lines had been established, the companies kept on building after they had reached a point where they could have joined. Many miles of parallel railroad were built until the meeting-point was fixed at Promontory Point near Ogden, Utah, where the famous Last Spike, completing the transcontinental railroad and connecting the Union Pacific and the Central Pacific, was driven on May 10, 1869. It had taken only a little more than five years to build the great artery.

During the course of construction across Indian lands there was some trouble with the tribes, notably the Sioux. But many of the Union Pacific men were ex-soldiers, and all were supplied with firearms. There were many raids and fights, but their nature was rather more that of harassment than battles.

Even before the transcontinental railroad was completed, the two companies instituted nationwide campaigns to promote emigration to the territory. Popula-

tion, with its commerce, industry and traffic, is, of course, the lifeblood of any railroad. But also the two companies had large holdings of real estate to sell and one element helped the other. The more land sales, the more traffic—the more traffic, the more the land was worth. Every possible promotion and circulation device was used not only in the East and Middle West but in Europe as well, and all sorts of inducements were made, including special "emigrant trains" at fantastically low fares.

Now the tide of emigration rolled west in great swells. This time it covered the land that had been hopped over by the Oregon Trailers and the gold-seekers. Now it was not only the Pacific Coast that won new population, but also the Northern Plains and all the country between the Missouri and the Pacific.

What was natural in this mass emigration, especially that resulting from European advertising, was the "national" or "foreign colony" character of it. Scandinavians would settle in one area—notably Minnesota, Germans in another—notably Wisconsin, and so on. There was hardly a European country that did not have a "colony" somewhere in the West. In time all these Europeans

The Golden Spike ceremony at Promontory Point, Utah, May 10, 1869. At the meeting of the Central Pacific (*left*) and the Union Pacific (*right*) the last spike, a golden one, was driven, the transcontinental railroad was a fact, and the locomotives were christened with wine. Montague, chief engineer of the Central Pacific, shakes hands with Grenville M. Dodge, chief engineer of the Union Pacific. *Photo by C. R. Savage.*

The Golden Spike. The names of the officers of the two companies are inscribed on one side. Other inscriptions read: "The Pacific Railroad—ground broken January 8, 1863, and completed May 8, 1869," and "May God continue the unity of our Country, as this Railroad unites the two great Oceans of the world."

THE TRAPPER'S BRIDE. Mountain men celebrating after a wedding in the Indian country. *Painted by Charles Banks Wilson.*

LIFE ON THE PRAIRIE—The "Buffalo Hunt." *From a Currier & Ives print, 1862.*

CHIMNEY ROCK. *Painted by Alfred Jacob Miller.*

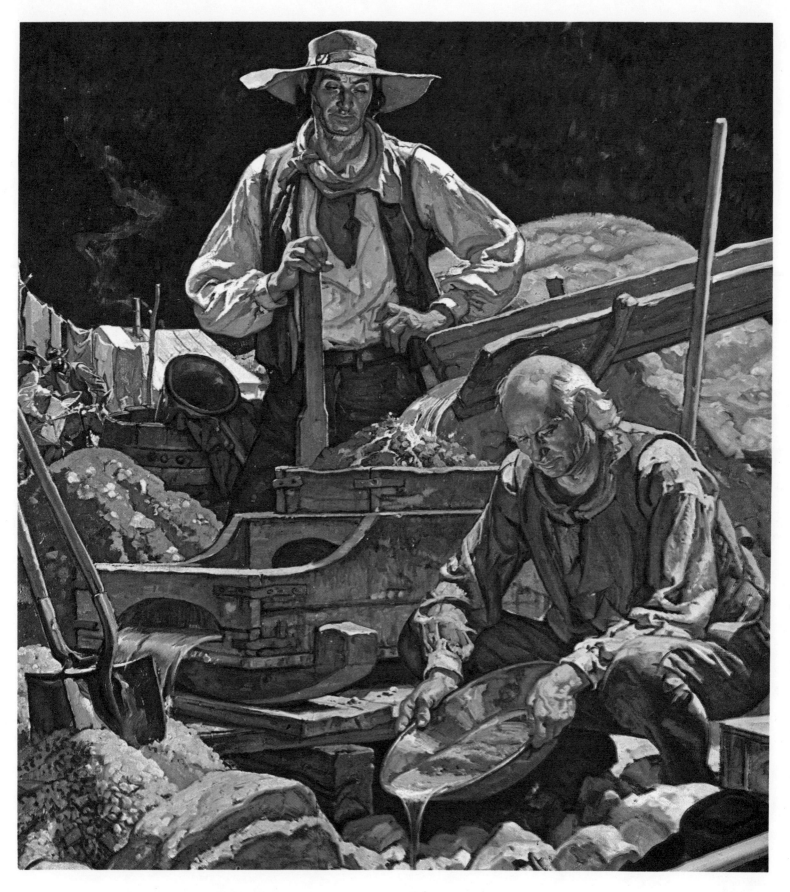

GOLD MINING AT SUTTER'S MILL. *Painted by Dean Cornwell.*

VIEW OF THE ROCKY MOUNTAINS. *Painted by Charles Bodmer.* These are not really the Rocky Mountains. Bernard De Voto commented in *Across the Wide Missouri,* "The peaks on the horizon must belong to either the Little Rockies or the High-wood Mountains, more likely the former."

YOSEMITE VALLEY, CALIFORNIA. *From a Currier & Ives print, 1866.*

LIFE ON THE PRAIRIE—THE TRAPPERS DEFENCE "FIRE FIGHT FIRE." *Painted by
A. P. Tait for a Currier & Ives print, 1862.*

KANESVILLE CROSSING, NEAR COUNCIL BLUFFS. This was where the Mormon vanguard crossed the Missouri. *Painted by W. H. Jackson.*

THE ROCKY MOUNTAINS. *From a Currier & Ives print, 1866.*

THE ROUTE TO CALIFORNIA. *From a Currier & Ives print, 1871.*

The Eads Bridge over the Mississippi at St. Louis. James B. Eads was the engineer of this bridge which, completed in 1874, was a vitally important link joining Illinois and Missouri, East and West. *Painted by Louis Bouché.*

became assimilated as Americans, but they still retained many of the traditions and folkways of the mother country, and in turn American culture took over and absorbed many of them.

As other main railroads—notably the James J. Hill rail empire, including the Great Northern, the Northern Pacific and the Burlington—were built in the West, the process of stimulating land sales and new emigration was repeated again and again, and the population multiplied. The West was well on its way to filling in and growing up, delayed only by the hazards of the wild Indians and the wild bad men.

James J. Hill. *From a painting by Alfonso Muller-Ury.*

From a brochure of the Chicago, Kansas and Nebraska Railway, St. Joseph and Iowa Railroad Co., Lessee—the Rock Island Route, 1888.

An early palace car.

The Utah Northern bridge across the Snake River. In the background is a toll bridge, and farther back are the original machine shops of the railroad. Formerly known as Eagle Rock, this is now the town of Idaho Falls.

[81]

An Englishman's View of an Emigrant Train

(From an unpublished diary of an Englishman who toured the West in 1876)

September 28, 1876. Arrived at Ogden about 8, where we exchanged from the Central Pacific to the Union Pacific. Left Ogden in a sleeper at 10. Passed several emigrant trains. Emigrants pay half the usual fare, and they are crowded about and treated by the officials like wild beasts. Both the Union and Central Pacific Railway trains rarely travel faster than 17-18 miles per hour, and as they have no competition they are renowned for being the most exorbitant, rude and disagreeable companies in America.

Laying ties and rails. *Photo by Alexander Gardner.*

First train into Boise, Idaho, September 12, 1887.

Central Pacific train on Long Ravine Bridge. *Photo by Thomas Houseworth & Co.*

Royal Gorge, Grand Canyon of the Arkansas. *Photo by W. H. Jackson.*

Snow sheds on the Central Pacific Railroad, near Donner Pass. *Photo by C. R. Bierstadt.*

The summit of Frémont Pass on the Colorado Railroad. *Photo by W. H. Jackson.*

Marshall Pass. *Photo by W. H. Jackson.*

Hanging Rock. Pike's Peak Railroad. *Photo by J. G. Hiesland.*

The Indian Wars

Government Management of Indian Affairs

THE Civil War and postwar troubles with the Indians focused attention on the national policy toward Indians, caused a re-examination of the methods of dealing with them and the establishment of a new system.

As early as 1775 the Continental Congress set up departments of Indian affairs to deal with the various tribes. The first formal treaty between the United States and an Indian tribe was made in 1778 with the Delawares. This policy of making separate treaties with the different tribes, each considered a nation, continued for about 90 years during which time some 360 treaties were made. Though some of these were respected and effective, on the whole they overlapped each other, were generally little understood and even less observed.

In 1789 the United States government assumed charge of the Indians and Congress ordered the War Department to administer Indian affairs. In 1793 the President was authorized to appoint agents to live among the Indians, help them, win their friendship and supply them with animals, tools, merchandise and money. Some of these agents were in control of tribes, some in charge of districts, where they set up headquarters known as agencies with full staffs and with Indians as policemen of the area.

Parallel with the administrative agent system in the early years was the factor system to control trade with the Indians and to protect them from being cheated by ruthless traders. Trading posts or "factories" were established at various frontier centers of Indian population, each with a superintendent of Indian trade in charge.

Kit Carson, famous scout, and the oath of office he took on his appointment as Brevet Brigadier General in the Army, January 4, 1866. *Photo by Mathew Brady.*

These factories supplied all sorts of merchandise to the Indians in exchange for furs, without profit. The government supplied the original capital which was replenished when the furs were sold.

When reputable and responsible private companies like the American Fur Company came into the field, the government withdrew, and in 1822 Congress ended the factor system.

In 1834 Congress passed a law establishing the Department of Indian Affairs under the War Department, providing for rules and regulations to govern the Indians and defining the powers of the various officers.

In 1849 the Department was transferred as a Bureau to the newly established Department of the Interior where it has remained except during crises or Indian wars when an area or a reservation might be placed temporarily in the Army's charge.

After the Civil War two important revisions were made in Indian policy:

Reservations: It was decided to get the Indians, by treaty or by force, to stop roaming and to live permanently on selected reservations of land which would be their own property. From the earliest days some such reservations had been established by treaties, but there had not been an active reservation policy. But in 1868 the reservation plan was pursued vigorously and within 20 years or so all tribal Indians were on reservations. A source of great trouble, as will be explained in later chapters, was the encroachment of the whites on the Indian lands, the breaking of the treaties and the lack of permanence of the reservations.

Wards of the Nation: In 1869 President Grant, at the suggestion of General Sheridan, embarked on a peace policy toward the Indians. No longer would the Indians be considered as members of a tribe or nation to be dealt with through their tribes or nations. Rather the Indians became direct wards of the United States and treaty-making with tribes or nations was abolished.

The Postwar Army

The treaty had been signed in Appomattox's white clapboard house. Lee's weary troops moved homeward for spring plowing, while the men in blue returned to the cities of the North. At first a great stillness fell over the bruised and bleeding land; then it was followed by a national restlessness, a feeling of discontent with familiar places and things.

As happens after almost all wars, many of the returning

A photograph taken at Fort Laramie, 1868, at the time when Red Cloud and his warriors met Sherman and his officers to arrange a peace treaty. *Left to right:* A. H. Terry, W. S. Harney, W. T. Sherman, a Sioux squaw, N. S. Taylor, S. F. Tappan, A. C. Augur.

General George Crook. *Photo by Mathew Brady.*

General Nelson A. Miles.

soldiers found it hard to fit in with the old way of life at home. They missed the excitement, the violence and the adventure. In the South, for many there was no old way to fit into. Homes had been destroyed, property looted and, above all, they had to knuckle under to a government that wasn't their own.

The exodus of ex-Confederates was great. There was a steady stream of them westward, and each year for a while there was an increasing number who had GTT ("gone to Texas"). But there were plenty of Northerners, too, who pulled up stakes and made their way to the new country in the West to seek their fortune and a new way of life.

In the beginning there were four transcontinental routes: southward over the ancient Santa Fe Trail; westward over the Kansas Trail to Denver, westward on the Oregon Trail to Nebraska and Salt Lake City to Oregon or the gold fields of California; northwestward on the Bozeman Trail through Wyoming to Montana. The Union Pacific was building along the Oregon Trail and the Kansas Pacific along the Kansas Trail to Denver. With the railroads operating only short distances, the only method of travel was the horse and the familiar prairie schooner.

In 1866 public sentiment for Army protection against the Indians mounted. Editorial writers in leading papers of the nation and the politicians began calling upon the government to furnish an army that could provide security for the settlers on the frontier.

But an army that could stand up against the aroused Plains tribes had to be sizable, tough, mobile. Now, after Appomattox, there were only 26,000 on the Army rolls. War casualties had taken their toll and they had not been replaced. Unlike that for drafted recruits there had been no bounty for the Regular Army man during the War Between the States.

After the gallant Army of Northern Virginia passed into history, replacements began to move back into the Regular Army. Men in gray and blue who could not return to the good life after four years of war—misfits, bored Easterners who wanted adventure, "galvanized" Yankees, drunkards, thieves and murderers—filled the ranks. Southern officers, who by law could not hold a commission, became top sergeants, corporals and even members of the regiment band. In the Regular Army, non-commissioned officers who had won battlefield promotion for heroic conduct stepped back down to their old rank.

Before the Indian wars would end America would have its own Foreign Legion—the toughest, hardest-riding cavalry in history. It would outfight and outride the greatest horsemen of the plains, including the Comanches.

Like the Foreign Legion, it was an army composed of men of many nationalities: Irish, German, French, Italian, Jewish. Negroes, many fresh from the slave quarters of southern cotton fields, flocked to the cavalry. Because of the thick, furry buffalo robes they wore in the winter, the Sioux called them "Buffalo Soldiers." In Montana and Nebraska General Carpenter's colored regiment was called "Carpenter's Brunettes." The all-Negro 10th Cavalry was one of the best in the West.

Indians themselves were also a part of the army fighting the Indians. Every regiment had its own company of scouts—Pawnees, Crows, Shoshones and Rees (Arikaras), all minority tribes who hated the powerful Sioux. When the Sioux were conquered some of the warriors turned on their own people and donned the blue. In Crook's campaigns against the Apaches some of his best scouts were Apaches.

The general-in-chief of the postwar Army was General Ulysses S. Grant, with William Tecumseh Sherman as chief-of-staff and hard-riding Phil Sheridan commanding the Department of the West. Under the command of these "big three" the Army marched and fought under its field commanders: Terry, Custer, Crook, Gibbon, Mackenzie, Miles, Howard, Merritt, Carpenter and the rest.

Some of the high-ranking officers were tyrants and drunkards, but the majority were sensitive, intelligent and well-educated. The troopers were mounted on excellent horses, tough western mustangs. The artillerymen were a small group who cared for their howitzers with as much care as they gave their horses. They were always treated with a great deal of respect by the new recruits after they had experienced their first fight with the Sioux. They soon learned that the sharp slam of the howitzer and the whir of the shell over their heads from the reinforcements coming over the rise was the most welcome sound in the world. The Plains tribes feared the guns and usually scattered when they opened up. Accompanying the troops were the mule-skinners or bull-whackers, civilians who could flick a fly off a mule's ear with their long whips.

The posts were reminiscent of the forts in the Mohawk

Signing the treaty at Fort Laramie, 1868. General Sherman is shown second on the right of the right-hand pole.

Brown's Hotel, Fort Laramie, 1868. *Photo probably by Alexander Gardner.*

The old Mormon fort at Bridger in ruins.

Lieutenant Colonel Baker and officers at Fort Ellis, Montana Territory, 1871.
Photo by William H. Jackson.

Soldiers' barracks at Fort Hays, Kansas, 1873.

U. S. Cavalry, early 1870's.

At Fort Maginnis, Montana Territory.

A company of the Fifth U. S. Infantry, Montana, 1878.

Fort Sill, Indian Territory, 1876. *Photo by W. P. Bliss.*

A pack outfit at Fort Custer, 1878.

General Miles and staff, Tongue River, Montana, 1877. This photograph was taken just before mounting, for the expedition against Sitting Bull and Crazy Horse. The temperature was 20° below zero. Miles is in the center.

Valley during the Revolution. Square, built of untrimmed logs, the tops pointed with axes, they included officers' barracks—usually log cabins—and log barracks for the enlisted men. Other buildings usually included a guardhouse, storehouse, quartermaster's headquarters, hospital and corral. Outside the quadrangle were the quarters for the married men, dubbed "Sudsville" because the women usually augmented their husbands' pay by taking in washing. There was also the sutler's store, which was a combination officers' club, enlisted men's canteen and general store.

There were always women on the post, wives and daughters of officers and men. They were a clannish, gossipy lot divided by feuds and jealousy, but united the moment their men moved out. It was then that their long wait began. It ended when they heard the bugles in the distance or listened with pounding hearts to the report of the weary dispatch rider that most of the troop had been exterminated.

The war with the red men was not a war of great battles of large masses of men meeting head on. It was a succession of sorties, ambushes, sieges and short and savage attacks in which stealth and cunning were demanded of its leaders. It was a war of no quarter, although the do-gooders in the East were constantly writing letters to the editors of big dailies denouncing the cavalry for needlessly killing the poor, bewildered red man.

From 1866 to 1875 more than 200 pitched battles would be fought, with the Army outnumbered in all of them. From 1882 to 1887 the Army was at constant war with the Apaches. One regiment participated in 97 field actions.

What Easterners failed to realize was that this foe was terrible, relentless and as dangerous as an aroused rattlesnake. Actually, no one could blame him; the Plains Indians knew they were fighting a war of survival, for land that had been theirs for centuries. What they were really fighting to maintain was an age that was vanishing like woodsmoke in the wind. The westward movement had started; it was moving like a juggernaut from the cities of the East. It could not be stopped.

It is not within the purpose of this book to detail all the Indian battles, but some of the more important engagements are described to indicate the nature and the scope of the conflict.

Officer's tent (B Company, Seventh Infantry), typical of the frontier in 1880.

The Sixth U. S. Cavalry training horses at Fort Bayard, New Mexico.

Target practice on the range.

First U. S. Infantry Band at Fort Grant, 1882.

Company B, 25th Infantry (Carpenter's Brunettes) at Fort Snelling, 1883.

Camp of the Sixth Cavalry, near Fort Fetterman, during the rustlers' war.

Camp of the Fifth Infantry in Yellowstone Valley, Montana, during the campaign against the Sioux.

B Company, Whipple Barracks, 1880's.

The great saga of the Indian Wars began in 1866 when the government commissioners at Fort Laramie began negotiating with the Sioux and the Northern Cheyennes for the right of emigrants to pass through the land which had been ceded to the Indians by the Harney-Sanborn Treaty of 1865. It was at this meeting that Red Cloud, the Sioux chief, denounced Brigadier General Henry B. Carrington as the "White Eagle" who was attempting to steal the Indians' land by force. After a violent speech he left the meeting to take the warpath.

The one concession the Army wanted from the Sioux was the unhindered construction of military posts to protect the Bozeman Trail. The Brulé Sioux under Spotted Tail and Standing Elk favored the concession. The older chiefs under Red Cloud, who feared that one concession would only lead to another and yet another, fought to the last against the posts. But the Army was determined to build the posts. No Indians were going to stop them.

In May, 1866, General Carrington, with a force of some 700 men, fully equipped, and guided by Jim Bridger, the mountain man, left for Kearny in Nebraska to establish a new post called the Mountain District. Included in the equipment were the saws and materials for two sawmills to be used in preparing the lumber for the new forts.

At the time there was only one garrison in the area, known as Fort Reno, some 160 miles from Laramie. The latter fort was manned mostly by "galvanized Yankees." Carrington was ordered to march there, then move to a point some 40 miles northward and establish another post on the Bozeman Trail between the Big Horn Mountains and Powder River. The War Department's reasoning was that such a post could command the valley used by the

General Henry B. Carrington.

tribes. A subsequent order had Carrington establish two more posts, one on the Big Horn, the other on the Yellowstone.

Carrington was one of the Army's finest frontier officers. A graduate of Yale, a scientist, Ohio's Civil War Adjutant General, and vigorous foe of the Copperheads, he was also the author of an impressive work on George Washington.

Carrington's force reached Reno in mid-June. A month later he established the command on the Big Piney Creek, about four miles from the Big Horn Range. The air was soon filled with the sound of axes, hammers and saws, while on Big Piney Island, seven miles away, the assembled

Spotted Tail.

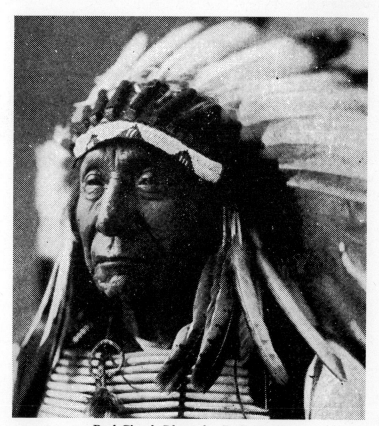

Red Cloud. *Photo by D. F. Barry.*

[93]

sawmill was trimming the logs. Carrington knew he was under constant surveillance by the Sioux scouts, so he established observation posts on nearby Pilot and Sullivan hills. The small garrison was constantly harassed by Sioux war parties. Stragglers were found scalped and mutilated.

The work on the fort continued through the long, hot summer. It was a rectangle, 600 x 800 feet, with a stockade of pine logs eight feet high with a loophole in every fourth log. Enfilading blockhouses were erected on diagonal corners with portholes for the cannons. Besides the barracks there were also officers' quarters and warehouses. Outside the fort itself was a log stockade surrounding the corral in which the livestock, hay and wagons were kept. In the center of the parade was a tall flagpole, planed and smoothed by the regiment's carpenter.

In August Carrington dispatched Captain Kinney with two companies 90 miles to the northwest to erect a second post, which eventually was called Fort C. F. Smith. In design it was Kearny in miniature. Carrington refused to build the third; there just weren't enough men left.

The main fort was finished in September. General W. B. Hazen, who inspected the garrison, called it the "best I have seen outside the one built by the Hudson's Bay Company in British America." It had been built at the staggering price of 150 men and officers killed and scalped, the wounding of 20 more and the capture of 700 animals against a backdrop of constant vigilance, both day and night.

The armed groups that made the round trips to the sawmills never made a trip without fighting off the swift-raiding Sioux. Five out of seven days the bugler sounded the alert upon a signal from Pilot Hill.

On December 6 the wood train was attacked by Indians in full force, and Captain William J. Fetterman was dis-

patched with a relief force. The Indians, however, instead of fleeing, turned on Fetterman with a wild ferocity. The raw troops broke and fled, but the ground infantry stood firm. The cavalry, with Carrington himself in the lead, swept over a hill to clash with the Indians; a wild melee followed and the troops finally drove off the redskins. Two days later President Johnson was assuring Congress that now all was peaceful in the West. . . .

But of course the raids continued. Then disturbing news filtered through the log gates that 3,000 bucks were encamped on the Powder River, whetting their scalping knives.

Despite the raw recruits and too few bullets the young officers at that frontier fort possessed an arrogance that was hair-curling. Fetterman was constantly begging Carrington to lead an attack on the main Indian camp, swearing that with "eighty men I can walk through the Sioux camp."

On December 18 the wood train was attacked again and Fetterman got his chance. Upon his plea of seniority Carrington reluctantly gave him the command with strict orders to drive off the attackers but on no condition to chase them across Lodge Trail Ridge.

Fetterman, however, did follow the redskins beyond the ridge and fell into ambush. To rescue him Carrington stripped the post of almost every man, arming his prisoners, cooks and civilians.

Captain Ten Eyck, who had been sent in relief, brought back sad news that afternoon. In his wagons were the bodies of 49 of Fetterman's men, but 32 were still unaccounted for. All the bodies were bristling with arrows; the corpses had been horribly mutilated and in some cases decapitated after shocking tortures. One-fourth of the command was buried secretly that night.

The next day Carrington rode out to recover the rest

Captain Fetterman.

Captain Ten Eyck.

of Fetterman's command. The officer left behind in command of a skeleton army was ordered to raise a white lantern if all was well and a red one if the fort was under attack.

By noon Carrington came to the scene of the battle and found the rest of the bodies, mutilated like the others. One officer had 120 arrows in his body. That night there was a raging blizzard and the temperature dropped to 30° below. Carrington knew that the Sioux were confined to their lodges by the storm, but he also knew he had to get help for his gravely depleted garrison. On his return to the fort he called for volunteers to ride to Laramie for help, and a civilian scout named John Phillips stepped forward and was accepted for the mission.

Phillips, called "Portugee," was given Carrington's own horse, a magnificent Kentucky jumper. At dawn Phillips reached Fort Reno, but it had no telegraph nor was there enough manpower to dispatch a force to Kearny. Portugee rode on through the snow. A few hours out of Reno he was spotted by a force of Indians but outrode them. At daybreak he reached Horseshoe Station and a wire was sent to Laramie. Acting on a hunch that the wires might be down and Laramie would not receive the message, Portugee insisted on riding on. (He was right—the message never got through.)

At Laramie that night a sentry shouted a command as a horse stumbled out of the storm. It crumpled to its knees, dying. The rider slid off, faltered, then staggered forward.

"Courier from Kearny. . . . Important dispatches. . . ."

Men jumped forward to support him, but he waved them away and handed the dispatches to the commanding officer. Then his tremendous stamina and will-power broke. He started to fall, but gentle hands lowered him to the floor and a doctor came on the run.

Portugee Phil had finished one of the most thrilling rides in western history. In three days and nights he had ridden 236 miles through a raging blizzard and through the lines of one of the largest Indian forces in the West. Within a few hours the First Battalion of the 18th Infantry moved out of Laramie.

The news of Fetterman's massacre aroused the nation to a great fever of anger and criticism. Carrington was the Army's scapegoat and was relieved of his command. He was ordered forthwith to transfer himself and his men to Fort Casper.

The one constructive thing that the sad frontier affair brought about was the erection of another fort between Laramie and Reno. It was called Fort Fetterman to honor the rash young officer. The War Department did not see fit to disclose that such a post, built with reinforcements, had been urged by Carrington many months before the fatal battle.

Map of the Fetterman fight.

"Today We Must Fight for Our Lives."

After Carrington departed, Fort Kearny was under constant siege by the Sioux riding with Red Cloud, now the unanimous choice of the bucks as their leader. To go on a logging expedition was to invite almost certain death.

In August Red Cloud, weary of skirmishing and small patrol battles, decided once and for all to come to grips with the issue; he would launch a major attack on Kearny or die in the attempt. In August, 1867, he gathered about him 3,000 braves, the flower of the Sioux Nation, and began an advance on the garrison.

As his ponies moved forward, Captain James W. Powell, a hero of Chickamauga, had arrived at Piney Island with a small party to guard the log-cutting operations at the saw-mill. He ordered the wagon bodies that were used in hauling the logs to be arranged in a wide oval. Two-inch holes were drilled into the sides of the wagons. The spaces between the wagons were filled with bags of hay and wheat and stacks of soft pine which would stop a bullet and not cast off flying splinters.

On August 2, Red Cloud's warriors attacked the saw-mill camp as the first step of his strategy to wipe out Kearny. The loggers retreated to the wagon oval after Powell, in a bold sortie, had drawn the Indian cavalry to himself, then retreated to the wagons without loss of a man.

After burning the camp the Sioux attacked the wagon-fort. It was 32 against 3,000. Fortunately, the soldiers were well armed; the best shots had the most rifles. One old Indian fighter had eight rifles beside him, while a poorer shot was assigned to do nothing but keep them loaded.

Red Cloud first sent his best horsemen forward, while behind them on their horses sat the impassive chiefs—Unkpapas, Miniconjous, Ogalalas, Brulés, and the Northern Cheyennes.

Crouched in the wagon-bodies, the troopers, loggers and scouts caught their targets in their sights and waited for Powell's shot, the signal for all to fire. The young officer had made no speeches and had given few instructions. He had said only, "Today we must fight for our lives."

The raiders were now 100 feet away . . . now 50. Powell's rifle cracked, a buck spun out of his saddle and the whole oval belched flame and smoke. That solid sheet of steel from the most rapid firing the Indians had ever encountered stopped them cold. As their comrades fell out of saddles or slumped over, they retreated quickly, leaving behind the writhing wounded and the screaming horses. When Powell counted noses he found his command had been reduced to 28.

"Look to your posts, gentlemen," he said. "They will be back."

This time they returned on foot, wriggling through the grass. Again there was a vast silence from inside the wagon-fort as the Indians poured into it a merciless fire. When they thought they had wiped out most of the defenders, they charged. Again the wagons belched flame as wave after wave crumpled within feet of the wagons. Again they broke and retreated.

The Wagon Box fight.

Forsyth's fight on the Republican River. *From a painting by Frederic Remington.*

Three times Red Cloud's warriors charged and each time retreated with heavy casualties. Finally he had enough and ordered a full retreat. It wasn't until a year after the battle that Powell learned he and his men had killed 1,137 of Red Cloud's warriors.

In the fall of 1868 a new treaty was made with the Sioux, and Fort Kearny was abandoned. The Indians promptly burned it as the camp of "the bad medicine fight of the white men."

A second classic siege of white men by Indians took place in 1868 when the gallant Major George Alexander "Sandy" Forsyth and 28 men fought off an army of Sioux at Beecher's Island on the Arickaree Fork of the Republican River in eastern Colorado.

The braves, under Roman Nose, hit Forsyth's forces when the troopers were resting their horses on the bank of the river. In the center of the river was a sandy island, smooth as a plate, 20 yards wide and 60 yards long. Due to a drought, the river bed was dry and hardened by the sun. However, on either side of the island, a creek less than a foot deep ran over the rocks and gravel.

The alarm was given as the advance party of redskins, blowing whistles, whirling rattles and beating drums, rode down the slope trying to stampede the trooper's horses. While his men poured a heavy fire into the advancing horsemen, Forsyth ordered a retreat to the tiny island. There they frantically dug shallow firing pits with hands, cups and pots. Roman Nose himself led the first charge of 500 warriors, the pick of the combined tribes, while his main army fired down from the slopes into the crouching men on the island. The surgeon was killed, Lieutenant Beecher, second in command, badly wounded, and Forsyth was hit in the leg, thigh and head. But, with his own blood filling his tiny firing pit, Forsyth ordered his men to hold their fire until he gave the order.

It was the wagon-box scrap all over. At 50 feet the valley shook with the blast of the rifles and revolvers. Volley after volley tore holes in the ranks of the braves. Roman Nose himself was knocked off his saddle and riddled with bullets. The charge broke and they retreated.

At two o'clock and at six they charged again—only to be repulsed. When night came Forsyth counted his casualties; his command was now reduced to 23. Among the dead was young Beecher, whose name would be given to the island.

That night Forsyth sent out two troopers to crawl through the Indian lines and reach Fort Wallace, a hundred miles away. At dawn the fighting resumed and for five days more the island was under attack, with the men chewing the putrid meat of the dead animals. Forsyth's wounds were gangrenous, and he seemed doomed when help was sighted. It was an ambulance, the vanguard of a force from Fort Wallace. The two scouts had slipped through the lines of the Sioux.

When Colonel Louis H. Carpenter, the officer commanding the relief expedition, rode up he found Forsyth, his rifle across his lap and his revolver nearby, calmly reading a copy of *Oliver Twist*. Later Forsyth said he knew he would break down at the sight of his friend and therefore had taken the worn copy from his saddle bag and made a pretense at reading.

Forsyth was burning with fever. Although the surgeon said he had to amputate at once to save his life, the young officer refused. It took four days to get to Wallace, four days of hell in the bouncing, jolting ambulance. It would take more than two years before his wounds healed completely.

On the trip back General Carpenter's "Brunettes" reported a large movement of Sioux on Beaver Creek, and this word was dispatched to General Sheridan at Fort Hays, Kansas. Brevet-Major General Eugene A. Carr and the Fifth Cavalry joined Carpenter's Tenth at Wallace and moved out three weeks after the rescue of Forsyth's men.

Carpenter's scouts found the Indians, who turned and attacked. Like Powell, the general formed his wagons in a double column, six on one side, five on the other with mules inward, and met the charges with devastating rifle fire from seven-shooter Spencers.

The battle lasted eight hours, with the Indians suffering heavy losses. Finally they retreated. On their way back to Wallace, Carpenter and his men rode through tough Sheridan City, terminus of the Union Pacific, and the men who

Captain Louis H. Carpenter.

ran out of the saloons gave the troops a "rousing welcome."

In the winter of 1868 Lt. Colonel George Armstrong Custer, the frontier's glory-hunter, leading the famous Seventh, four companies of foot soldiers and the Nineteenth Kansas Volunteer Cavalry, attacked the Cheyenne under Black Kettle in the valley of a small river in the Indian Territory called Washita.

The troopers fell on the village to the accompaniment

Roman Nose leading the charge against Forsyth. *From a painting by Charles Schreyvogel.*

George Armstrong Custer.

[98]

of their regiment's tune, "Garry Owen." It was a massacre, with Black Kettle among the dead. The remainder of the united Kiowas, Arapahoes, Cheyenne "dog soldiers" and reportedly even some wandering Apaches counterattacked. Led by the Kiowa Santana and Black Kettle's successor, Little Rock, they almost had Custer's back to the wall when fresh ammunition arrived. The troops managed to drive off the Indians, following which Custer burned the village and shot more than 700 Indian ponies.

A year later General Carr, leading the Fifth and with the flamboyant Buffalo Bill as his scout, defeated Tall Bull at Summit Springs, Colorado.

Sitting Bull, the Sioux's medicine man, and Crazy Horse, probably the ablest war chief in western history, now had taken a position in the Valley of the Big Horn near Powder River. Forts and federal agencies for Indians encircled them. The Missouri was on the east and north; on the south were the military posts along the Union Pacific, to the west were the mountains. Three expeditions were to be launched against the Indians simultaneously; one was to march eastward from Montana, another was to advance northward from southern Nebraska and a third was to strike west from Fort Abraham Lincoln.

Only one expedition got off, that led by General Joseph Reynolds, who captured Crazy Horse's village, but retreated ignominiously when the Indians counter-attacked. It was not until years later that the Army proved effective against Sitting Bull and Crazy Horse.

Santana (White Bear), the Kiowa sub-chief, wearing the uniform given him by General F. S. Babcock at the time of the signing of the treaty at Medicine Lodge, Kansas, in October, 1867.

The "People"

The wiliest, the cruelest and perhaps the toughest enemy the cavalry ever encountered was the Chiricahua Apache. They made up for their lack of numbers by a fierce hatred of the white man and an almost fanatical kind of courage. During the Civil War they ravaged the Arizona Territory many times, driving the settlers back into the larger towns. Even Tucson was menaced.

After the reorganization of the Regular Army, General George Crook was given the task of subduing "People," as they called themselves. Crook insisted from the beginning that an offensive campaign was the only way to dislodge the tribes from their *rancherias* in the mountain strongholds. In 1871 his methods began to produce results. In the spring of that year Eskiminzin and his band left the mountains and surrendered to the Army at Fort Grant. The burly Indian said simply, "We are tired of fighting."

The citizens of nearby Tucson, who had felt the brunt of the Indian raids in the bleak years of the war, were aroused. On April 28, 1871, a mob raided the Indian camp in Pantano Wash, east of Tucson, and massacred 108 Apaches, mostly women and children. The leaders of the mob were later tried and acquitted.

In Christmas week, 1872, a patrol sent out by Crook bivouacked in a small canyon near Cottonwood Creek. An Apache scout, Nantaje, had reported that there was a large body of Apaches in a big cave on Salt River nearby, that they must march at night; if they were seen in daylight, not a man would return alive. Major Brown, in command, gave the orders and at dusk the column set out.

An advance scout reported that the Apaches, just back from raiding the settlements on the Gila, were dancing in the large cave. The soldiers crept from rock to rock.

Major General Eugene A. Carr.

Soon the *rancheria* was completely surrounded. At a signal from Brown a deadly fire poured into the cave. The canyon shook with sound. From the cave came screams and cries. After a time Brown ordered a pause in the firing. An interpreter called for unconditional surrender, but the answer was defiant; the Apaches were ready to fight to the death.

The lines were ordered to aim at the roof of the cave so the bullets would ricochet into the huddled Indians behind their ramparts. The strategy worked. Warriors attempted to rush forward, only to be cut down.

Another command to stop firing was issued. In a lull the dust and the black powder smoke hung in the air. Then from the cave rose the death chant. Brown reluctantly gave his order. Rifles crashed in solid volleys until there was no answering fire from the cave.

The troops moved forward cautiously, but soon it developed that out of the entire band only 12 women and small children, some badly wounded, were alive. Seventy-six men and boys had been killed in the battle.

Crook's offensive warfare was too much for the Apaches. On April 27, 1873, the last band surrendered at Camp Verde.

Cato, a Chiricahua chief.

General Crook with two Apache scouts. *Left*, Dutchie; *right*, Alchise. *Probably a photo by Camillus Fly.*

[100]

Gold in the Black Hills

In 1873 and 1874, two large expeditions were sent out for the purpose of exploring the sacred Black Hills of the Dakotas. The first, in 1873, was under the command of General Stanley. Custer and his Seventh were included.

The following year, Tom Custer, General Custer's brother, captured Rain-in-the-Face at Standing Rock Agency, 20 miles from Fort Abraham Lincoln. But the chief escaped from the jailhouse with a civilian prisoner. He swore he would someday eat Tom Custer's heart.

His revenge was just over the rim of the next hill. . . .

The following year the second Black Hills expedition, this time under George Custer, set out from Fort Lincoln. It was a long train of a thousand troopers and scientists.

Although the Black Hills, sacred to the Sioux, were in the center of their nation, Custer was not discovered. His force skirted the Black Buttes of Wyoming, continued across the valley, and camped near Inyan Kara.

Custer and his staff climbed to the peak, then marched on to nearby "Floral Valley."

He wrote: "Our march was amid flowers of the most exquisite colors and perfume." But Custer found something more important than wild flowers; there was gold in the Black Hills.

Captain Tom Custer.

The Custer family at home, 1874. George Custer is standing at the piano; his sister, Mrs. Calhoun, is playing, "I'm Waiting, My Darling, for Thee"; Mrs. Custer is fourth from the left; Tom Custer's head shows at the right as he leans forward.

Rain-in-the-Face. Taken at Fort Yates.

fearless, resourceful and experienced frontiersman, was elected "trail boss" of the expedition.

Christmas week, 1874, the party camped near the present site of Custer City and on French Creek, where gold had been found. A large stockade and a fort were built and the party settled down for some mining and hunting, but in April, cavalry from Fort Laramie found the party and escorted them out of the hille.

Other parties tried to slip into the Hills after the Gordon Party. One wagon train was found and burned by the troops.

However, it was impossible for the cavalry to hold back the flood of gold-mad men. In the next year the Hills were open and Deadwood was founded. And from the rims of their sacred Hills the Sioux and Cheyennes looked down at the mushrooming gold towns with bitterness.

Some members of the Gordon Stockade party.

Shortly after Custer made his report, Charles Collins, editor of the Sioux City (Iowa) *Times*, went to Chicago for the purpose of outfitting an expedition to prospect and mine. But he had no sooner reached Chicago and stated his intentions when Lieutenant Sheridan issued an order forbidding anyone to go into the hills until proper treaties were made with the Sioux. Although Collins was stopped, he went back to Sioux City and started to organize a new company "on the quiet."

On October 6, 1874, 26 men and one woman set out for a secret trip to the Black Hills. For deception, the lead wagon was labeled "O'Neil's Colony"—a homesteading colony on the Elkhorn River, Nebraska. John Gordon, a

A reconstruction of the Gordon Stockade.

OFFICIAL COMMUNICATIONS RECEIVED DURING THE MONTH.

[See Army Regulations as to the mode of obtaining *missing* orders.]

NOTE 4.—Communications will be acknowledged in the following order: 1st, "Letters;" 2d, "General Orders;" 3d, "Special Orders" from the A. G. OFFICE; 4th, "Letters;" 5th, "General Orders;" 6th, "Special Orders" from HD. QRS. OF THE ARMY; 7th, "Letters;" 8th, "General Orders;" 9th, "Special Orders" from DIV. HD. QRS.; 10th, "Letters;" 11th, "General Orders;" and 12th, "Special Orders" from DEPT HD. QRS. All orders will be arranged according to their numbers, and without reference to the date when they are received at the post.

DATE.	WHENCE ISSUED.	WHEN RECEIVED.	PURPORT.

August 2" 1874 — Companies C & K 7" Cav. accompanied by a Detachment of Engineers left the main camp for the purpose of exploring the North Fork of the Cheyenne River. The Prospectors accompanying the expedition found gold this morning.

August 3" 1874 — Companies A. C. L. of 7" Cav. and scientific party left main Camp for the purpose of exploring the South Fork of the Cheyenne River. Chas Reynolds a scout in the employ of the Government left Cheyenne River with the mail for Fort Laramie.

August 5" 1874 — The Detachment returned from exploring the North and South forks of the Cheyenne River.

August 14" 1874 — Traveled down the hills into the open prairies and arrived near the base of "Bear Butte"

August 15" 1874 — Six Indian Scouts left Camp for Fort Lincoln with the mail.

August 16" 1874 — Indians intercepted by our Scouts who sent word that six (6) bands of hostile Sioux were encamped on the east side of the Little Missouri waiting to attack this command.

August 17" 1874 to 25" — Traveled over a burnt prairie. Grass found in isolated places.

August 30" 1874 — Arrived at Fort A. Lincoln D.T.

SEPT 16 1874
ADJUTANT GEN'LS OFFICE

G. A. Custer
Brevet Major General U.S. Army,
Commanding the Post.

Part of Custer's field report for the month of August, 1874. Note the laconic statement of August 2: "The prospectors accompanying the expedition found gold this morning."

The Hostiles Strike Back

The Custer Massacre

IN the winter of 1876 the Army had been reorganized. In May, under General Crook, it moved out from Fort Fetterman, Wyoming. Its object was the camp of Sitting Bull and Crazy Horse on the Rosebud. The long train moved up the Bozeman Trail past Fort Reno, and past the ghosts of Fort Kearny, now a charred ruin.

At Tongue River Crazy Horse sent a message to Crook not to cross the river, but the tough frontier fighter answered that not all the Indians in America could stop him. This was the temper of the Army; they were out to show the clever Indian chief that they were not the same as the troopers under General Reynolds, who had fled like squaws.

On the morning of the 15th Crook stripped his army down to fundamentals, left a garrison behind to guard the wagons and sent his flying columns to the Rosebud. On the evening of the 16th they crossed the Tongue River and marched to the Rosebud, where they made camp. The next morning they moved forward, and at eight, "the ball opened," as they said, and Crazy Horse attacked. One estimate put Crazy Horse's warriors at 6,000—undoubtedly exaggerated—with not all taking part in the attack.

The battle lasted for three hours. Crook camped the night on the battlefield, buried his dead and marched back to his base on Goose Creek. In a sense it was a victory for Crazy Horse. He had fought Crook to a standstill and forced him to return to his base camp and, in fact, had halted the army's expedition. He also had protected his villages and retired in good order under heavy fire. Crook sent his wounded back to Fort Fetterman and ordered more supplies and reinforcements.

While Crook was battling furiously on the Rosebud, Custer was testifying before a Congressional Committee investigating the alleged sale of tradership posts by Secre-

Sitting Bull. *Photo by D. F. Barry.*

General Custer and Colonel Ludlow with a grizzly bear they killed during the Black Hills Expedition of 1874-75. *Photo by W. H. Illingworth.*

tary of War Belknap. As General George Forsyth stated in 1902, "Custer, who was a good hater, hated Belknap and volunteered to testify against him." When his testimony turned out to be hearsay, an enraged President Grant ordered General Sherman not to allow Custer to take the field against Sitting Bull. It was only on the insistence of General Sheridan that Custer was "necessary" that Grant revoked his order and Custer was assigned to the campaign against the Sioux.

On June 22, 1876, the famed Seventh Cavalry under Custer, left its camp on the Powder River at high noon. With them were 50 Arikara auxiliaries, some Crows and some newspaper correspondents.

Custer was under orders from General Terry to move up the Rosebud, find the trail of the Indians and follow it until he found Sitting Bull's Camp. Terry would rejoin him a few days later on the Little Big Horn.

The soldiers moved off according to plan, and on the evening of June 24th they camped in the valley of the Little Big Horn. The Indians knew where Custer was; their scouts had reported the movements of his troops. But Custer apparently did not know where the Indians were or how many there were. Though he repeatedly boasted that he himself was going to destroy the whole Sioux nation he failed to achieve proper scouting and reconnaissance.

On the morning of June 25th a detachment of about 200 men under Major Reno crossed the river and headed up the hillside in the direction of the Indian camp. They kicked up a great deal of dust, made no effort at concealment, and were sitting ducks for the Indians above. There was a fierce burst of gunfire from the Indians, and the troop was half wiped out, half dispersed as the survivors fled into the woods, pursued by Indians.

At this point, another detachment of troops reached the other end of the Indian camp and started shooting. The alarm was raised, and the warriors rushed over in great numbers. Soon the soldiers were surrounded, struck at

The telegram notifying the Adjutant General of Custer's disaster. Dated June 27, it was received in Chicago July 6, 1876.

from every side, and wiped out in a last, furious hand-to-hand charge by the redskins.

Some of the soldiers who had reached the bluff above the river held out and resisted every effort of the Indians to drive them off. These men were besieged and attacked all night, but in the morning, the Indians broke off the attack. They set fire to the grass and, protected by the resulting smoke screen, rode off into the Big Horn Mountains.

Two hundred and sixty-six soldiers died in the Battle of Little Big Horn, a few escaped, and 54 wounded were recovered. Custer was not found, but later it was established that he had been killed. He had not been identified because the day after leaving Fort Abraham Lincoln he had a trooper cut his long yellow hair, and his body was not recognized.

The Battle of Little Big Horn is one of the West's most controversial. Was Custer outrageously careless and foolhardy; had he arrived at the Little Big Horn too soon before the arranged time of rendezvous with the other troops so that he could achieve the victory himself, had he planned a brilliant, flanking tactic that had not come off? The matter is still debated. For a time Custer was regarded as a

The bluff where some of Custer's men were driven into the Little Big Horn. *Photo by S. J. Morrow.*

An Eye-Witness Account of the Custer Battle

BY GALL

(Gall, an Indian who had taken part in the fight gave this account as reported in a pamphlet edited by Usher L. Burdick, *Indian Notes on the Custer Battle* by D. F. Barry. Barry was a well-known photographer of the West. In the company of some Army officers and Indians who had been in the battle, he visited the Little Big Horn battlefield ten years after the event. He reported what Gall said.)

It took about thirty-five minutes to wipe out this bunch of soldiers (Custer's), and I never saw men fight harder. They were right down on their knees firing and loading until the last man fell. I never saw any soldier offer to surrender. The smoke and dust was so thick that we could not always see the soldiers. The soldiers were fighting on foot, so finally we rode over them with our ponies. Our ponies were well rested and fast runners, but the soldiers' horses were so hungry that they were eating grass while the battle was going on and our braves had no difficulty in catching all of them. While making our way to Poplar River these horses were not much good and we left a lot of them on the Missouri River.

On the morning of the 25th away to the East we saw soldiers marching down the divide in our direction. They passed out of sight behind the rough land several miles from the river. Just how these soldiers were divided, I do not know. We never saw the pack train (McDougall's Command) until it joined Reno on the hill.

We first noticed several companies of soldiers about two miles east of our camp, marching along the bluffs in the direction of the lower end of our camp. These soldiers kicked up lots of dust and they came in sight the second time about two hours after noon. They were mounted on white horses and it was a nice sight to see this parade across the river to the east. We watched these soldiers and were rounding up our pony herd so we could fight if the soldiers attacked us. . . .

The soldiers we were watching were headed for the camp of the Cheyennes. While we were thus watching them, some boys who were out Southeast of the camp ran into the Blackfoot camp and told them soldiers were coming from the Southeast and had shot at them. Very soon we heard a great amount of shooting in that direction. Crazy Horse rushed through our camp headed in the direction of the shooting and his men followed; I started that way too, and so did Crow King. We paid no attention to the soldiers marching toward the North end. About two thousand warriors finally gathered down where the shooting was (Reno's Command).

There was one force of Arikara scouts with this band of soldiers and they were on our right as we sped in that direction. We charged them first because it made us mad to see Indians fighting us. They ran first and we never saw them again. We turned toward our left to fight the soldiers. They were hard to drive out because they were on foot and in the brush and grass. We could not shoot them, so we charged them and soon they were successful, ran a most straight east and crossed the river and got up on a high hill, (Reno Hill). We killed many while they were fighting with their horses, and we killed many while they were running as our ponies were more speedy. . . .

As soon as we had chased these soldiers out, (Reno's force), we did not fight them again right away. Crow King and Crazy Horse were afraid the soldiers that we had seen march in the direction of the north end of the camp, might kill our women and children. They went back the way they had come; their ponies were racing. Crow King turned to the right before he got to the North end and got in a deep gulley and those soldiers (Custer's), could not see the warriors. Ride down there and you will see that this gulley is so deep that no one can see you from here. This gulley, the upper part, brought Crow King very close to the soldiers. Crazy Horse went to the extreme north end of the camp and then turned to his right and went up another very deep ravine and by following it, which he did, he came very close to the soldiers on their north side. Crow King was on their South side.

It was about a little after 2:30 p.m. when this part of the battle began. Crow King shot from the South and Crazy Horse from the North. The soldiers were trying to get back up the hill, but Crazy Horse and his warriors were behind the top of the hill shooting. Soldiers were falling all around; they were on foot and their horses were in the upper end of the ravine where Crazy Horse was.

I saw what was going on and left the hill, Reno Hill, and ran for the battle. I struck the train the soldiers had made as they had marched down to the North end and soon came up to some of them to the east of where the rest were. (He meant east of Custer.) We either killed or ran over these and went on down to where the last soldiers were. They were fighting good. The men were loading and firing, but they could not hit the warriors in the gulley and the ravine. The dust and smoke was black as evening. Once in a while we could see the soldiers through the dust, and finally we charged through them with our ponies. When we had done this, right here on this ground, just a few rods South of us; the fight was over.

Gall, who fought against Custer and told the story of the Little Big Horn massacre. *Photo by D. F. Barry.*

A letter written by Major Marcus A. Reno in 1885, reporting the discovery of his own diary, found lying on the grass after the Custer massacre.

hero, admired for the courage of his magnificent last stand on the bluff. Indian chiefs who had taken part in the battle testified that Custer and his men died gallantly. But as the evidence mounted, it began to appear that, as in the noble charge of the Light Brigade, someone had blundered.

The news of the annihilation of Custer's command swept across the plains like a grass fire. At Pine Ridge Reservation, a thousand Cheyennes broke out and went on the warpath, visualizing, no doubt, the plunder and the scalps just waiting to be collected.

The Fifth under General Wesley Merritt with "Buffalo Bill" Cody as its chief scout, made a forced march of 30 hours to head off the hostiles at War Bonnet in southeast South Dakota. In a brief battle Yellow Hand was killed by Buffalo Bill, another western incident which has almost as much controversy about it as Custer's last stand. The Cheyennes were finally chased back to Pine Ridge.

Crook, meanwhile, after the action at Rosebud, took out after Crazy Horse. It was days of marching and finding nothing. The Indian army seemed ghostlike as it

Major Marcus A. Reno.

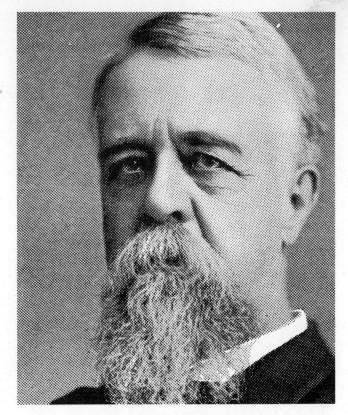

General Alfred H. Terry.

slipped away before the doggedly marching white men. By mid-September, there were only two and a half days' worth of supplies left in the entire train. Crook sent young Captain Anson Mills with 25 troopers of the Third to Deadwood City to get provisions—"any kind," as Crook put it.

On his way back Mills discovered a small Sioux camp at Slim Buttes. A surprise attack wiped out the village, found to be the camp of American Horse. The dying chief finally surrendered after holding out in a canyon with his surviving braves and women and children. Mills was delighted to find supplies and forage in the camp which he immediately sent back to Crook's main base.

The season was changing, and Crook returned to Fort Fetterman to plan his winter campaign. On November 4 Colonel Ronald S. Mackenzie, with ten troops from the Second, Fourth and Fifth, set out to attack the Cheyennes in Willow Creek Canyon in the Big Horn Mountains. After a stubborn battle Mackenzie's troops routed the Cheyennes, killed their leader, Dull Knife, and set fire to the villages. The starving survivors sought out Crazy Horse, who, short on rations himself, refused to shelter them. It was poor diplomacy, and the Cheyenne bucks, after terrible hardships, entered a reservation. In the spring they would ride with the troopers against their traditional ally.

Curly, known to his Crow tribesmen as Ash-ish-ish-e.

General Wesley Merritt.

Captain Jack Crawford (x on hat), the scout poet who served with Merritt, shown in the Black Hills, 1876. *Photo by S. J. Morrow.*

Red Cloud, Buffalo Bill Cody, American Horse.

In another phase of the winter and fall all-out Indian campaign, General Miles' foot soldiers defeated but did not capture Sitting Bull on the Yellowstone. Crazy Horse, with 400 bucks, escaped; others had promised Miles to surrender at the Red Cloud Agency, which they did.

In December the relentless Miles moved against Crazy Horse. In a spectacular battle in January, 1877, in which troopers climbed the walls of a steep cliff of the Tongue River south of the Yellowstone, he defeated the great war captain. After his camp, baggage and supplies were captured, there was nothing left for Crazy Horse but to surrender.

Dull Knife.

American Horse. His buckskin shirt is trimmed with scalps.

In May, Miles captured the village of Lame Deer and Iron Star, and in the melee both chiefs were killed. Now only Sitting Bull remained and he escaped, leading a small band of followers into British Columbia.

On September 7, 1877, Crazy Horse was killed in a fight near the guard-house. Now it seemed that peace had come to the Great Plains. As one old chief told Miles: "We are poor compared to you and your force. We cannot make a rifle, ammunition or a knife. In fact, we are at the mercy of you who are taking possession of our land. Your terms are harsh and cruel, but we are going to accept them and place ourselves at your mercy."

It would be a fleeting peace at the most.

A letter written by Chief Red Wing of the Sioux, "through hand of white maiden"
to the President of the United States, "Father Grant."

To the great father in the council house of the people;

Red Wing, from the Dakota country of the Black hills, one of the Sioux, coming from the upper hunting grounds of the good Spirit, makes this appeal in behalf of his red brothers.

Many, many moons ago, the tribes of the Red man was visited by a council of palefaces, who bartered for their fine land, and sent the red man way towards the setting sun, but the blankets, and the shooting irons that the paleface gave, were soon used, and the redskin had no way to live but, as he had before the white man came, (on the chase, seeking game).

The red man settled in his new territory (in one little spot of the great country that the good Spirit gave to the Indian moons before the paleface knew of it), but he had no peace, the white man, eager for more land, more game, eager to drive the red man off, came; our lodges were destroyed, our council fires broken up and the red children of the plains were scattered like the leaves of the forest.

The Indian, burning from his wrongs, made fierce by the treatment of the whites, rushed upon the palefaces; and not making distinction, scalped and tomahawked all he found, believing every paleface to be treacherous and mean, unfit to live in the vast country which the great Manota gave to his children, where they live in their lodges free children of the forest and the lake, and so, he scalped the whites, as snakes, believing that the smile of the Great Spirit, shone on them in the beams of the morning sun, for it.

But, Red Wing no come to tell of this, Red Wing come to whisper to the great father of the white people, of the treaty he made (some time ago) with the Red man when he made the reservation of the Black hills country to the Sioux.

Not yet, has the Summer sun shone, or the winter snow fell, eight times since the treaty was made by Chief Sherman, and other chiefs on the great sachem's side, and the chiefs of the Sioux on the Red man's. Not yet have the leaves of the forest fallen eight times, since the provision ("No persons, except such officers, agents, or employees of the Government as may be authorized to enter on Indian reservation territory, in discharge of the dutys enjoined by law, shall ever be permitted to pass over, settle upon, or reside in this territory," and, "the honor of the government of the United States is pledged to keep it." treaty.

When this treaty was made by big chiefs sent out by strong Sachem at Washington, Sioux, expect white man keep it, but no, squads of palefaces come, search the country, want to drive red man away, and seize the country, what, Redskin do, if he drove from Dakota, where go? Paleface drove game from other parts of country, Red man no want starve, no want see paleface take lodge and blankets from papoose, go further West, he find the sun setting there, no go south, it no be his home. And so he get fierce, he sharpening his tomahawk, he fixing shooting irons, he get ready to steal on palefaces, when moon hides her face and the stars grow dim. And Red Wing calls upon the great father to prevent the bloodshed of the whites, and the extermination of the Indians, to preserve his treaty, to allow no one to settle in Sioux territory who no belong there.

Red Wing come way east to white maiden to ask mighty father to look after his red children, he has granted heap big sum for the red man's use, heap wampum, but white man greedy, he give red man poor blankets, rusty shooting irons, damp powder, bad beef, musty flour, take wampum big Sachem say for Indian, and spect Indian be satisfied.

Indian no satisfied, he calls of great Spirit to help him, Great Spirit hear, and sends Red Wing to the father at the council house to ask father, to see to red children, to send out brave, good palefaces to distribute stores to Sioux, and Cheyennes and Arapahoes and others. Send chiefs to look after the wants of the red children, send out talking sheet over the country forbidding white man invade Black hills in search of shiners, send words to chiefs at forts no to allow braves to fire on redskins.

This what Red Wing want, this what great Spirit want, the good father at Washington to make his council a council of Peace, want him to protect Red man, then the Indian troubles will subside, and the Red man will pass away, quite and natural from his lodges, to the hunting ground of Manota beyond the setting sun, leaving the country to the paleface, and the glory of father Grant will surround his life like the glory of the sun at noon day heat.

Red Wing, Sioux, through hand of white maiden

Red War in the Lava Beds

While the bluecoats were fighting the Sioux and Cheyennes on the western plains, the United States was engaged in one of its most costly wars—fought in the lava beds of Oregon—during the winter of 1872-73. Here 50 Modoc Indians under the leadership of Kientpoos, better known as Captain Jack, not only held off a force of cavalry and infantry several times their number but defeated the soldiers time after time.

The Modocs first became a major problem to the military in 1852 when they wiped out an emigrant train near Tule Lake. The entire company was murdered, many subjected to hair-raising tortures. One man, left for dead, managed to escape and tell his story.

A Californian named Ben Wright gathered together a large posse and chased the Modocs, who escaped from them in the lava beds. Wright then sent out word to Schonchin, the Modoc chief, to come in for a peace parley. When they arrived Wright and his party opened fire and killed most of the Indians. After the Civil War a treaty was made with the tribe. Under Schonchin, their chief who had led them in the wagon-train disaster, they settled on the reservation only to find to their dismay that they were quartered with the larger Klamath tribe.

There was much friction and Captain Jack, Hooker Jim and Curly Headed Doctor left the reservation to camp on their old hunting ground, the Lost River Country. The Modocs, a shiftless, transient band, frightened the settlers in the region, who protested to the Army. General Edward S. Canby was ordered to return the Modocs to their reservation, "peaceably if you can, forcibly if you must."

Captain James Jackson and 40 troopers were ordered to round up the Modocs and bring them back to the reservation. On the morning of November 28, 1872, after an all-night ride through a downpour, Jackson arrived at the Indians' camp and, in his own words, "jumped" it.

The Indians surrendered, but Jack stayed in his tepee. When Jackson demanded that the Indians surrender their weapons Scar Face Charley, who had seen his father hanged by the white man, refused. Others joined him. When an officer and some men tried to take away their rifles, the battle started. Meanwhile, across the river some civilian volunteers had opened fire on Hooker Jim's camp only to be driven off. When the smoke cleared Captain Jack and the remnants of his people had disappeared in the hills, leaving 15 warriors, women and children dead on the field.

He retreated to the lava beds, where he was joined by Hooker Jim, who had killed 17 settlers on the way. The combined tribes counted 50 warriors and a large number of women and children.

Detachments of the First Cavalry and Twenty-First Infantry, along with units from the Oregon and California Militia, were sent out to bring back the Indians, who were now boasting they could hold off a thousand troops in

Captain Jack of the Modocs.

Shacknasty Jim, Hooker Jim, Steamboat Frank, Judge John Fairchild.

the rugged lava beds. They made good their boast as they moved like shadows among the ridges and cross-passages which they knew as well as the backs of their own hands.

The soldiers stumbled from ridge to ridge, their shoes cut to pieces by the flint-sharp rocks. From out of nowhere rifles cracked, men dropped. Volleys would be turned against the spot from where the shot had come, but when the troops charged they found only emptiness. After a fruitless campaign the army's commander returned to his base with one-fourth of his command killed or wounded. He said he would need a command of a thousand men armed with artillery and mortars to blow the small band of Modocs out of their hiding places.

The First Cavalry was put into the field; reinforcements brought the command to the thousand mark. Artillery was also included, and General Canby himself took to the field. First he tried peace negotiations, promising to put the Modocs on Angel Island in San Francisco Harbor until they could choose another reservation, but this the Indians refused. It was Lost River country—or nothing. Captain Jack wanted to settle on his own terms, but his warriors called for all-out war. In one of their councils legend has the warriors putting a woman's shawl on Jack's shoulders to show their contempt. This action brought Jack to his feet. "If you want war you shall have it," he cried angrily.

The first step which they thought would make the white man withdraw was to agree to a peace meeting with the white man's commissioners, then murder the

Toby Riddle, the Modoc wife of Frank Riddle.

commissioners, who besides Canby included Colonel Gillem, the Reverend Dr. Eleazar Thomas, a Methodist minister well known to the Modocs, H. B. Meacham, a former Indian agent, and another agent, L. S. Dyer. Riddle, a squaw man who had married a Modoc woman, urged Canby to call off the meeting. He said he was sure Jack could not be trusted.

On the lookout for an attack in the lava beds.

WILD HORSES. *Painted by Charles Banks Wilson.*

THE MOUNTAIN OF THE HOLY CROSS. *Painted by Thomas Moran. Reproduced from an L. Prang & Co. print, it was the first successful mechanical attempt to reproduce color, 1876.*

THE TOWERS OF TOWER FALLS, YELLOWSTONE. *Painted by Thomas Moran.*

A Cavalry Charge. Based on "Custer's Last Fight," a painting by William Leigh.
Painted by Samuel H. Bryant.

Sɪᴛᴛɪɴɢ Bᴜʟʟ. A portrait made in September, 1890, shortly before his death.
Painted by Gilbert Gaul.

QUANAH PARKER, 1890. *Painted by Julian Scott.*

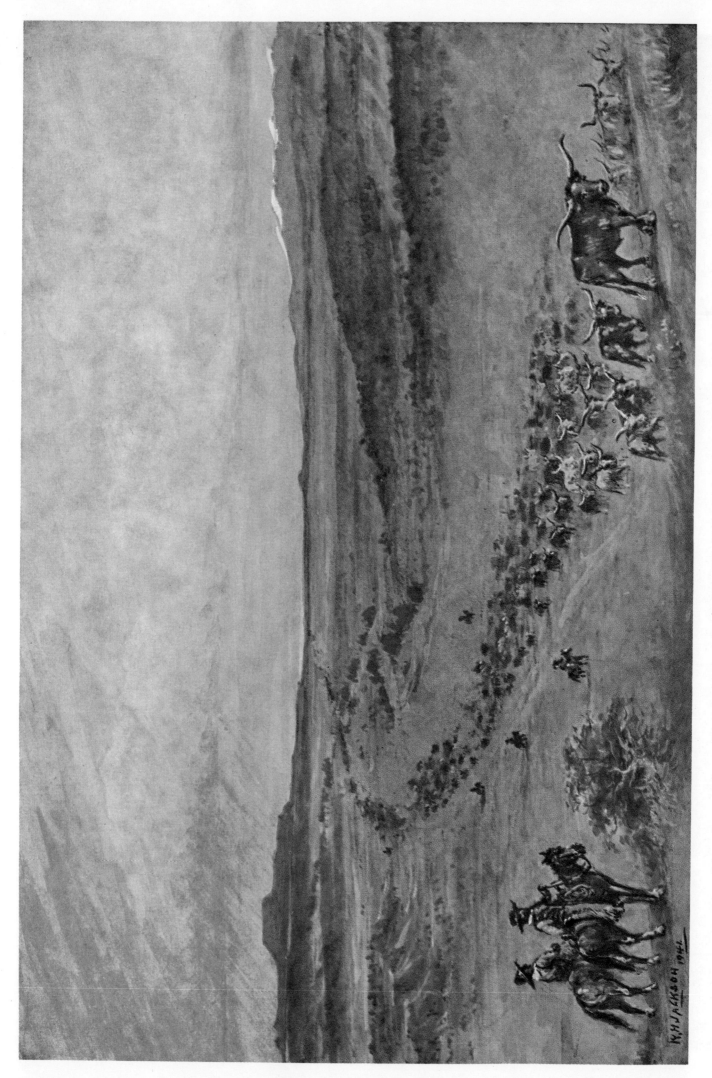

Texas Longhorns Driving North Over the Chisholm Trail. *Painted by W. H. Jackson.*

The Stampede. *Painted by John Henrici.*

On the morning of April 11, 1873, Canby and his party met Captain Jack and his warriors in the large peace tent. Riddle, the squaw man, felt so strongly about the council that before he agreed to act as interpreter he made the commissioners accompany him to the bedside of Colonel Gillem, who had been taken ill, and at the sick bed made a violent protest against holding the council. But Canby, who was not swayed, ordered it held.

The council was brief and tense. The Indians were insolent and savage. It was clear they meant trouble but, unruffled, Canby continued the council. Suddenly Captain Jack shouted an order and each Indian in the tent who apparently had been assigned a victim opened fire. Canby was shot in the face by Jack, while Boston Charlie shot Dr. Thomas as he was kneeling. Dyer and Riddle, who at the last minute had slipped derringers in their pockets, escaped with the Indians after them. Hooker Jim was about to grab Dyer when he turned and fired his revolver. The surprised Indians, seeing their intended victims were now armed, broke off the chase after firing several rounds.

The Indians stripped the bodies of Canby, Thomas and Meacham and Boston Charlie prepared to scalp them. He had slit the scalp of Meacham when Riddle's Indian wife cried, "Soldiers are coming," and the Modocs fled.

Colonel Jefferson C. Davis with officers during the Modoc campaign.

The cowardly murder of General Canby aroused the Army; it was clear that Jack and his people had to be dug out of the lava beds even at bayonet point. On the 14th Colonel Gillem left his sick bed to lead a large force in an attack against the beds. Mortars zeroed Jack's stronghold with a curious effect. One shell failed to explode and one curious Indian tried to pull out the plug with his teeth; result: seven dead Modocs. Realizing that the mortars had made his position untenable, Jack retreated back in the maze of crevices and underground passages in the beds.

On April 21 a party of soldiers and Warm Springs Indians set out after them. They were ambushed and many of the soldiers panicked, leaving behind most of the command. When the Modocs had slipped away 22 soldiers and officers were dead and 18 wounded. Not one of the 20 warriors had suffered a scratch.

Colonel Jefferson C. Davis (the Union officer, not the Confederacy's President), commander of the Department of Columbia, was finally given command and ordered to close the shameful campaign at once. Davis, a strict disciplinarian, reorganized his troops, gave them new provisions and weapons and, adopting the Modocs' own tactics, began to tighten a cordon around the lava-bed area.

A Modoc War correspondent, McKay of the San Francisco *Bulletin*, in the lava beds.

The Indians had split into two parties, one under Jack, the other under Hooker. They were now suffering from lack of water, supplies and ammunition. There was also friction in their councils, and finally it was agreed to leave the beds.

On May 10 the Indians, united into one command, launched an attack on the camp of the Fourth Artillery, mounted for this campaign. The surprise was at first successful, but the troops rallied to give the Modocs their first clear-cut defeat in addition to capturing their mules and ammunition.

They now fled from the beds, and Colonel Davis ordered a vigorous pursuit. One large band of 100 families was captured, and Davis offered them their lives if they would disclose the hideout of Captain Jack and Hooker Jim.

A redskin Judas led the troops to where his comrades were hiding. Jack and Hooker Jim were at last taken into custody and Davis prepared to hang them. Washington officials, however, stopped him after a discussion of the legality of the execution. A trial was ordered and Hooker Jim, Bogus Charley and Shacknasty Jim became government witnesses. Jack, without benefit of defense counsel, made a long speech defending himself, but the evidence that he had committed cold-blooded murder was too strong. He was found guilty and sentenced to hang along with Schonchin John, Black Jim and Boston Charlie. Two of their co-defendants had their sentences commuted to life imprisonment by President Grant. The quartet was hanged at ten o'clock on the morning of October 3, 1873, in full sight of their people.

Just before he was executed a chaplain came to comfort Jack with the advice that he was going to a far, far better land. Jack looked thoughtful. "You say, Mr. Preacher, that the place I am going to is a nice place. Do you like this place you call Heaven?"

After the preacher added a glowing description of Heaven, Jack nodded and said with an impassive face, "I tell you what I will do. I'll give you twenty-five head of ponies if you take my place. As you say, Heaven is such a nice place. Because I do not like to go right now."

There were no takers and the four walked the steps to the gallows.

After the hangings, while Jack's preserved body was taken on a tour of the East, the remainder of his tribe was transferred to a small reservation near Baxter Springs, Kansas. The Army totaled up its casualties with a red face; the Modocs had lost 14 dead in the campaign, four hanged and one suicide. The soldiers and white settlers' casualties were 168, of whom 83 were killed. The cost of the campaign was estimated at a half-million dollars.

The Western Scene in Photographs

ONE of the first photographers to penetrate the West was S. N. Carvalho, who accompanied Frémont on his 1852 expedition. But Carvalho's plates were all, or almost all, lost to posterity in a fire. Carvalho sent his plates to Mathew Brady for processing and Brady returned them to Frémont, who sent them to Mrs. Frémont for safekeeping in their home. The Frémont home burned down and all the plates in it were destroyed. But in the Brady studio a plate was found showing an Indian village (reproduced on page 47). It could not have been Brady's or any other eastern photographer's, and many experts, including Paul Vanderbilt, formerly of the Library of Congress Prints and Photographs Division, believe the daguerreotype could have been made by Carvalho.

In the fifties Robert H. Vance made many excellent plates of the California gold-fields, scenes in Oregon, Washington, Colorado and probably Nevada. Alexander Gardner, one of Brady's wartime assistants, made a number of fine western photographs after the War.

But it was Tim O'Sullivan, another Brady battlefield assistant, who was the great photographer of the West. In 1866 and again in 1867 and 1869 he went out as official photographer of the U. S. Engineer Department's Geological Exploration of the 40th Parallel, led by Clarence King. In this, and in the Wheeler Expeditions of 1871, 1873 and 1874 O'Sullivan photographed everything of possible interest. He even contrived an ingenious magnesium flare arrangement for the first photographs of underground mining scenes ever made.

The roster of famous photographers of the West is long and honorable: William H. Jackson, John Hillers, L. A. Huffman, D. F. Barry, Charles R. Savage, C. C. Pierce, A. J. Russell, John Carbutt, S. J. Morrow, Camillus Fly, W. P. Bliss and many others. There were also innumerable local commercial photographers.

But until the development of halftone engraving in the 1880's none of these photographs could be reproduced economically for magazine or book publication. Many did achieve wide circulation in the form of stereoscopic views, which had been made enormously popular by Mathew Brady and Edward Anthony. These were double-prints pasted on cardboard and viewed through a stereoscopic lens to achieve three-dimensional effects.

The sale of stereoscopic "Rocky Mountain Views," "California Scenes" and a host of other such pictures was tremendous and served to stimulate interest in the West.

Probably because they were a convenient 4″ x 7″ size and backed by cardboard, a great quantity of these views, including many by O'Sullivan and Jackson, have been preserved. But the great wealth of original photographs of the 1865-1890 period of the West has been lost. Only a few collections exist and, as explained in the foreword, a number of these were "lucky finds."

In addition to the photographs shown in the following pages, many other examples of the work of these famous photographers are included in their appropriate sections. The picture on this page was taken on the Wheeler Expedition of 1871. The pictures on the following 14 pages were taken by O'Sullivan on the King Expedition.

Pack mule, pack and packers. A facsimile of a stereoscopic view card. *Photo by Tim O'Sullivan.*

Mount Agassiz.

View on the Snake River.

Shoshone Indians.

Paiute Indians, Pyramid Lake.

[126]

Officers' quarters, Fort Ruby.

Company quarters, Fort Ruby.

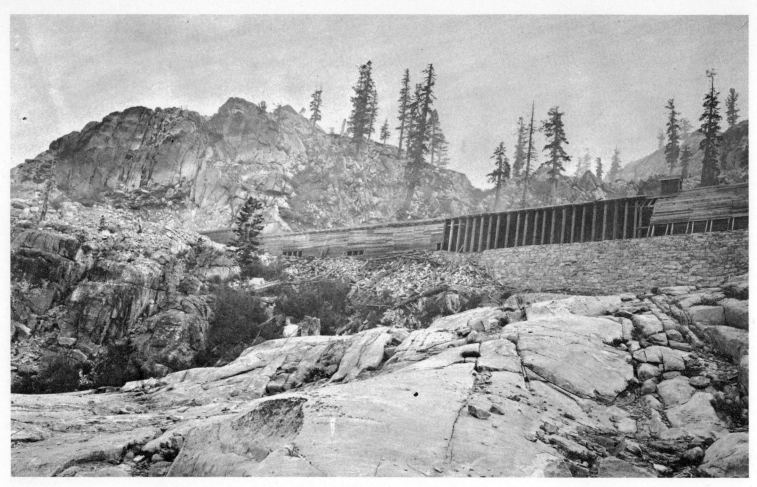

On the Central Pacific Railroad. Wall and snow sheds east of Summit between tunnels 7 and 8.

Livermore Pass, Central Pacific Railroad.

Donner Lake.

Eastern portal of Summit Tunnel, showing old wagon road east of Donner Pass.

Virginia City, Nevada.

The Virginia Mines, showing the Curtis Shaft (*top left.*) The other three pictures are underground views, the first photographs ever taken in a mine by magnesium light.

Gould and Curry Mill.

Sugar Loaf, near Virginia City.

Gold Hill.

Montezuma Works at Oreana, Nevada.

Pyramid Lake, Nevada.

Alkali lake, near Ragtown.

Shoshone Falls, Idaho.

Humboldt Hot Springs, Nevada.

Steamboat Springs, Nevada.

Sand dune, near Sand Springs.

Astronomical observatory.

Headquarters U. S. Geological Exploration, 40th Parallel.

King's camp, near Salt Lake City.

On the Truckee River.

Ridge of Trinity Mountains, Nevada.

City of Rocks, Idaho.

Uintah Mountains, head of Bear River, Utah.

Summit of East Humboldt, Nevada.

Pyramid Lake island (lime tufa).

Cottonwood Canyon, Wasatch Range.

Sawmill in Cottonwood Canyon, Wasatch Range.

Glacial lake, East Humboldt Mountains.

Uintah Mountains, Utah.

Big Bend, Truckee River.

Austin, Nevada.

Wasatch Mountains, east of Salt Lake City. Camp Douglass on the left.

ROBERT H. VANCE

Vance, called the "Mathew Brady of the Gold Rush," was one of the earliest photographers of the West, an expert at large-scale views. He operated a studio in San Francisco in the 1850's and made many pictures of the gold camps and of San Francisco.

The view from Poverty Bar to Oregon Bar.

Forest Hill, under the Hill.

Garland's Mill, Placer County.

A. J. RUSSELL

Russell (whose name is sometimes spelled Russel) worked for Brady early in the Civil War. In 1862, at the request of General Haupt, he joined his Railroad Construction Corps as a "special artist." His adventures as a Civil War photographer included being blown up by a shell and landing unhurt, with his camera intact. He went west as a Union Pacific photographer.

Laramie Valley, from Sheephead Mountain.

Malloy's Cut, Sherman Station, Laramie Range.

Dial Rock, Red Buttes, Laramie Plains.

Conglomerate Peaks of Echo.

Serrated rocks of Devil's Slide, Weber Canyon, Utah.

Hanging Rock, Echo City.

Wilhelmina's Pass, showing Devil's Slide at right, Weber Canyon, Utah.

Bitter Creek Valley, near Green River.

C. E. WATKINS

Watkins, originally a New Yorker, went west with the '49ers to the gold fields of California. He was introduced to photography by Robert Vance and took over Vance's gallery in San Francisco in 1854. His photographs of the Yosemite—spelled Yo-Semite at the time —taken in 1861 became nationally known. The plates were taken with his huge homemade camera under the most primitive conditions. All were destroyed in the San Francisco earthquake and fire, including those from which these prints were made.

The Grizzly Giant, 33 feet in diameter, Mariposa Grove, California.

Forest scene, Yosemite.

Yosemite Falls.

River scene, Yosemite.

JOHN K. HILLERS

Hillers, who accompanied the Powell Survey of 1872, was appointed chief photographer after illness had forced the former chief to return to civilization after a few days on the plains. According to Frederic S. Dellenbaugh, whose series on the survey made Hillers' photographs the talk of the country in the 1870's, the photographer descended the unknown Colorado River "in one of the greatest feats of exploration ever executed on this continent."

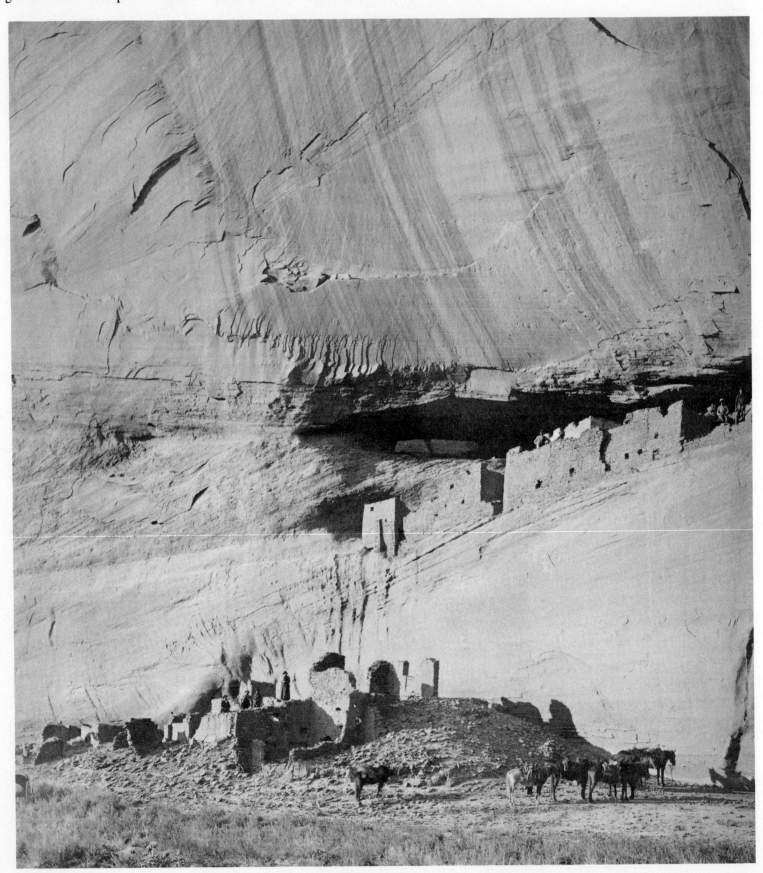

Ruins of cliff dwellings, Canyon de Chelly.

View in Canyon de Chelly, Arizona, looking west.

Navajo Church.

Uintah Ute scout, western slope of Wasatch Mountains.

Bend in the river.

JOHN CARBUTT

Carbutt's series on the building of the Union Pacific and the famous "Excursion to the 100th Meridian" were personally ordered by T. Durant, vice-president of the railroad. Carbutt accompanied the party which included "two brass bands, two kinds of the most distinguished citizens of America, reporters from practically every important newspaper in the country, a staff of chefs, a French marquis, an English earl, government commissioners and Union Pacific directors." The series is extremely rare.

Engine house and workshops.

Laying the rails—two miles a day.

Landing of the guests for the 100th Meridian excursion.

The way west.

[147]

TIM O'SULLIVAN

O'Sullivan is without a doubt the greatest of western photographers. He served his apprenticeship with Mathew B. Brady and was at Gettysburg on the third day. After the King Expeditions he served as official photographer for the Wheeler Expeditions of 1871-74, and took the pictures shown here. He died on Staten Island, January 14, 1883.

The start from Camp Mojave, Arizona. The boat expedition under Lieutenant Wheeler was the first to ascend the Colorado through the Grand Canyon.

Marble Canyon on the Colorado. The cliff is gray, the slope below a brilliant red sandstone.

Mojave Indians.

Northern wall of the Grand Canyon.

Baldy Peak, Colorado, 14,234 feet high.

Navajo squaw and child. Canyon de Chelly, Arizona.

Jicarilla Apache brave, northern New Mexico.

Zuñi Indian braves at their pueblo, New Mexico.

Navajo squaws weaving blankets, Canyon de Chelly.

Apaches ready for the warpath.

A Ute squaw, northern New Mexico.

Ruins of the Pueblo San Juan, New Mexico.

Roman Catholic Church, Guadaloupe County, Colorado.

One of a group of Pagosa Hot Springs.

Navajo brave with his mother.

Jicarilla Apache brave and his squaw.

Ute braves in "full dress," New Mexico.

[149]

WILLIAM HENRY JACKSON

Jackson is one of the best known of all western photographers. When he died in New York City in 1942 he was one of the last of New York's four Civil War veterans. His father was an amateur daguerreotypist and by 1857 young Jackson was his assistant. He was official photographer for the F. V. Hayden Surveys, 1870-1879, and his photographs of that territory, now Yellowstone National Park, were instrumental in the establishment of the park. He retired in 1929, devoted himself to painting scenes of the West, and achieved a notable reputation in that field also.

Grand Canyon of the Arkansas.

Leadville, from Capitol Hill.

Aspen, Colorado.

GENERAL JOHN T. PITMAN

Pitman began photographing western scenes after he entered the Regular Army in 1866. His collection of glass plates, now in the possession of the author, records the life and times on the frontier from Fort Snelling, Fort Abraham Lincoln and the Dakota Territory to the arrival of President Roosevelt's "Great White Fleet" in New York Harbor in 1907-08. Pitman was in charge of the team that developed smokeless powder for the army at Frankfort Arsenal, Philadelphia. Some of his plates include scenes of life at the Arsenal.

Sioux burial platform. Note ropes holding the body to the platform.

Standing Rock Agency. Note the "ant blankets." This was a device copied from the Sioux. The ants destroyed any vermin in a blanket left on the ground.

Bismarck, Dakota Territory, 1880.

On the porch of Custer's house at Fort Abraham Lincoln.

Fort Snelling, Minnesota.

The famous *Helena* of Omaha.

D. F. BARRY

Barry, a superb craftsman among the western photographers, is best known for his gallery of portraits of Indian chiefs and warriors. He began his career in Bismarck, Dakota Territory, in 1875 and was soon known to the Sioux as "Little Shadow Catcher." He persuaded Gall to let him take his picture but the chief returned the next day, threatening to kill Barry if he didn't destroy the plate. Barry hid the plate although Gall drew a knife and went on a rampage in his studio.

Crow Foot, Sitting Bull's son.

Indian Commission at Fort Abraham Lincoln, Dakota Territory, 1889. *Left to right:* General Crook, Governor Fasler, and Major Warner, sitting in front of "Custer's house," which was occupied by Custer in the 1870's.

[155]

C. E. WATKINS

In his later years Watkins operated chiefly in the Northwest. His Columbia River series is a rare record of the Oregon-Washington country and his Yellowstone photographs are among the best of that area.

Polar bear, taken at the Columbia River.

Cascades of the Columbia River.

Cascades Canal.

Spokane Falls, Washington Territory.

Morning Glory Geyser.

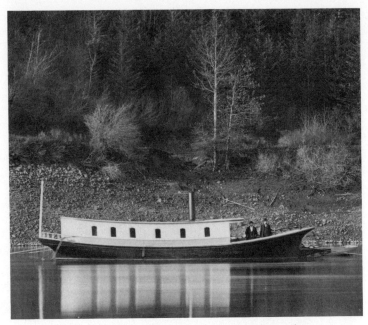

Steam launch, government locks, Cascades.

Golden Gate and bridge, Yellowstone Park.

Salmon wheel boat.

Hell's Half Acre and Five Hole River.

I. W. TABER

San Francisco's Chinatown, its colorful side streets, Seal Rock and early Los Angeles were the favorite subjects of Taber, who became well known in the 1880's for his experiments in lighting and background.

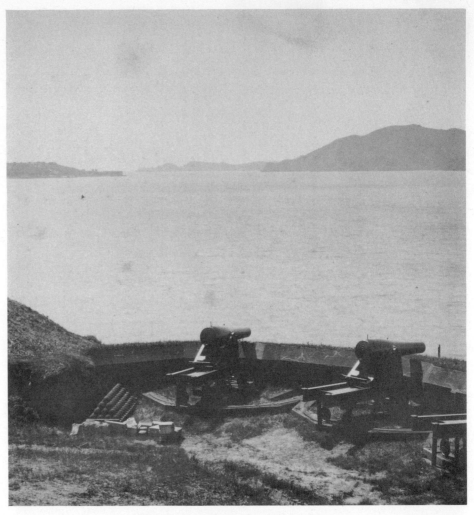

The Golden Gate, from Fort Mason.

The garden of the Santa Barbara Mission.

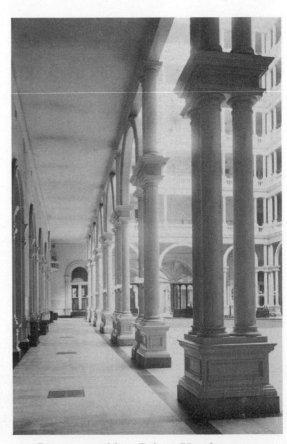

Lower corridor, Palace Hotel court.

The Three Brothers (4,000 feet).

Table Rock, Glacier Point.

A fallen tree, 300 feet long, Mariposa Grove.

L. A. HUFFMAN

Huffman learned photography as apprentice to his father and began his career as a western photographer with Frank J. Haynes in Moorhead, Minnesota in 1878. He became fort photographer at Fort Keogh, and then opened a studio in Miles City, Montana. He made a fine record of the era, with his excellent photographs of Indians, cowboys, soldiers, buffalo and other wild life. He died in Miles City in 1931.

The chase.

Roped.

Held down.

Examining a dim brand.

CHARLES R. SAVAGE

There is scarcely a schoolboy in America who hasn't studied one of Savage's most famous photographs—the meeting of the transcontinental railroads at Promontory Point, Utah, May 10, 1869. Savage was an Englishman who went west, settling in Nebraska, where he opened a daguerreotype gallery in 1860.

Ute squaws, Utah.

Yucca brevifolia, Mojave Desert.

W. H. ILLINGWORTH

Illingworth, an aggressive and hard-working frontier photographer, was well known in St. Paul, Minnesota. He is famous for his series on the Fisk expedition of 1866 to Montana and for his series on Custer's expedition to the Black Hills.

The Fisk expedition, which escorted emigrants to the Montana gold fields, 1866.

[163]

STANLEY J. MORROW

Morrow, believed to have been trained by Mathew Brady, went west in 1870 to open a daguerreotype gallery in Yankton, Dakota Territory. In 1873 he accompanied the General D. S. Stanley Expedition, which protected the construction parties of the Northern Pacific Railroad. He is best known for his photographs of the Crook expedition and the Custer reburial expedition.

The Crook campaign, 1876. A wounded lieutenant being transported by travois.

CAMILLUS S. FLY

The Tombstone, Arizona, photographer who is best known for his series on the peace councils held by General Crook with Geronimo, was also an eyewitness at the famed Battle of the O.K. Corral.

Geronimo, Nachez and Geronimo's son.

Cattle

Cattle trail. *Photo by C. D. Kirkland.*

The Drives North

WHILE the story of cattle in the West began with the *conquistadores* and their introduction of longhorns to the plains, the story of the cattle kingdoms and their fabulous cattle ranches really began after the Civil War.

The first "cow hunts," forerunners of the round-ups, were conducted by men who had returned from the wars to find the land teeming with wild cattle which roamed the plains, much like the wild horses, but in far greater numbers. Cattle could be sold in the beef-hungry North for a fantastic profit. The one problem was how to get the steers to the nearest northern railhead. The answer lay in cattle drives.

Cattle drives were not unique to the Texas frontiersman. The *Tenth Census, Statistics of Agriculture,* paints a vivid picture of those early cattle drives. The report was completed in 1880 by Robert Gordon, a member of the Department of Agriculture, after he had traveled across the West, interviewing scores of pioneering cattlemen and Army officers attached to frontier posts.

Gordon tells of the first cattle drives, some as early as 1837 when cowboys gathered herds ranging in size from 300 to 1,000 in the Nueces and Rio Grande country "and drove them to interior cities for sale."

In 1842, cattle drives were extended to New Orleans with a large herd shipped by Morgan steamer in 1848. The line plied between Galveston, New Orleans and Mobile. However, outlets for the drovers were few and the cattle herds continued to grow larger and larger.

Gordon said "a report" had a drive going north to

Missouri in 1842, but the earliest authenticated account of a drive was by a man named Edward Piper in 1846, who took a thousand head to Ohio, "where he fed them and sold them."

One of the most spectacular drives was made, not to the Border States, but to New York City. In 1853, with the nearest railheads on the Mississippi River, Tom Candy Ponting set out for New York with a herd that stretched along the prairie for miles. In the autumn he halted in Illinois to winter and fatten the herd. In the spring he resumed his drive. At Muncie, Indiana, where the trail met a railroad, Ponting decided to put the herd on the "cars"—a brand-new idea in cattle driving. On July 3, 1854, Ponting and his herd reached Bergen Point in Jersey City and were ferried across to the slaughterhouses in Manhattan. The bellowing longhorns caused large crowds to collect, and more than one carriage horse ran away.

Ponting's pioneer method of getting beef to the New York market caught on, and within a few years Texas longhorns were a common sight on the streets. The western cattle drives continued to expand both in the size of the herds and the distances they covered. By 1856 herds were being taken directly to Chicago, Arizona and New Mexico Territories as well as to New York.

Compared, however, to the postwar drives, these early irregular journeys were insignificant. By the time the war had ended and the Texans were back home, the cattle in their state numbered 4,000,000. During the war there had been a few drives for the Confederates, but that was stopped when the Union forces won control of the Mississippi River.

After the war even greater herds of wild cattle ran freely over the state. They were a far cry from today's cattle. The longhorns were tough and short-tempered. As Colonel Dodge wrote in 1876, "Any sportsman on foot would eye with uneasiness the long-horned beasts pawing the earth and tossing their heads in anger at his appearance."

James MacDonald, a Scot, described them as: "Nothing less than Spanish cattle, direct descendants of those unseemly rough, lanky, long-horned animals reared for so long with large herds by the Moors on the Plains of Andalusia." Their meat was "teasingly tough" and they were almost as wild as the buffalo they were soon to replace on the western plains.

These ornery beasts could not be driven by a boy with a stick and a dog as was done on eastern stock farms. Only a physically tough, excellent horseman could do the job. He soon found that to bring a longhorn to the corral he would have to use a rope and a smart horse.

In 1866 the Texas cattleman was not the powerful rancher he would be within a few years; he was usually a cotton or corn farmer as well as a stockman. When he heard of the gold ready to be paid out by the North for beef, he began looking about at the wild herds and began computing figures. On paper he found himself to be a rich man. He lost no time in staging his "cowhunts."

In 1866 more than 200,000 head crossed the Red River

Shipping beef from Montana in the 1880's.

"Rounding 'em up." *Photo by C. D. Kirkland.*

Putting cattle aboard a steamboat.

and headed for Sedalia, Missouri, then the neareast rail-head to St. Louis. But the drivers found the southwestern roads leading to Sedalia blocked off by former guerrillas and bushwhackers who forced the owners of the cattle to pay bribes. These early trails were scenes of horror where Texans were tied to trees and flogged until they begged to ride back home and leave their herds to the outlaws.

If the Texans showed fight and had enough guns to back them, the outlaws would use other methods mostly to stampede the herd. The bandits would then corral as many of the scattered cattle as possible and hide them. The more brazen agreed to "sell" them back to the orig-inal owner at large prices. If the drover didn't have the entire price, the thieves would take as much as the traffic would bear and return some of the herd, keeping and selling the remainder.

In addition to the outlaw bands, the cattlemen found themselves faced with indignant Indian tribes when they entered the Indian Territory. The tribes resorted to the law instead of the gun.

The Five Civilized Tribes, whose wealth lay in their own herds and their rich grazing lands, realized that if they allowed unrestricted grazing, they might find them-selves in a land so barren it could not support their own cattle. So they turned to the Indian Act of 1834, which ordered the white men to pay a toll for each head passing across the red man's land.

In 1867 the Cherokee National Council quickly passed a law demanding ten cents for each head. Other tribal councils followed suit, toll gates were erected and Indian representatives held out their hands.

Quarantine laws proved to be another roadblock. The tough longhorns were immune to Spanish fever, but the domestic cattle of Missouri and Kansas could not with-stand the fever, so in 1867 both states passed a law for-

Cow-hunts

Lee Moore, a Texas driver, later foreman of a large outfit in Wyoming, gave a vivid description of early cowhunts:

We didn't call them roundups in those early days. We called them cow-hunts and every man on this cow-hunt was a cattle-owner just home from the war and went out to see what they had left to brand up. . . . I was the only boy on this cow-hunt . . . and was looking out for cattle that belonged to my father before the war. We had no wagon (chuck wagon). Every man carried his grub in a wallet on behind his saddle and his bed under his saddle. I was put on herd and kept on herd when we had one, and I don't think there was ever a day on this hunt when we didn't have a herd, and I carried a lot of extra wallets on be-hind my saddle and a string of tin cups on a hobble around my pony's neck. A wallet is a sack with both ends sewed up with the mouth of the sack in the middle. I just mention this for fear some of the cow men don't know what a wallet is. Whenever the boss herder couldn't hear those cups jingling, he would come around and wake me up. We would corral the cattle every night at someone of the owner's homes and stand guard around the corral. I didn't stand any guard, but I carried brush and corn-stalks and anything I could get to make a light for those who were on guard to play poker by. They played for un-branded cattle, yearlings at fifty cents a head and the top price for any class was $5 a head, so if anyone run out of cattle and had a little money, he could get a stack of yearlings. My compensa-tion for light was twenty-five cents per night or as long as the game lasted. Every few days they would divide up and brand and each man take his cattle home, as we now call it—throw back.

This cow-hunt continued all summer and when I wasn't going to school, I was picking cotton or cow-hunting.

bidding Texas longhorns from entering the states during fall and summer. In addition to the fee-demanding Indians, the outlaws and the quarantine laws, there were the home-steaders, who banded together and forced the drivers to flank their farm lands or settle for the damages done to gardens and fences.

All these obstacles tended to bend the trails further north so that the Texas Panhandle and the eastern part of Colorado became the doorway to the northern ranges. It was a period of trial and error. Some drovers turned to the Missouri-Kansas border toward another railroad east of Sedalia. The trails were rough and the herds usually fin-ished in poor condition. Other cattlemen drove as far as Wyoming, others to Illinois and Iowa.

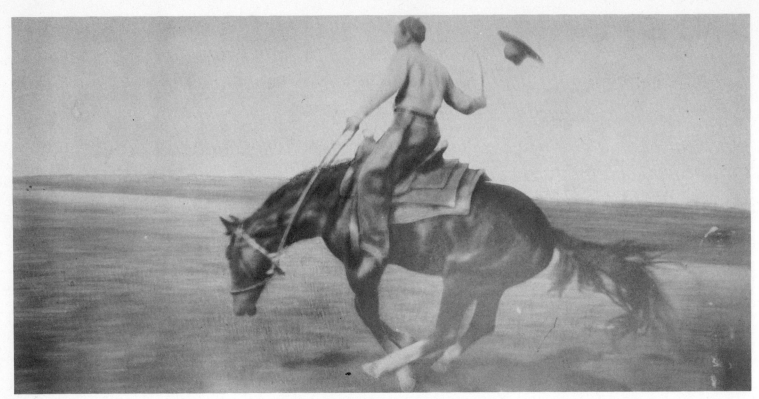

A "bucker." *Photo by C. D. Kirkland.*

It was the famous Texas drover, J. G. McCoy, who ended the cattlemen's nightmares. A dreamer with a practical bent, McCoy wanted to find a point which would meet the herds coming north and the westward-moving railroads. As he said, "the plan was to establish at some accessible point a depot or market to which a Texas drover could bring his stock unmolested and failing to find a buyer, he could go upon the public highways to any market in the country he wished."

After being turned out of some railway offices, McCoy did sign a contract with the Hannibal and St. Jo Railroad granting favorable rates for shipping cattle from the Missouri River to Chicago.

McCoy now returned to Kansas to pick his spot. He finally found the quiet little town of Abilene in Dickinson County. As McCoy first saw it, the town was a collection of a dozen log huts, covered with dirt for roofing, while the "whole business of the burg was conducted in two small rooms, mere log huts, and of course the inevitable saloon."

But despite its poor appearance, McCoy found what he wanted, a well-watered countryside with grass suitable for the grazing of cattle. McCoy brought in lumber and within 60 days he had pens that could hold thousands of cattle. Meanwhile he sent out a woodsman to scour the plains and tell the drovers what was waiting. After a few weeks of wandering, this man found a herd in the Indian Territory owned by a man named Thompson.

The Texan was suspicious and felt sure this was a trap. But with his hand near his gun and his men ready to go into action, he followed McCoy's man. Before they could reach Abilene, Thompson had sold the herd to some northerner who drove it to Abilene.

Bronco-buster. *Photo by W. G. Walker.*

Another large herd stopped long enough to graze near Abilene and was sold on the spot.

On September 5, 1866, the first herd was shipped to Chicago. Cattlemen from several states shook the town with their celebration.

With the establishment of Abilene as a convenient stockyard and shipping port, the cattle business flourished and an enormous system of cattle ranches developed. The first year 260,000 head were shipped; by 1880 the cowtowns had shipped more than 4,000,000.

Each ranch was a sort of barony, with a spread of thousands of acres in its domain, and in a sort of informal league with its neighboring ranches. For most of the year the cattle roamed the open range—the vast acreage of the area was not fenced off—grazed where they chose and found their own water.

Each steer was branded with the distinctive mark of its ranch owner. These marks were respected by all other honest ranchers, and later on, all brands were registered. But the open range provided opportunity for the cattle thief, "the rustler," who would drive off the cattle, re-brand them, and claim them as his own.

The ranch staff lived in the ranch-house area, which was essentially self-sufficient and consisted of a main house, bunkhouses for the cowboys and the foreman, barns, corrals for the horses, blacksmith shops, and other buildings and equipment in accordance with the size of the ranch.

At round-up time extra hands would be hired by each ranch, and almost the entire crew would go out to the range where they would join the cowboys of the neighboring ranches to round up the steers for the drive to market. Each ranch would obtain possession of the cattle marked with its brand and would brand the calves running with its cows.

Then came the drive north to the cattle shipping point.

The cattle business required a new way of life and especially a new sort of skilled craftsman—the cowboy.

As a result of books, magazine articles and newspaper accounts, ranch life, the "wide open spaces" and especially the cowboy achieved a glamorous, idealized glorification and became a "national institution."

In retrospect the drives north sound thrilling and romantic, but actually it was grueling work that required being in the saddle 15 hours a day, seven days a week. The drovers were usually young, tough ranch hands and excellent horsemen. The ramrod, or trail boss, was older and more experienced. After weeks on the trail, worn by the long hours in the saddle, it is little wonder that the cowboys turned into whooping hellions who sought to hurrah the town with gunfire for relaxation.

The makeup of the outfit consisted of a chuck wagon which carried the food, bedding and tents. From its tailboard, food was served which had been cooked over an open fire. The "hoodlum" wagon carried the outfit's supplies, such as branding irons, water barrel, wood for pens, or for firewood. A herd of horses was known as the *remuda* (a word borrowed from the Spanish). The outfit's boss was the horse wrangler, usually a youngster.

Cow horses were well trained. Not only did they help

A Texas cowboy in the 1880's.
Photo by F. Hardesty.

A Montana cowboy in the 1870's.

A rest on the drive.

A Wyoming cattle ranch in the 1880's.

Livery stable, Abilene, 1871.

their owners in roping a steer, but would be "tied" when the reins were let down—ground-hitched. The reason for this training is twofold: the cowboy usually had to leap from his saddle and work fast; secondly, there weren't many places to tie a horse on the plains. Every cow hand furnished his saddle, bridle, saddle blankets, spurs and "hot roll"—his bedding and tarpaulin, a piece of canvas doubled and composed of "quilt or suggans."

The staff of the outfit consisted of a wagon boss, usually foreman of the ranch, cook, hoodlum driver, horse wrangler and the straw boss, who was next in command to the wagon boss.

The *point* of the outfit was the reconnaissance man, who sought out possible Indian ambushes, water and suit-

able grazing country. The least desirable of the posts was the drag rider, the rider at the rear of the herd who swallowed the dust.

The fear of stampede always hung over the outfit. The longhorns were a scary lot, and even the drop of a pan could stir them up and turn them into brawling, runaway herd whose hoofs shook the plains. When a man was caught in a stampede, there was seldom anything left to bury.

The night watch literally rode on tip-toe. He kept his voice down, and to calm the sleeping animals and to defy his own loneliness he would croon like a mother to her young. Thus were born our western ballads.

The most popular trail to the railhead was the Chisholm

San Antonio, 1876.

Martin Garretson measures a longhorn.

Junction City, Kansas, 1876.

Branding on the round-up, Telluride, Colorado. *Photo by W. J. Carpenter.*

Trail, believed to have been laid out by Jesse Chisholm, a legend that has as much controversy about it as Little Big Horn. But whoever found the trail really laid out the Golden Highway of the western frontier. It was level and had plenty of grass and water. The latter was highly important to the success of any drive.

There were numerous other trails that are as important historically. For example, west of the Chisholm were the Panhandle Trail, going to Kansas and Colorado, and the

Looking for a place to land.

Controlling a Stampede

(From *Prose and Poetry of the Livestock Industry*)

BY COLONEL CHARLES GOODNIGHT,
famous Texas pioneer and cattleman

The task of the men was to gain control of the herd and gradually turn the cattle until they were moving in a wide circle. Then, although they might break each other's horns off and crush one another badly, the great danger was past. The well trained night horse needed little guidance and knew that if the herd came his way, all he had to do was to lead. The speed of the herd was terrific, but the position at the head of the stampede was what the trail man desired, for he was in the position to start the herd turning.

In the excitement of a stampede a man was not himself and his horse was not the horse of yesterday. Man and horse were one and the combination accomplished feats that would be utterly impossible under ordinary circumstances. Trained men would be generally found near the *point* at both sides of the herd. When the man on one side saw the herd bending his way, he would fall back and if the work was well done on the other side of the herd, the stampede would gradually come to an end; the strain was removed, the cowboys were the happiest men on earth, and their shouts and laughter could be heard for miles over the prairie. . . .

Cowboys at a corral near Helena, Montana.

Pecos Trail up the Pecos Valley into New Mexico and on to Wyoming and Colorado.

Drives were usually started in the spring when the grass appeared on the plains. The herd did not move like eastern stock but in a long snakelike line. The herd moved out at dawn, with the *point* usually using hand signals, many of which had been adopted from the Plains tribes. An average good day's trek was 15 miles. The first day's mileage was usually twice that in an effort to break the herd from its home-range habits and to tire the confused, protesting steers so that they would not be too much of a problem to the night riders.

Branding a steer. *Photo by C. D. Kirkland.*

One of the most terrifying parts of the drive was the so-called "dry drive," which was simply a drive across a waterless tract of land. For example, a trip across the Llano Estacado, the Staked Plains of Texas, was a dry drive. The 100-mile trip took the herd from the mouth of the South Concho River to the Pecos. In 1855 a survey team headed by Brevet-Captain John Pope of the Topographical Corps was ordered to sink wells across the southern portion of the Staked Plains, but nothing came of it.

Gold strikes helped boost the cattle business. Perhaps a solitary prospector could live off the land, but a community needed beef. In Virginia City the poorest beef was auctioned off at 25 cents a pound in spirited bidding.

News of these prices drifted back to Kansas, Missouri, and Texas. In 1866 Nelson Story came over the Bozeman Trail to Gallatin Valley with a herd of 600 longhorns he had driven up from Dallas. Two years later there were 18,801 cows and calves in and around Virginia City.

When the rails of the Union Pacific began to inch across the plains the buffalo-hunters like Buffalo Bill supplied the crews with buffalo steaks. But the rancher found as ready a market for his steers in the rail camps as he had found in the mining camps and in the emigrant trains.

With the combination of the expanding railroads and the return of the military posts, which alleviated the Indian problem, the cattle industry began to boom. In the

Horse herd. *Photo by C. D. Kirkland.*

The mess wagon. *Photo by C. D. Kirkland.*

Cowboys of the N Bar N ranch on the prairie, during a drive moving 7,000 head
of cattle 300 miles. Northwest Montana, late 1880's. *Photo by Dan Dutro.*

beginning the business was haphazard; a drover never knew where he would find a buyer for his herd. It wasn't unusual for a deal to be made around a campfire on the plains and the gold counted on a blanket. By 1870 a Kansas City bank was handling more than $3,000,000 in cattle money.

The country was opening fast, the tribes were being defeated and the ruthless extermination of the buffalo was well under way. The Union Pacific naturally was a booster for the northern ranges. In 1870 the Omaha *Herald* carried a series of letters from a Doctor Latham, a surgeon for the railroad, boasting of the "succulent grasses" that could feed a continent of beef cattle so that the price would come down and the poorest family could live on steaks. The following fall the letters appeared in pamphlet form and gained wide circulation in the East. There also appeared the typical tenderfoot story about the storm-bound freighter who was forced to turn loose his team of oxen to die. Imagine his surprise and joy in the spring to find them well fed, sleek and fat. The wild yarn would be incorporated many times in the prospectus by new cattle companies.

By 1875, ten years after the first steers had splashed across the Red River, the cattle industry was booming beyond McCoy's wildest dreams. The *Rocky Mountain Husbandman*, quoting the Buffalo *Live Stock Journal* in 1875, wrote exuberantly: "Cotton was once king but grass is now. If grass is king, the Rocky Mountain region is its

throne, and fortunate are those who possess it."

The West, with its free "boundless, gateless pasture," was there for the asking. All a man needed to make a fortune in cattle were a few cowboys and a branding iron. By 1881 the Northern Pacific reached the Yellowstone and before long, names that rang like bells in the Indian Wars became routine stops on the timetables.

As Granville Stuart, one of the West's superior cattlemen, put it, "There were 600,000 head on the range that was now devoid of buffalo, with the elk and the antelope indeed scarce. The cowboy had become an institution."

Not all the capital in the booming cattle companies came from American sources. A large part was foreign. The stockmen's boom was the talk of Europe, and before 1880 no less than an estimated 20,000,0000 head of cattle in Texas, Colorado, Missouri, New Mexico and Arkansas were owned by foreigners.

Edinburgh was a Cheyenne in miniature, and as John Clay, an agent for English investors, was to write in the London *Economist*: "Drawing-rooms buzzed with the news of the last of these bonanzas, and staid old gentlemen who didn't know the difference between a steer and a heifer discussed it over their port and nuts." It is amusing to contemplate the doughty Scots, with their mutton-chop whiskers, in the funereal quiet of the best clubs, arguing over rangeland that only recently had known the tread of a moccasin.

Omaha, Nebraska, 1870.

Dodge City, Kansas, 1867.

El Paso, Texas, 1880.

Congress Street, Tucson, Arizona. *Photo by Buchman and Hartwell.*

The Cowboy

The nature of the work determined the character, behavior, appearance and even the language of the cowboy. It was tough work that required energy and youth. Only the best riders, the most skilled in roping and marksmanship, were hired by the outfits. The cowboy took great pride in these skills, engaged in all sorts of contests—shooting, horse-breaking or bronco-busting, roping—and looked down with contempt at the inept, soft-muscled newcomer whom he called a "tenderfoot."

It was lonely, monotonous work; loquacious men were a rarity. Many of the words he did use were borrowed from the Spanish, who were there and dealing with cattle before him: lariat, remuda, arroyo, mesa, rancho, pueblo, canyon.

His costume was Spanish in origin—the high heels, the chaps, the spurs, the boots, the bandana. But the hat, the five-gallon or ten-gallon Stetson, was American.

Among the many who have depicted the life of the cowboy perhaps the two most famous are Frederic Remington, the great painter of the West, some of whose pictures are shown here, and Theodore Roosevelt, who wrote from long personal experience many books and articles about life on the plains and also took a number of photographs of cowboy activities. A few of these rare pictures are shown here, and serving also as an illustration of ranch life is the following bit of the Rough Rider President's personal history.

The Cowboy Who Became President

The young bespectacled tenderfoot named Teddy Roosevelt had anything but good luck when he went buffalo hunting for the first time in the badlands of Dakota in 1883. First of all, it rained for a week. When it finally cleared he and his guide found the remnants of a herd late in the night. In the moonlight Roosevelt wounded a bull, but when he tried to finish it off the buffalo turned and charged, almost finishing Roosevelt.

In addition the horse bolted and the heavy rifle barrel made a deep gash in his forehead. Miles from their camp on the Little Cannonball, Roosevelt and his guide, Joe Ferris, decided to camp for the night. In the early hours a wolf frightened their horses and they had to search for them in the darkness. When they found the animals at last and rolled up in their blankets, it began to rain.

In the morning they found another herd. Roosevelt crept close, fired and missed. The herd stampeded and his chance to get a "buffer" was gone. The world's most famous hunter never forgot that shot.

The rain continued for several days, a lashing cold rain that numbed both men. They rode all day and spent miserable nights trying to sleep. The first clear day Joe's horse narrowly missed a rattlesnake's fang, and a bluff weakened by the rain broke under them, sending men and horses tumbling down the steep slope. A few hours after they had set out again, Roosevelt's horse stepped into a

A bend in the river (The Little Missouri). *All the pictures in this series, except the last, were taken by Roosevelt in 1882.*

Cattle on a sandbar.

The saddleband in the rope corral.

The midday meal.

gopher hole and made a complete somersault, pitching Roosevelt almost ten feet. While Joe held his breath Roosevelt got up, adjusted his glasses and remounted. They had ridden but a few feet when the earth gave way under Roosevelt's horse and it sank into the gluelike mud up to its withers. After a back-breaking hour they pulled the frightened horse out with lariats.

Joe, the veteran plainsman, began to eye Roosevelt with a sort of awe. At night beside the campfire he was stunned to see "Four Eyes," as he called him, take up a book as if he were in a comfortable living room. It was during this rough hunting trip that Roosevelt casually told Joe that his lungs were bad and that the doctors hadn't given him much more time to live.

They finally returned to the ranch run by Gregor Lang. There Joe Ferris discovered that he was mistaken in thinking the rough days and nights had finally cured the tenderfoot. Rather he had fallen in love with the raw, vast badlands. Roosevelt told Lang that he had made up his mind to run cattle there and wanted him to recommend someone to take charge for him. Lang suggested Bill Merrifield and Silvane Ferris. The next day after a short talk with these two men Roosevelt took out a checkbook, wrote a $14,000 check and he was in the cattle business.

High noon.

Branding calves.

In the corral.

Roosevelt never forgot his years as a ranchman in the Dakotas. As he told Hermann Hagedorn, who wrote the excellent *Roosevelt in the Badlands,* his years on the plains were a "kind of idyll." Someone once said of him that he had "a weakness for murderers," and certainly the future President of the United States met his full quota of desperate men in the wild and woolly town of Little Missouri. There were gunfighters, outlaws, cattle thieves, horse thieves, gamblers and confidence men.

One of the most exciting chapters in his life in the West centers around an outlaw named Red Finnegan. A stocky man with a brick-red complexion, he boasted that he was from 'way up Bitter Creek "and the further up you went the worse people got."

In March, 1886, as Roosevelt prepared to go out on a long-planned hunting trip he found his skiff gone. A torn red mitten, identified as belonging to Finnegan, was found nearby. Footprints showed that Finnegan had been joined by two other men.

Roosevelt boiled at the theft, but since travel by horse was impossible he got his ranch hands to build another boat. In three days the craft was finished. Meanwhile he sent some of his men to Medora to get enough supplies for a two-week journey.

With Wilmot Daw and Bill Sewall, two Maine frontiersmen he had taken to the Badlands, Roosevelt set out in the crude craft down the Little Missouri. The region through which they passed was bleak. The weather was bitter cold, and occasionally the wind stung their faces with particles of ice.

On the third day they rounded a bend and saw Roosevelt's original boat on the bank and the smoke of a cook fire shredded by the wind. They flung off their coats, and while Sewall swung the boat in toward shore Daw and Roosevelt knelt in the bow, rifles ready. They knew Finnegan was "a shooting man" and could pick them off from the bushes.

Gathering the day herd.

Elkhorn Ranch.

Fortunately, he and his companions were out searching for game and had left the boat in the custody of a halfwit who told them Finnegan was accompanied by a halfbreed outlaw and killer.

They disarmed the halfwit and waited. After a short wait they heard the two men coming through the sagebrush. Roosevelt waited until they were within twenty yards, then jumped up.

"Hands up!"

The halfbreed dropped his rifle, but Finnegan went into a crouch as if to get off a hip shot. But Roosevelt stared down his rifle barrel and said calmly, "You thief! Put up your hands."

After they had searched the pair Roosevelt told them, "If you try anything we'll shoot you."

The next day they started downriver but were stopped by a great ice jam which had been moving along the river for days since the thaw had set in.

Their provisions ran out, there was no game in the bleak country and they were reduced to eating unleavened bread mixed with the muddy Little Missouri water.

A few days later Roosevelt set out on foot and found

Elkhorn ranch house.

Ready to start.

a small ranch, where he borrowed a horse which turned out to be a half-broken bronc. After a rough ride he tamed the horse and rode 15 miles to a larger ranch at the edge of the Killdeer Mountains. There he hired a covered wagon, provisions and a rancher, who drove the wagon to the camp on the ice-bound Little Missouri.

The thieves were put into the wagon, and Roosevelt and the driver set out for Dickinson, which had the nearest jail. His journal gives a brief account of the stages of that 300-mile journey:

April 7.   Worked down to the C. Diamond Ranch. Two prairie chickens.
April 8.   Rode to Killdeer Mountains to arrange for a wagon which I hired.
April 9.   Walked the captives to Killdeer Mountains.
April 10. Drove captives in wagon to Captain Brown's ranch.

Captain Brown looked puzzled when Roosevelt drove in. "What I can't understand," he said, "is why you made all this fuss instead of hanging them offhand."

The next night Roosevelt turned the prisoners over to the United States Marshal in Dickinson.

The prisoners.

Barbed Wire

Joseph Glidden, a dour, thin-lipped farmer, was fascinated by the exhibit in the De Kalb, Illinois, County Fair. He had returned three times to stare at the invention of Henry Rose, a farmer who had a place north of his. It was simply a rail fence topped by a row of sharp spikes.

Back home, Glidden sat on the back porch brooding. Finally he borrowed his wife's coffee grinder and, with the aid of an old grindstone to bend the wire, he made the first practical barbed wire fence. He was granted a patent on November 24, 1874. The patent, number 157,124, is one of the most important in western history.

Barbed wire is as completely American as pumpkin pie or wild turkey. The strands which stretched across the plains of the early West helped to change its history. It bred lawsuits, feuds, violence and murder, but it played a major role in bringing the West to agricultural preeminence.

The history actually begins with an angry German farmer who had a fruit grove a few miles north of San Antonio. The longhorns were still roaming at will and were ruining the farmer's fruit crops. He finally built a fence and studded its top with large spikes. Then the next day he took a seat in the nearby tree to see the fun.

The longhorns arrived and for a moment eyed the fence. Then with a roar they charged. They retreated licking their wounds. The jubilant German ran into town and in the saloon told his triumphant tale. He was astounded to see his listeners give him a cold stare and leave. That night a delegation of flint-eyed men with shotguns and six-shooters paid him a call.

"Get that cruel and inhuman fence down, mister, or you'll leave town in a box," was the warning. The fence came down at dawn and it was many years before another barbed fence was erected.

After Glidden began manufacturing the wire a 25-year-old salesman named John W. Gates decided to augment

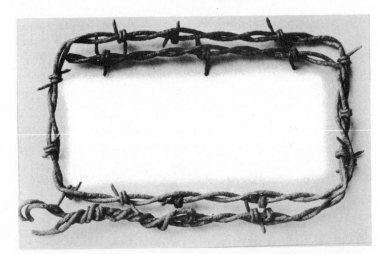

First piece of double-strand barbed wire. Made in 1874 by Joseph F. Glidden, who used the crank of a grindstone.

Part of the "coffee mill" used by Glidden to form barbs for his first barbed wire.

CAVALRY OFFICER. *Painted by Frederic Remington.*

THE COWBOY. *Painted by Frederic Remington.*

The Fight for the Water Hole. *Painted by Frederic Remington.*

Arizona Cowboy.
Painted by Frederic Remington.

THE CAVALRY CHARGE. *Painted by Frederic Remington.*

John W. Gates Introduces Barbed Wire to the Rangeland.

WHERE THE GREAT HERDS CAME TO DRINK. *Painted in oil, 1901, by C. M. Russell.*

At the End of the Rope. *Water color painted by C. M. Russell.* Charles Manion Russell was one of the great artists of the West. He worked in oils, water colors, pen and ink, and made many sculptures of western subjects in bronze. He was a cowboy in Montana in the 1880's, lived for a while with the Blood Indians and from time to time simply roamed the plains and the mountain country with only his horse for company. Though his earliest painting dates back to 1880, when he was only 16, the main body of his work was done in the early 1900's, when he achieved his great fame. An early sketch, "Waiting for a Chinook," shown on the next page, helped him to gain national recognition.

WAITING FOR A CHINOOK, or THE LAST OF 5,000. *A water color re-creation by Russell of his famous early sketch.*

UNSCHEDULED STOP. A hold-up scene in water color, dated 1926. *Painted by C. M. Russell.*

Poster distributed by Washburn and Moen and I. L. Ellewood about 1877.

his weekly salary of $25 by going west and selling the idea of barbed wire to Texas cattlemen.

In San Antonio they laughed at him as he spread his samples across the bar. Finally he forced them to agree to an experiment. In the town square he built a large corral. The next day 25 of the toughest longhorns in the county were driven into the corral by excited, whooping cowboys. Tails raised, eyes wide, they charged at the fence. It held. They backed off, pawed the ground and charged again. This time they retreated for good. Before nightfall Gates—later famous as "Bet-a-Million" Gates—had more orders than he could fill.

For a long time Texas ranchers had realized that the tough, angular longhorn was not the best of beef cattle. He didn't have the weight, the docility or the low feeding-cost factor that other cattle had. The new wire seemed the answer to their problem. New breeds could be introduced with the assurance that each breed would be controlled (within the wire) and unmixed. At first the cattle barons, who considered the range free, refused to accept the wire. Cowboys with cutters were sent out. Fence wars started and men died, sprawled across the cut wire.

The violence was so great that the Governor of Texas in 1884 summoned a special session of the legislature and passed a law making wire-cutting a felony. The passage of the law ended wire-cutting and now to the grazing herds came the Herefords, Durhams, Shorthorns and Polled Angus Brahmas—all fine breeds.

On one section of the famous King Ranch, the Gertrude Ranch, were errected 1,500 miles of barbed wire. Inside this enclosure was developed one of the world's finest breeds, the Santa Gertrudis, three-eighths Brahma and five-eighths Shorthorn, combining the natural beef qualities of the latter with the hardiness of the Brahma.

The rapid growth of the barbed wire business in the West is underscored by the following table of wire sales from 1874 to 1881:

Year	Pounds Sold
1874	10,000
1875	100,000
1876	840,000
1877	12,863,000
1878	26,655,000
1879	50,337,000
1880	80,500,000
1881	120,000,000

A ton of wire made two miles of staunch three-strand wire. In 1876 the adoption of Bessemer steel created a revolution in the wire business. Now wire could be produced cheaply and the price dropped from 18 to 8 cents a pound. Now even the humblest sodbuster could fence in his quarter.

Curiously, wire also helped to bring law and order to many a wild section of the West. It encouraged land

John W. ("Bet-a-Million") Gates.

Part of the first wire drawing frame, which could produce 2,500 pounds of wire a day. Previous equipment could produce only 50 pounds a day.

investment and improvement. Crops now could be grown and rustling dwindled to a nuisance crime.

The following table sums up the meteoric history of barbed wire:

1874   Joseph Glidden obtains his patent and forms a company in De Kalb, Illinois.

1875   Actual production of barbed wire begins.

1876   Washburn and Moen Company, Worcester, Massachusetts, obtains all patents on the wire, and with the adoption of Bessemer steel produced a cheaper and more durable material.

Windmills

Like barbed wire, windmills played an important part in the development of the American West. Without them the cattle business could not have survived. They appeared on the great plains in the early 1870's when the cattleman was faced with the grave problem of supplying water for his rapidly expanding herds.

The simple fact is that the range land, the Great Plains country—once called the Great American Desert—is very dry, with annual rainfall much nearer the arid desert level of less than 10 inches than the satisfactory level of 30 inches or more that prevails in good farming areas. In addition the natural water-storage conditions are unfavorable. Often, when the rains do come they come in great storms and the water runs off quickly so that not enough is retained. Rivers, streams and springs dry up.

In the West, from the days of the *conquistadores* even until now, water has been the crucial factor, determining the economy, welfare and growth of any section. If sufficient water was available, or could be obtained by well-digging, irrigation or other means the area could support more life, could flourish and grow. Without more water there could not be more life. But there was more life—increasing population and expanding herds—and so besides the search for water there was and is the continuing fight in the dry parts of the West for water. There were constantly scraps, lawsuits, battles and war about the control of water supply, the diversion or damming of streams, the construction of aqueducts, tunnels and reservoirs.

Since the Spanish, men in the West have tried everything including snake dances and prayer to induce rainfall and to increase the supply of water. In the post-Civil War years the artesian well—the word is taken from Artois, France, where it originated—was the talk of the plains. In an artesian well the water, once reached underground, flows to the surface by itself. Cattlemen were wildly enthusiastic when they heard that such wells, ranging in depth to as much as 400 feet, had been drilled in dry Kansas. Large bonuses were offered to drillers. Test drills were made, only to reveal that the condition of the plains earth and its topography made artesian wells virtually impossible. The water could be reached, at one depth or another, but it would not rise to the surface by itself. It would be an ordinary well—ground water that had to be drawn or pumped to the surface. Ordinary wells provided only a scant supply. If it was necessary to go 200 feet down or more to find water (as was the case in most of the Great Plains area) it was just about impossible to obtain a sufficient quantity of water by hand pumping. Power pumps had not yet been perfected and were not a practical solution at that time.

Finally, someone recalled that windmills could be used to pump water. Soon windmills became an important factor and a major industry in the West.

The Aermotor Company of Chicago was one of the

Early western windmill.

The first steel windmill.

pioneering windmill companies. This company made the first iron windmill in the 1880's. It became extremely popular among the cattlemen and before the century had turned, its iron fan was catching the four winds wherever they swept the western plains.

Windmills are still a very important part of western life. In 1957 the Aermotor Company reported sales of 7,000 complete windmill outfits for pumping water, with most of them going to Texas, New Mexico, Nebraska and Arizona.

With the introduction of the windmill came a little-known western figure who, although not so romantic as the cowboy, was just as necessary. This was the itinerant windmill builder. Little if anything has been written about him.

One of the earliest was George Strait, who in 1870 left his home in New York's Tioga County in the rural serenity of Condor, to seek his fortune building windmills on the western plains. He was a faithful correspondent in his letters to his family. They not only describe the trials and

tribulations of a pioneer windmill builder but also give an interesting picture of the times.

Most of the letters are addressed from Missouri Valley, Iowa, and cover the years 1874-76. After leaving Condor, Strait built windmills in Nebraska, Omaha and the Dakota Territory. But he finally settled with his wife, Fanny, and two small children in Iowa, "the finest state in the Union." As he said in his first letter, "My only regret is that I did not come out here ten years ago."

He averaged about $200 a month. In one letter he outlined what it cost a family in the way of food. "The best kind of flour costs $1.25 per sack, cornmeal $.75 a pack, good wheat for $.60 a bushel. Pork is $5 a hundred pounds and beef about the same." He added, "Fanny and the children love the land, and they have all the wild duck, geese, prairie chickens they want to eat . . . last night I was lucky and came home with seven wild ducks. . . ."

Writing to his parents on January 3, 1875, he tells them he is so busy erecting windmills that he can't even find time to send them some wild game for the holidays.

Fifty years of windmill-blade arrangements.

Another type of windmill.

The same day Strait's son wrote in a childish scrawl to "Grandma and Grandpa" that he liked the frontier and observed casually that 275 Cherokees "were around."

On February 14 Strait wrote his parents, giving them "an account of the events of the past weak (sic)." One of the most important, he wrote, was the erection of a windmill "in the timber about twenty miles from here where the Indians are thick. We stayed all day in a little cabin and had to roll up in blankets, and one of the men stayed awake to keep a fire going. We was there one day and one night and they come for us to bring us to put in another water works (windmill). We stayed there one day and one night. We had plenty of wild hog to eat, and there is plenty of wild game. But it was so cold that the Indians kept to their wigwams. Came back Thursday and expect to go out again. Last week clear for my share was $62."

On March 7, 1875, Strait, in writing to his father, described how the cattlemen were virtually standing in line begging him to put in windmills. "This weak (sic) I have three artesian wells to put in and three windmills to erect if Bell (his helper) is well enough to be away from home.

One of the windmills is for a stockyard about one mile out of town. They keep from 2 to 300 head of cattle and I am going to put them up a windmill to pump water for them. I got all the business I can attent to."

Apparently Strait's reputation as a windmill builder was getting around because he described "a man who has been around after me to go out to Montana to put in windmills to pump water for the gold mines. I don't think I shall go there as I have plenty of windmill work here." Then as an afterthought he added, "The Indians are much too ruff (sic) there. There is too much risk to run in such a trip."

His last letter of April 23, 1876, proves beyond any doubt that the Union Pacific was using windmills to draw water for its engines. Strait's home was now in Little Sioux, Iowa, and in his letter to his sister, Elisa, who had been ill, he described how "I have been out on the Sandy Desert on the Union Pacific putting in waterworks for them."

Apparently the railroad had been satisfied with his work and contracted for more mills, for Strait had moved to Little Sioux "to be nearer to my work." Again he points out he has more work than he can attend to.

The End of a Western Era

The first major disaster in the western cattle industry came in 1873 when the eastern banking firm of Jay Cooke & Company suspended payments and closed its doors. A panic swept the nation. Confidence was destroyed. Banks and businessmen from the foremost industrialist to the smallest local merchant were afraid to buy or invest. Prices plummeted. Many factories closed and people were afraid to spend money on anything except absolute necessities. The panic was particularly disastrous to the market for beef. Prices were ridiculously low. A single cattle company lost $180,000 in three weeks. Many others could not even raise the cost of the transportation when they sold their herds.

It took three years for the cattle market to get back on its feet. Finally came the great boom of the golden eighties. Money was plentiful once again. Railroads had criss-crossed the country. The tribes were reduced to the status of beggars. The range was wide and free. Towns were rising and the great tide of immigration from Europe was at its peak.

By 1882 cattle was selling for $35 a head; a profit of 300 per cent could be made. In 1883 a terrible drought swept the West. Thousands of dead cattle littered the over-stocked, dried-out range. Prices went even higher because of the scarcity. But two years later in 1885 when there was no drought and plenty of supply, prices dropped sharply. There was a rush to unload, and beef hit the market at any price.

In 1886 the severest winter in the history of the West struck the plains with unprecedented savagery. Snow was roof-high, the temperature sub-zero. In the fenced areas, steers whose instinct made them move before the storm, found their way blocked by barbed wire. Armies of them died on the ugly strands. People in frontier towns recalled many years later how they had clapped their hands over their ears to drown out the cries of the dying cattle wandering through the snow-choked streets.

In the spring the cattlemen rode slowly across their domain. As the late "Cimarron" George Bolds, once Bat Masterson's deputy, remarked just before his death: "You could weep at the sight of them . . . one outfit near Garden City (Kansas) had a handful left. Some didn't have any ears or tails . . . we couldn't stand it, we had to shoot them."

The dripping of the icicles over the bunkhouse door was the death knell of an era.

Dodge City, snowbound, 1870's.

Homesteads

The Nester

THE cattleman accepted the fickleness of his long-horns, the uncertainty of the weather, the natural danger of the ambushing hostiles, but he did not accept the homesteader, the sodbuster or the "nester" as he contemptuously called him.

In return, the homesteader hated the often tyrannical cattle barons. Their conflict is one of the true dramas of the West. On the side of the cattleman was his long struggle to conquer the land; he usually had an aching wound from an arrowhead or a Cheyenne bullet to prove that he had put his life on the line for his spread. But in the end it was the homesteader who won out. He not only had the law on his side, he also was the forerunner of a new era that could not be halted. It was irony to top irony; the cattleman in his own time had heralded the end of the free life of the Plains tribes. Now it was his turn to face the fact that his day and his time were ending.

The peak of homesteading came at a time when the range was being overcrowded and at a time when the stockmen themselves were divided. The smaller rancher was now bucking the Stockmen's Association that con-

A homesteader's cabin in Colorado.

trolled and regulated the cattle business. The newcomer found it almost impossible to obtain admission to the charmed circle. It was true that any stock grower was eligible for admission, but to be admitted was another question. The investigation committee almost always turned down the new applicant. Rather than risk doing without the many advantages of belonging to the powerful organization, the stranger usually tried to find a less

A homesteader alongside an adobe hut.

Sir:

The bounty land claim of *Robert Hayne No 8726* filed under the act of 3d March, 1855, for services rendered in the removal of the Cherokee Indians under *Capt. Haywood Weir — Tenn —* United States volunteers, has been examined. As it is shown by documents on file that said company was part of the forces raised under an act of Congress passed May the 23rd, 1836, and served exclusively in the removal of said Indians, with whom no war existed during their enlistment, and as the benefits of the above and all other bounty land acts extend only to those who were called into service BY THE AUTHORITIES OF A STATE, OR TERRITORY, and have been paid for the same by the United States, or who served in some one of the several wars in which this country has been engaged since 1790, said claim cannot be allowed.

A rejection of a bounty land claim.

crowded area where his chances of survival were greater.

To admit more cattle was to endanger the cattle industry, but to allow the homesteader to move onto the open range and interfere with their grazing cattle was to the big ranchers almost unthinkable.

With the introduction of barbed wire, the cattlemen had begun to fence in public domain land, land that belonged to the government and was available to homesteaders only. In the early eighties the situation bordered on the fantastic. Routes of travel were wired off, even mail deliverers complained that they were forced to detour around some cattle king's empire, sometimes at rifle point. Many times homesteaders and small ranchers closed ranks as they watched the encroachments of the big cattle companies.

The San Antonio *Drovers' Journal* in 1884 reported that the Texas governor was forced to ask the legislature to help free the county seat of Jones County, which had been cut off from the rest of the state by cattlemen's wire fences. In 1884 Colonel Goodnight's Red River Ranch had 250 miles of fence. The wire of Goodnight and his neighbors stretched from the western border of the Indian country straight across the Panhandle and clear into New Mexico for 35 miles! In Colorado one cattle company had 40 townships cut off by wire fence, an area of more than a million acres. Signs warned the trespasser what would happen to him.

The homesteader at first tried to ignore the fences, but no sooner would he start housekeeping when he would receive a visit of a dozen or more hard-looking cowhands who gave him just a few hours to clear out. If he didn't obey, he was either shot down or driven out and his cabin and belongings burned.

Settlers started to send in complaints to the Land Bureau in Washington. The Bureau conducted its own investigation and the testimony of the hearings was staggering. In 1883, after an outbreak of violence, the Secretary of the Interior advised the settlers to cut the wire fences on the land they had filed for.

Actually it was no easy matter to sell the eastern farmers the idea of a Utopia in the western plains. For too many years the West had been pictured as a terrible, arid place which couldn't grow an apple. As far back as 1775 Edmund Burke was telling the House of Commons that the Great American Desert was a deadly menace, that it was a desolate land which would breed a race of "English

Application }   Homestead
No. 1.   Land Office
               Brownville N.T. January 1st 1863

I Daniel Freeman of Gage County Nebraska Teritory Do hereby apply to Enter under the Provissions of the act of Congress aproved May 20th 1862 Entitled, an act to Secure Homesteads to actual Settlers on the Public Domain The South half of N.W¼ & NE¼ of N.W¼ & S.W¼ of NE¼ Sec. 26. in Township (4) Nine Range Five East containing 160 acres Having filed my Pre Emption Declaration thereto on the Eighth day of September 1862

                     Daniel Freeman

       Land office at
               Brownville N.T. January 1st 1863

I Richard F Barret, Register of the Land office do Hereby Certify that the above application is For Surveyed Lands of the Class which the applicant is legally Entitled to Enter under the Homestead act of May 20th 1862 and that there is No Prior valid adverse Right to the Same

                   Richard F Barret
                       Register

A Nebraska homestead application and certification.

A railroad poster.

Tartars, a fierce and irresistible cavalry, [who would] become masters of your governors and your counsellors."

Early Western explorers brought back the same picture of the West. In 1810 Pike described the West as a vast, treeless wasteland. This was confirmed by Stephen H. Long's expedition of 1823. The terrible experiences of the emigrant trains was further evidence to the East that only sand and sage grass could exist in the West. Even Francis Parkman was convinced that the western plains country was sterile. He wrote: "Sometimes it glared in the sun, an expanse of hot, bare sand; sometimes it was veiled by tall coarse grass. Huge skulls and whitening bones of buffalo were scattered everywhere. . . ."

It was not a picture that would send eastern farmers hurrying west even though they were given a free quarter-section, 160 acres of land.

Subsequent government surveys, principally that of Ferdinand V. Hayden, did not materially change the nation's thinking. Then Charles Dana Wilber, an amateur Nebraska scientist, coined the phrase that was echoed time and again in Washington: "Rain follows the plow." Wilber took to the lecture platform and told large audiences about the fabulous possibilities for the western homesteader.

After the panic of 1873 homesteading began to increase. America recalled Greeley's famous remark, "Go West, Young Man, go forth into the Country." Now the unemployed were being advised that if they "made a farm from Uncle Sam's generous domain, you will crowd nobody, starve nobody. . . ."

However, although the settlers did increase up to the panic of 1887, they never did fulfill the Republican Party's great dream that the West would one day develop into a vast agricultural region. Large grants of land to railroads, failure to enact a realistic land program, speculators and cattlemen's frauds failed to make the homesteading program the success it should have been. From 1862 to 1890 only 372,650 Americans took advantage of the Homestead Act. Actually the Union Pacific sold more land at $5 an acre than was conveyed free under the government's public land program.

Congress passed many acts in an attempt to induce the farmer to go westward. The Land Office sold Congress the idea that if enough trees were planted, rainfall would increase to such an extent that the sage grass country would yield vast fields of crops. The Timber Culture Act was passed in 1873 by which a homesteader, in addition to his original quarter-section of 160 acres, was given another quarter-section to plant 40 acres of trees.

In 1877 Congress, still determined to move the eastern farmer westward, passed another law giving him an additional 640 acres on the condition that he irrigate the whole section within three years. Both acts were far removed from reality. It was big politics and nothing more.

One of the most important reports on the land itself was that submitted to Congress by Major James W. Powell

A homesteader family and their sod-house.

in 1878. In his *Lands of the Arid Regions of the United States* Powell advocated a revolutionary plan to classify the West in such sections as those fit only for pasturage, for minerals, timber and so on. Congress refused to move, but the report did result in the establishment of the United States Geological Survey, whose main purpose was to make such classifications.

In addition Congress created a Commission on Public Lands. The Commission toured the western country, in-terviewing both homesteaders and cattlemen. The Commission's report confirmed Powell's contention that some sort of classification should be made.

By the late seventies the cattleman was still king of the frontier. In 1879 the Land Office reported to Congress that vast tracts of public land were being denied to home-steaders by cattlemen who had fenced them off and that water rights were being granted to the beef men by the worst kind of fraud, conspiracy and bribery.

A sod-house in the Dakota Territory, 1880's. *Photo by General John T. Pitman.*

Finally Congress acted in 1885, passing a law making it a crime for anyone to fence public-domain land. The cattlemen tried to beat this by paying their cowboys to stake out claims along the stream sites. Thus for twenty-five cents an acre, they had exclusive control over the section for three years. At the end of that time, by paying a dollar an acre and running a plow here and there they could retain the land permanently.

In some sections the homesteaders, by weight of numbers, controlled the community. In the late eighties in western Nebraska they boldly killed cattle that wandered on their land. As they became part of the local communities, cattlemen found the tables had turned; in Wyoming they might control the judges and the juries, but in Nebraska it was an all-granger grand jury that was refusing to return a true bill against a farmer accused of wantonly killing some stock.

But no matter how strong their numbers, the homesteader's life was poles apart from the romantic picture painted by the Washington politician and Greeley's editorials.

It was a hard life, a constant battle against the arid land, against drought, grasshoppers and loneliness. Women aged

A half-completed sod-house near Eagle Butte in the Dakotas. The sod will be built up about the walls. *Photo by P. T. Peterson.*

The Life of a Dakota Homesteader

An old friend of the author, Pat McDonough, recalls homesteading with his family at Langtry, midway between Eagle Butte and Dupree in Central South Dakota. The McDonoughs' first home was a sod hut on their quarter.

"Fuel for a fire was a problem," Pat wrote. "There were no trees for miles around. The Sioux sold berries and wood. When we were out of wood we used cow chips, deposits by the wild cattle which roamed the plains near us. There were stock yards down near the railhead, but instead of corraling the cattle, they let them roam for free forage.

"I was five years old at the time and my brother was seven. When we got up at the crack of dawn to walk to school we first climbed a small hill and looked around the land. If there were no cattle in sight we would continue on to the school which was about a mile's walk. If we saw the steers we would return; they were dangerous and would charge when they saw or smelled a human.

"School was a small shack; the class had about a dozen kids.

"Mother used to bake bread for men who were 'batching it' on the claims. They would provide the flour and Mother did the baking while they sat around outside.

"Later my father and uncle and neighbors built a larger house, which was composed of three rooms. Immediately a family of rattlers built a house in one corner. It's an understatement to say it was a hazard walking to the outhouse.

"Our sport was simple and born of the frontier. In the winter we used as a sled a mortar box, about four feet wide and six feet long, with a couple of boards nailed across for seats.

"We had a handyman by the unlikely name of Arthur Murray, who called my mother chief cook and bottle washer.

" 'I'm the sod-packer,' he would say when we would ask him what he was.

"He never forgot those days. For years while he lived he would send the family cards celebrating certain anniversaries, such as the first day he came to work for us.

"There were plenty of Sioux bucks around. One day Mother got the scare of her life. She turned and there was one big as life.

"All he would do was grunt and say 'minnie.' Mother wanted to give him what he wanted because stuck in his belt was a murderous-looking knife. Finally, by pointing and sign language, she found out all he wanted was water from our pump for his horse.

"We didn't have Mass every Sunday. The priest traveled over a wide area of the frontier. Sometimes he would say Mass in the settlers' homes. I can recall he once said Mass in our house. I also can recall him telling us how he said Mass for the tribes in a tent.

"One thing I can recall of those days was our first house. It was so small we had to put the bed outside in the daytime and the table at night."

in months and many times went mad from the endless space, the great quiet broken only by the high keening winds, by the feeling of desperation and hysteria that settled over them with each dawn.

In the end, after working from dawn to dusk, the homesteaders' reward was a miserable sod hut and crops ravaged by the elements; a dreary present, a hopeless future.

Sheep

Another object of the cattleman's hatred was the western "woolies"—sheep. Like the cow pony and the longhorn, the plains sheep were the product of the Spaniards. They had been raised by the missions and had accompanied the Spanish colonization attempts on the frontier.

Colorado was the principal sheep state along with Montana and Wyoming, all beef territories. In 1880, according to the *Tenth Census Report*, there were 1,820,945 sheep in these states. The woolies also invaded Kansas, Nebraska and the Dakotas, but never in such numbers.

The disastrous winter of 1887, which broke the back of the cattle industry in the West, enabled the sheep business to prosper. Although the cattlemen of the 1880's bitterly opposed the sheep herds on the theory that they cropped the grass too short and killed it, that their smell drove away cattle, and that sheep destroyed young trees, they soon found no alternative but to turn to sheep-herding. By 1890 a large number of former beef men were in the sheep-raising business.

The sheep drives, with all their color and drama, were not so widely publicized as the cattle drives north from Texas. However, there were extensive sheep drives from as far south as California to as far north as Nebraska, or from the Rocky Mountain areas to Kansas. The California drives took several months but the profits were large.

The herds could be easily controlled by one man and well trained dogs whom sheep men valued as much as cowboys did their ponies. When the herd was on the move, the dogs circled its flanks constantly, nipping at the heels of the woolies who refused to stay in line.

Just as the cattle drives had their grub wagons, so did the sheep-herders have their own vehicle. This was a large

A Colorado sheep ranch.

A freighter loaded with wool. Montana in the 1880's.

Sheep-shearing on a Monterey County, California, sheep ranch. *Photo by I. W. Taber.*

wagon with a covering of canvas several layers thick. Inside the wagon were a stove, chairs, tables, and so on. In other words it was a sheep-herder's home on wheels.

The owner of the herds, called the flockmaster, usually stayed in the main camp, which was on land leased either from the railroad or from the county. One of his hands was constantly contacting the moving camps of the herds, bringing supplies, news and orders.

Armed with a staff as he followed his thousands of woolies, his sheep dogs circling the herd, this lonely, usually bearded man could have stepped out of a Biblical picture. When the herd stopped he would rest on a high point gazing out over the feeding animals, watchful always for the wolves.

July was shearing time for the sheepmen. Teams of professional shearers went from ranch to ranch, shearing by hand. After the shearing, the sheep were "dipped" by being driven into a vat containing sulphur and tobacco.

In the 1890's war between the sheepmen and the cattle-men exploded. Cattlemen sent raiders to clean out the sheepmen by killing the sheep, shooting the herders and burning their homes. Men with sacks over their heads, called "gunny sackers," did most of the damage to the sheep camps. In Wyoming the sheepmen fought six years against the raiders, who not only dynamited the camp but stampeded the herds until they ran over cliffs and were smashed on rocks below.

Besides the cattlemen, the prairie wolves and the gunny-sackers, the most feared enemy of all the sheep-herders was the prairie fire. The first sign was the smell of smoke, then the faint, far-off wisps of smoke. Dogs and men would make frantic efforts to save the herds. The fright-ened animals would mill about, falling and tumbling over each other in utter confusion. Often enough, the shepherd had all he could to save himself and his dogs. He would return the next day to find the plains littered with the blackened bodies of his beloved woolies.

A sheep-herder's "dipping station," Wyoming, 1880.

A sheep-herder's camp, Wyoming, 1880.

The Buffalo's End

THE journals of Coronado's men, the letters, copybooks and reports of the early western trappers and explorers and the journals of the Forty-Niners constantly point up the general wonderment and awe at the great herds of buffalo which roamed the Western Plains.

Ironically, the American buffalo is not a buffalo at all, but rather a bison. Scientists point out that the term "buffalo" should be applied to the water buffalo, the carabao, or African buffalo. But scientists or not, the word, "buffalo" will stand forever in western history.

At the time of the discovery of the American continent the buffalo herds covered one-third of the North American continent. It is generally believed that there were herds north of Great Slave Lake, while to the south they extended into Mexico. To the west they ranged as far as the Blue Mountains of Oregon, and in the East there were abundant herds in Pennsylvania and New York, up to the Canadian border.

The buffalo is the largest and most distinctive game animal on the North American continent. In height a full-grown bull stands five to six feet at the shoulder and weighs about 2,000 pounds. The buffalo differs from the common cattle because it has 14 ribs and a smaller weight of viscera; cattle have 13 ribs, Brahma cattle only 12. The flesh of the buffalo is similar to beef. The hunter always tried to kill a fat, dry heifer or cow, as its flesh was tender and more pleasant than that of the bull. Plainsmen agreed that the hump was the choice part, and that a constant diet of buffalo meat was less tiresome than that of any other animal. Hunters were also of the opinion that a man on a buffalo meat diet seldom missed bread.

The buffalo's coat is dark brown but grows paler towards spring. Trappers' journals tell of rare roan animals, while the white buffalo, which were revered by the Blackfeet and Sioux, occurred about one in two million.

In the spring and summer the buffalo would paw the turf and wallow in the holes to rid himself of vermin and loose hair. The buffalo wallows had the appearance of a large saucer. The buffalo's natural habitat was the treeless plains, and when a tree was discovered by the herds, it would be quickly destroyed by the shaggy hides pressing against the trunk. Hunters called them "rubbing posts."

There have been cases recorded of explorers and trappers finding a large, solitary rock on the plains and a ditch around it worn down to a depth of three feet by the circling beasts who rubbed against its sides.

When the first telegraph poles were strung it was not considered necessary to raise the wires high off the ground.

American bison bull.

A typical buffalo wallow.

Buffalo skulls and bones.

This view changed when the buffalo used the poles as rubbing posts and knocked them over. When the harassed wiremen drove in spikes the buffalo fought among themselves to get near the spiked pole, so that method of stringing wires was soon abandoned.

A calf, usually born from April to June, would follow its mother for about a year, then seek its own way in the world. Its life span was usually about eight years, but Martin Garretson, the famous buffalo expert, reports that in some cases the buffalo lived to an age of fifty years, or more.

The buffalo was a sluggish sort of animal, mild, inoffensive and dull—except when a cow had a calf beside her. So dull were they that hide hunters usually established what they called a "stand"—and methodically wiped out an entire herd. In most cases the lethargic beasts did not stir from the spot but only stared stupidly at their dead or dying mates.

The stampedes were terrifying. Eye-witnesses tell us that it seemed the whole earth was trembling under the pounding of their hoofs. In 1867 a large herd tried to cross the South Platte River when it was low. The leaders were soon stuck in the mud, but those behind just continued to stampede so that in a few hours the entire mile-wide river was black with the bodies of dead or dying buffalo.

The buffalo had herd habits from which it never deviated. When it sought water, the whole herd followed in one mass, then after drinking, rested and returned to the feeding ground. Thus, when the early pioneers were seeking water they simply followed the buffalo trails.

The buffalo's instinct for direction also helped the western pioneers. At all times he followed the line of least resistance so that when the survey teams mapping routes for the railroads followed the trails left by the roaming herds, they could travel for miles without having to improve the grade. The Baltimore and Ohio Railroad, for example, followed the buffalo trail across the mountains to the Ohio River; the Union Pacific up the Platte Valley follows an old buffalo trail all the way from Omaha to the Rocky Mountains.

The estimated peak population of buffalo has been a matter for debate among scientists for years. A conservative estimate would be sixty million.

In Townsend's *Journey Across the Rocky Mountains*, published before the Civil War, he tells how he was awed by the sight of one vast buffalo herd "which covered a whole plain as far as an eye could see." The width of the plain was about eight miles. In 1871 plainsmen reported to Fort Larned that a herd was crossing a plain which was 50 miles long and 25 miles wide. The plain was completely covered.

Although the herds covered the western plains like one great rippling black blanket, they were quickly wiped out of each section as civilization advanced into it, and were just about completely exterminated as soon as the outrunners of civilization reached across the plains. The ex-

Cheyenne squaws dressing and stretching buffalo hides. *Photo by S. J. Morrow.*

termination of these vast herds is a chapter in history which most Americans view with shame and disgust.

In Pennsylvania the last herds were wiped out in 1799; in 1803 the last buffalo was chased out of the city of Buffalo in New York State; by 1820 they were practically extinct east of the Mississippi.

By the time of the Civil War there was a brisk trade in buying and selling buffalo skins for robes, hats and "buffer" overshoes with the hair turned inside. For a pound of cheap sugar a trader could buy from the Indians a buffalo robe worth ten dollars in the Missouri River towns. Tourists from the eastern cities paid fifty dollars for a prime robe; and more if an Indian squaw had decorated it with colored porcupine quills.

By 1870 some firms were selling as many as 250,000 robes. The next year there was a shed in Cheyenne, Wyoming, 170 feet long, 60 feet wide and 30 high, that was bulging at the joints with robes.

Buffalo tongues being cured or smoked by suspending them over a smudge fire.

It was the Union Pacific which split the herds in two—the northern and southern herds. By 1871 the range was overrun with hide-hunters. At one point there were more than 5,000 hunters in the field along with countless pleasure-seekers who simply shot down the great beast, perhaps took his horns and then left the carcass for the lobo wolves who were always harrying the herds.

For a time it seemed the nation had gone on a buffalo-killing spree. In two months, 260,000 buffalo had been slaughtered in one section alone. By 1875 there were so many skins the market fell to about a dollar a skin. When the herds drifted into Texas the hunters followed them, still wantonly killing them off. Near Fort Griffin a four-acre section was once covered with drying hides. By 1878 the southern herd had been wiped out. The few remaining buffalo fled to the Staked Plains, where the last four were shot down in 1889.

Not only the hunters but the government itself was part of the shameful conspiracy to kill off the herds. The Indians were on the warpath and it was commonly accepted that once the herds were wiped out, the red warriors would come back to the reservations. In an open debate in 1876, Congressman James Garrison openly charged that the Secretary of the Interior had told him he would "rejoice," as far as the Indian question was concerned, when the last buffalo had been shot down.

After the hide-hunters had done their bloody task, the bone-scavengers arrived. For 12 miles along the Santa Fe there were mounds of bones 12 feet high and 12 feet wide. The bones brought from $8 to $12 a ton and were shipped east for fertilizer, while buttons and combs were made from the horns. From 1868 to 1881 $2,500,000 was paid out for buffalo bones. It required 100 buffalo to make a ton of bones.

The northern herd soon met the fate of its southern mate. From 1876 to 1882 the hunters ruthlessly wiped out the herd. By 1883 there was one small herd left near the Cannonball River in North Dakota. In September of that year Sitting Bull led his hunters in a winter hunt, killing about a thousand in one day. By the fall of the next year there were no buffalo left.

The passing of the herds was a calamity for the tribes. They were truly the "Indian's cattle," for they provided him with food, shelter and clothing. No part of the beast was wasted; even the hair was braided into reins and the green skins were used as kettles. The hoofs were used to

Buffalo grazing in a National Park preserve.

"The valley was covered with buffalo." *From a drawing by M. S. Garretson.*

glue arrows to the shafts; the horns were made into drinking cups and part of the war bonnet. Even the buffalo chips, the dried excrement, called "prairie coal" by the settlers, were used in fire making. Thus, in the end, not only a species, but a nation had been exterminated.

Many attempts, going back to a James P. Swain of Westchester County, New York, in 1868 have been made to mate wild buffalo and cattle. Swain's attempts were successful and as he reported, the cows gave a surprisingly large amount of sweet milk and "they were so mild even a small boy could herd them."

Efforts were also made to preserve and perpetuate what few buffalo remained. At the turn of the century the total buffalo population in America had dwindled to about 1,000. There was a small herd in Yellowstone Park under federal protection, but poachers killed them off until there were only 20 left. In 1902 Colonel Charles J. Jones, the Kansas frontiersman, widely known as "Buffalo Jones" was appointed warden of the Park by Congress and given an appropriation of $15,000 to buy buffalo and to build up the herd. Twenty-one were purchased from private owners, including Colonel Goodnight. Under the leadership of Dr. William T. Hornaday, director of the New York Zoological Park, a new herd was started in Oklahoma with 15 of the finest pure-blooded buffalo—all from New York's Zoological Society.

In 1905 Dr. Hornaday also organized the American Bison Society. Among the achievements of the Society was the establishment of the Montana Bison Range in 1909 and the Wind Cave Herd of South Dakota in 1913. In 1918 the Society again saved the buffalo from disaster when it managed to suppress a cattlemen's campaign to open the Parks to grazing stock. Through such efforts, the American buffalo population has mounted slowly so that today it numbers approximately 10,000—a figure nearly ten times that of 50 years ago!

A hide-hunter's camp on Evans Creek in the Texas Panhandle, 1874. *Photo by George Robertson.*

Gold and Other Mining

AFTER the great strike at Sutter's Mill the prospector became a permanent western figure. His uniform of battered hat, boots, flannel shirt, pan, shovel and mule became as distinctive as the chaps and spurs of the cowboy. He moved about the West "looking for color" in every gulch, valley or canyon. In the diggings he endured frightful hardships, and there were times when he struck it rich only to sell his precious find for a fraction of its real value.

One of the first strikes after the California find was in Gregory's Gulch in Colorado. In the first week of May, 1859, John H. Gregory and two other men led their burdened mules out of Cherry Creek to look for a claim. They ended on Clear Creek, the present site of Central City. Gregory began washing a pan of dust and got a dollar's worth. The party took a bag of dust valued at about $15 to Denver, and the stampede was on.

1859 was also the year of the news of the fabulous Comstock Lode found in the Virginia Mountains of Nevada, some 20 miles from Reno. It was the richest silver deposit ever found, and there was plenty of gold in the hills also.

The influx of treasure-seekers was enormous and the town of Virginia City, founded the same year, became the boom-town hub of the whole mining camp area. In its early years it was probably the rip-roaringest mining capital of them all, with the biggest and best saloons and bars. By 1860, it even had a newspaper, the celebrated *Territorial Enterprise*, of which Mark Twain was an editor (1863-67). The fame of Virginia City lived on long after the gold and silver petered out. It has been restored now

A prospector with his "staff of life," the water donkey. *Photo by B. W. Kilburn.*

The rush to the Comstock Lode, Virginia City.

to the appearance of its liveliest days and is a tourist center, popular with all visitors to the area.

In 1863 the first big strike was made in Montana. That summer William Fairweather, Robert Vaughan and a small group were prospecting on a creek when Fairweather took his horse across to tie to some trees.

"There's a ledge over there we ought to try to get some money for a little tobacco," he said.

Vaughan returned to the spot with Fairweather. Fairweather dug and Vaughan washed the dirt. While his companion expertly panned the water and dirt Fairweather began scratching a ledge with his knife.

"Looks like I found a scad!" he cried.

"If you have one I have a thousand," Vaughan jubilantly replied.

The first pan contained $2.80 worth of gold. The next pan was worth over a hundred dollars. Day after day they continued to pan the gold, pledging among themselves to keep their find secret. But as at Sutter's Mill, such a secret could not be kept.

Soon one of the maddest gold rushes was taking place, with most of Montana's population hurrying to the gulch which Fairweather had named Alder Gulch from the grove of alder there. In a matter of hours, a new city, also called Virginia City, was born, and in a few years it became the territorial capital.

An 1865 broadside.

George Warren, discoverer of the Copper Queen mine. *Photo by Camillus Fly.*

A Black Hills miner guarding the camp. *Photo by S. J. Morrow.*

Statement of Deposits and Coinage

AT THE

Branch Mint of the United States, Carson City, Nevada,

During the Month of February 1872

	VALUE.
Gold Deposits	$ 307697.14
Silver Deposits and Purchases	252490.45
Total Deposits	$ 560187.59

COINAGE EXECUTED.
GOLD·

DENOMINATION.	No. OF PIECES.		VALUE.
Double Eagles	4000		$ 80000.00
Eagles	900		9000.00

From a statement of the Carson City mint, February, 1872.

Alder Gulch took on the aspect of an ant-heap, with prospectors virtually crawling over themselves to pan gold. So rich was the color that a poor average for a miner was a hundred dollars a day.

There were many other gold and silver discoveries, many other mining-camp boom-towns, notably Deadwood in the Black Hills of South Dakota, where gold was discovered in 1875, and Tombstone, where rich silver mines were found in 1877. Both of these towns, each founded a year or so after the finds, were notorious as hotbeds of wildness and reckless revelry.

Copper was discovered near Butte, Montana, in 1880, with some rather different consequences from the silver and gold discoveries. Copper mining was a much more mechanized operation than gold or silver mining. Large or well-capitalized companies had to conduct the actual mining and the area became more industrialized and somewhat more orderly than the other mining areas. Also, there was widespread speculation. Worthless lands and even options on worthless land were sold and resold at higher and higher prices. Copper-mining companies were formed with practically no assets, but they continued to sell shares at ever-increasing prices. The boom fever spread over the country, and when the bust came, there was much more money lost in the speculation swindle than was made in copper profits for many years.

As the people moved west, new riches—notably in

Mine entrance, Colorado, 1860's. *Photo by W. H. Jackson.*

Deadwood, South Dakota, 1876. *Photo by S. J. Morrow.*

Another view of Deadwood, 1876.

Idaho and Colorado, besides the areas already mentioned—were discovered on or under the ground—zinc, iron, coal, borax and many other metals and minerals. Each find drew new population from the East; each had its own peculiar impact on its era. But essentially the two extremes were the gold and silver towns on the wild side and the copper areas on the sober, industrial side. Naturally, the famous gold mines were the ones to capture the interest and imagination of the country. Everyone wanted to know about them. Stories about them found a ready market, and newspapers and magazines published many accounts about them.

In the early rushes there was a great deal of "salting" by fast-talking promoters. To salt a mine, a man would distribute gold dust over a claim. The best method was to load a shotgun with gold dust and fire the load into a hill or mound. In 1859 a group of solemn-faced miners watched Horace Greeley get down on his knees and wash pan after pan of dirt. In the end the famous editor had a small bagful of glittering dust.

Getting to his feet, he said, "Gentlemen, I have worked with my own hands and have seen with my own eyes, and the news of your rich discovery shall go all over the world as far as my paper can carry it."

He was cheered wildly by the gleeful miners, who had carefully salted the mine before Greeley had arrived.

Cabin of the "bottle fiend" of Deadwood, surrounded by kegs full of bottles. *Photo by S. J. Morrow.*

In the West booms rose and fell. In 1863 mere holes in the earth were being sold as mines in Colorado. Naive buyers in the East bought millions of worthless, so-called mines. So great was the transfer of property that the clerk and recorder of Gilpin County was forced to employ an extra staff to assist him in the paper work. In the spring the boom collapsed like a punctured balloon.

The boom towns of the West were as picturesque as they were dirty. At Helena, Last Chance Gulch, Virginia City, Alder Gulch and Bannock on Grasshopper Creek miners lived in holes dug into the sides of the hills or in tents made of anything from canvas to potato sacks. Chair bottoms were of rawhide or rope. Beds were mounds of straw covered by a ragged blanket.

Prices were fantastic. A straw boom cost $5, eggs, $3 apiece—$2 more than in the last days in Confederate Richmond; flour, $25 a sack; water, 50 cents a barrel; peaches 50 cents each.

The saloons were usually large tents which shared barber shop and grocery facilities. Such places were always madhouses of shouting miners trying to attract the attention of the harried clerk, gossiping prospectors with weeks of beard waiting for a chance in the barber's chair and drunken members of the local amateur quartet practicing at the bar. There were many bars but few churches.

Mail service was desired almost as much as whiskey and women. When a camp was set up, riders delivered mail to Fort Laramie for 25 cents a letter. Later the stagecoach would take over, cutting the cost of postage.

Sports were cruel and vicious: bullfights, dogfights and cockfights. Boxing matches ended only when one contender was beaten into insensibility. In 1865 in Virginia

Ready to blast in the West Stewart Mine, Butte, Montana, 1880. *Photo by N. H. Forsythe.*

Shaft scene in a Cripple Creek, Colorado, mine. *Photo by James A. Harlan.*

Placer mining at the Plowman Mine, Idaho City.

City one fight started at eight in the evening and ended at dawn after 185 rounds had been fought. The battle was declared a draw.

As the boom towns became more civilized, traveling circuses and road shows would appear. The New York *Tribune's* correspondent in 1866 reported that the Virginia City Theatre held 200 customers, a large stove, candles at the footlights and a green cambric drop curtain. The audience was apt to get wild and sometimes the performers also; one night in Tombstone Calamity Jane forgot the villain was only an actor and pegged a shot at him. Fortunately, she missed.

Cemeteries and Boot Hills were established almost as soon as a town was born, but undertakers took their time in arriving. In Denver's second year, six men died in a mine disaster. There was no undertaker, so the women of the town dressed the bodies and the miners buried them. It would be a long time before the formal black hearse would replace the bumping quartz wagon which took the crude pine coffins to the cemetery outside the town limits.

The men were rough in dress and manner, but a great many were highly educated. In 1862, when George Crocker and his party walked 150 miles to Colorado City to attend the Territorial Legislature, he arrived at the House of Representatives with a worn blanket, a six-shooter on his hip, a blue flannel shirt, trousers patched with buckskin, and an old slouch with its rim half gone. He was bearded and gaunt with weariness, but when he was elected Speaker of the House, he made a speech which would have been a credit to a polished diplomat.

Boom towns attracted professional gamblers, men and women and plenty of gunmen and bandits. Games of all kinds went on day and night. Fortunes were won and lost with the flick of a card. Men died in a game of cards, their blood staining the green baize tables.

An advertisement in *Samuel's Directory*, Portland and East Portland, 1874.

The dance hall was a favorite spot in the mining camps. Here a lonesome miner could buy a ticket for a dollar— the proceeds were usually split down the middle between the dance-hall owner and the girl—and dance around the room a few times. After a gay whirl, the miner could take her to the bar for a drink and, if he wished, arrange to spend some time with her alone.

The rough mining camps underscored the American knack for bringing order where chaos had existed. Before legislators or courts could be elected and established, vigilante committees and miners' courts took care of the swift administration of justice. Veteran miners had an amazing knowledge of mining laws and constitutional privileges, and it was difficult for the law-breaker to defeat justice in those early courtrooms. The majority of votes elected the judge in murder trials, and a jury was chosen from the spectators.

Like the cowboy, the miner left his own vocabulary on the western frontier; diggings, dust, shebang, color, pan out, lead, outfit, and apparently the favorite expression of all—"You bet!"

Ruins of the old Mexican smelter at Ouray, Colorado. *Photo by C. H. Clark.*

Timber-r-r!

STANDING side by side with the cowboy on his horse, the prospector with his pan and the painted Indian brave is the bearded logger with his double-bitted axe. He is as much a part of the American West as his companions. And, like the others, he has placed his stamp on our folklore, our ballads and our traditions.

Curiously, the logger paralleled the cattleman in his philosophy of the West. He paid no heed as to who rightly owned the land on which grew the timber he wanted. As far as he was concerned it was all an open range and whoever got there first served himself first.

The first loggers were usually small parties of one or two men who stocked up a canoe with enough provisions to last them a few weeks, then set out to reconnoiter the country for excellent timber sites. When one was found, a camp was made and the axe-men would be sent for.

The loggers spent the winter cutting and trimming the timber and sending it downstream on the ice. As early as the 1850's small logging parties "got out" as much as a million feet of lumber, using only 15 men and two yoke of oxen. The ice route had to be utilized because there were no roads and the Indian trails were too narrow for the yoke of oxen.

The camps that were established in the West were patterned after the "State of Maine" camp. There was but one building about 40 feet long and elevated two feet from the ground. The roofs were usually of evergreens, the walls of logs.

In a way the building resembled the long-house of the Iroquois in the East. In the center of the room was a large fireplace; above it was a fire hole. Sometimes wooden pine shakes were extended down from the roof to about a foot above the fireplace to act as a sort of funnel to catch the smoke.

The fire was used not only for cooking but for heat and illumination, as there were no windows. Berths were built along the sides of the walls. The loggers slept with their heads toward the wall. Between the logger's feet and

Early western logging camp showing wooden sled. *Photo by Martin's Gallery.*

Driving logs on the St. Croix River, 1870's.

the fire was a broad plank called the "deacon's seat," which he used as a step to get into his bed. Here he sat, dressed and gossiped.

At the end of the building was the pantry, the world of the cook. Here were the rough tables and chairs where the men were fed. Here also was the inevitable grindstone, which was always in use as the loggers ground fine their axes. Other standard items were the water barrel and the bucket used for washing.

Blankets were usually buffalo robes. At night a visitor might think he was in a laundry, with all the heavy woolen socks hanging on lines crisscrossing the room. Sometimes the loggers slept spoon-fashion under a single cover. When one logger got tired of sleeping on one side he would shout "Spoon" and the whole line would turn over.

In the pre-dawn darkness the cook's assistant would walk into the bunkhouse banging on an iron triangle and shouting for all to rise and shine. After a hearty breakfast they would move into the forest.

The logging party was divided into teamsters, who hauled the logs; choppers, who felled the giants of the forests; sawyers, who sawed the logs into sections; and swampers, who prepared the roads. Expert choppers were the heart of the camp. A man who was an expert with his double-bitted tool received as much as $75 a month in the pre-Civil War era.

A log jam on the St. Croix, 1870's. *Photo by M. Nowack.*

A bull team (oxen) on the skidroad. The skid-greaser is getting a new can of grease for the skids. The Douglas fir region on the north bank of the Columbia River, 1895.

A skid road.

In the early days of western logging, many of the Maine methods were used in preparing the logs. One was to "go-devil" the log or drag it whole to the river bank, where it was cut into sections. The double saw soon took the place of the double-bitted axe. With this tool two men always worked together. After a scaler selected a tree, they made a bite on one side with an axe, then started to saw on the other. It was an extremely risky business. Sometimes the tree trunk would split and the cry "Whip the saw!" would ring out. The saw was then turned to the other side and the men began frantically sawing to stop the split.

There was always danger in the felling of the tree. Sometimes the tree did not fall in the direction the loggers intended, or else in falling it hit another tree and the massive trunk would whip about. The first warning that a fall was near was the harsh, ripping sound that grew in intensity. Then the forest would echo with the traditional "Timber-r-r! Down the line. Watch out."

When they heard this cry, the loggers scrambled for safety as the giant of the forest plunged down, making the earth tremble as it hit. Out of the dust and falling leaves would come the sawyers, who first trimmed, then used their two-handed saws in an even rhythm to saw the big trunk into 16-foot sections. The cut loads were then put onto a sled with the aid of heavy chains and oxen. The next step was piling them on the ice for the trip "down-river."

The life of a western logger was hard and lonely. After supper each logger took his turn on the grindstone. Then they would settle down on the deacon's seat for an evening of smoking and telling tall tales. A camp that had a fiddler was considered first-rate. After eating he would take his stance in the middle of the room and begin playing. Sometimes, to relieve the monotony, the loggers would "hurrah." To cowhands this meant shooting up a town or "treeing it"; to loggers, this was an all-male dance. The men who would act the part of the ladies had a bandana tied around one arm. Then they kicked and swung their partners all night to the fiddler's tune.

Sunday was a day of laundering: washing and boiling clothes. In the afternoon card games would be held, or perhaps a new tenderfoot would be sent to beg of the cookie where he could find a "bean-hole."

As the cattle kingdoms expanded in the seventies and eighties, so did the logging camps. It soon became the custom of the larger companies to hire expert timber cruisers, who would go out alone and mark whole tracts of excellent timber to be cut.

Camps now numbered as many as 100 men, who would cut millions of feet of pine during one winter. Now the old Maine camps were gone. In their place were large bunkhouses, cook and pantry buildings and dining rooms. Fresh meat, vegetables and pastry took the place of the old pork and beans. New methods were also introduced, such as the "Michigan Road." This was a system used in Michigan in which a tank wagon would ride up and down the road, dousing it with water to insure a heavy coating of ice when the freeze came.

The number of logs on the river increased so that the lumbermen, like the cattlemen, produced their own brands, which they used to stamp the ends of their logs. Each logger registered his own brand.

One of the most exciting aspects of logging was the "drive" downriver. The pick of the camp put on their heavy caulked boots and overalls and selected their peavey, canthook and pike pole. At the landing they began breaking up the logs and soon were moving downstream. The logs, bouncing and floating at all angles, invariably piled up in a huge, grinding, crushing jam. The drivers would then start seeking the one log that had "frozen" the drive. A skillful driver could find this log and with his pike pull

it free. Then slowly, with a loud, wrenching groan, the jam would disintegrate and the logs would work free.

To prevent a recurrence the drivers would ride the logs, skipping from one to another, poling, pulling and guiding the timber through the rapids, over small waterfalls and along the sluiceways. There were also times when even the most skillful driver could not find the reason for the jam. Then dynamite would be used to break up the jam of twisted timber.

After the timber was cut into sections at the sawmill these also would be floated downriver. But now a "crib" was made of the sawed sections. This was usually a crate-like affair 16 feet wide, 32 feet long and up to 20 inches deep. In the middle and at the end of the crib were huge oars made from a tree trunk. Meals on the crib were prepared on a pile of sand. Just before the Civil War, tents appeared on cribs, later followed by shacks. It usually took a crew of 20 or more tough oarsmen to move the cribs downriver.

The logging crews were a colorful part of the western

A fallen giant redwood, 17½ feet in diameter at the stump, approximately 1,300 years old. Near Fort Bragg, California. *Photo by Frederick.*

A few of the several thousand company log-brands registered at Olympia, Washington.

Moving logs by horse team.

Moving redwood trunk sections by bull team.

Logs moving downstream.

Moving redwood sections by locomotive.

frontier. After a long, hazardous drive downriver they would "tree" a town as high on payday as any cow outfit after a drive from the Red River country up to Abilene. Huge, powerful men with thick beards, grimy, checkered mackinaws and insatiable thirsts, they often took a steamboat back upstream to the main camp. More than one skipper had to blow for help when his burly passengers decided to challenge each other in a fight on the lower deck—"for the fun of it."

After the Civil War, raft-tugs made their appearance, and soon the western waters were crowded with the tiny, blunt-nosed crafts towing the large rafts.

Puget Sound log-dump. Preparing to roll logs from the pier
into the water.

Moving logs by steamboat and raft. These logs are being towed some 1,200 miles,
from the Columbia River to San Diego.

The Bad Men and The Wild Ways

THERE were many hazards, obstacles and disadvantages that had to be overcome before the West could be fully settled and its resources properly developed. These included the nature of the terrain, the hostile Indians, the lack of water, the lack of trails, transportation and communication and—most publicized and probably least significant—the lack of law and order, the prevalence of outlaws.

For the most part the settlers of the West organized themselves and governed their affairs well. But as was to be expected in any frontier society, there was somewhat less order, somewhat more crime and banditry than in a seasoned long-regulated society

From 1866 to the late 1880's there was in the West an excess of outlawry and violence. Why the excess of crime and violence? Why the widespread prevalence of outlaws and the occasional outlaw society?

There are several reasons: the postwar influx of ex-soldiers and other restless young men inured to killing and violence, the peculiar nature of the mining towns, the peculiar nature of the cattle business, the romantic accounts in popular periodicals of the glamourized Robin-Hoodized bandits and their counterparts, the sheriffs and marshals.

As has been mentioned before, after the Civil War many ex-soldiers, Union and Confederate, bored or dissatisfied with the dull life back home, made their way West. Besides the families and the settlers who wanted new opportunities there were many single men seeking adventure and excitement. Some of these went out to the

A Pictorial Directory of Desperadoes and Lawmen of the West

The pictures shown in this directory are all made from drawings by H. O. Rawson. Early in this century Rawson set out to make sketches of every western personality of importance—outlaws, sheriffs, Indian chiefs, army officers and other men and women identified with the West. He worked mainly from authenticated photographs, but some of his drawings were made at first hand, directly from life. He published these drawings as a series of cards which had a very large circulation in the early 1900's. A comparison of his sketches with known photographs wherever possible, indicates his amazing accuracy, and it can be assumed that sketches of personalities whose photographs no longer exist were also accurate and true pictures.

The Apache Kid.

Arizona Joe.

Sam Bass, train and bank robber, 1870's.

John Behan, sheriff of Tombstone.

mining camps, some to Texas and the cattle country to become ranchers or cowboys, some joined the Army, but some became bandits. The outlaw life seemed a short-cut to easy money, which could buy women, liquor and a turn at the gambling table. And strangely enough, many outlaws were regarded as heroes, honored for their exploits, respected for their bravery and boldness.

In a strange way, the wave of lawlessness produced countless articles which helped to spotlight and romanticize the West in the periodicals of the time. Ned Buntline mixed his spurious heroes, blood and ink to reap a fortune in royalties, and the careful *Harper's* writer sat back in amazement as Wild Bill Hickok spun his wild yarns for gullible eastern audiences eager for lurid tales.

Heading the list of outlaws, of course, must be the James-Younger clan, who terrorized the Middle Border for years. They are a case in point of how outlaws could command an entire community by the use of fear and bribery and by playing upon partisan sympathies.

To the Southerners in the Missouri legislature, Jesse and his boys could do no wrong; they were the symbol of the "undefeated" Confederacy, the veterans barred from a chance to enjoy the good life by their former enemies, the Yankees. Overlooked, of course, was the fact that Jesse's first strike was at the Liberty, Missouri, bank that held his neighbors' funds.

A band as evil but more ingenious than the James-Youngers was that of the Reno Brothers of Indiana, who "invented" train robbery. Actually, they commercialized this form of outlawry; there had been reports of train robberies as early as 1850. The activities of the Renos ranged from robbing banks and trains to raids on public offices in Iowa, Indiana and Missouri. Lesser robber bands included the Farrington brothers of Missouri and later the Sam Bass, Dalton and Doolin gangs.

The early hold-up gangs were usually composed of blood relations, kissing kin, neighbors and former Army comrades. The technique was simple: they selected a train bearing a gold shipment, stacked ties across the rails and waved a red railroad lantern until the engineer jammed on the brakes. While some of the gang hurrahed the passengers by gunfire, the rest killed or wounded the Express

"X" Beidler, Montana vigilante.

Billy the Kid (William Bonney).

"Black Bart" (Charles E. Bolton), stage-coach robber and poet.

Henry Brown, member of Billy the Kid's gang.

Neil Brown, Dodge City lawman, late 1870's.

Laura Bullion (Della Rose) member of the Wild Bunch.

Company messenger guarding the gold and filled the grain or cotton burlap bags with the loot. A horse-holder was always stationed nearby. The riders either rode together to a hideout or split up to meet later at an appointed rendezvous. In later years larger bands such as the Wild Bunch used for their escape relays of horses hidden in canyons or gullies.

Frontier law-enforcement usually consisted of the Pinkertons and detectives for the railroads and cattle associations. There were many brave and fearless local sheriffs and marshals, but they were outnumbered by the cowards and bribe-takers. One wonders how Jesse James, the most wanted man in the Midwest, rode so casually in and out of Clay County. . . .

The records of the Pinkertons show without a doubt that the Pinkerton detective agency was the largest and most effective law-enforcement agency in the West. The founder, Allan, and the sons, William and Robert, trailed, fought, captured and killed outlaws all over the West. Joining forces with the Pinkertons—the agency represented the Adams Express Company, then the nation's largest carrier—were detectives employed by the Union Pacific, the Central Pacific, the Southern Pacific and many other railroads.

The detectives employed by the cattlemen's associations also did valiant work in breaking up the large gangs of rustlers, despite local apathy. In one case a detective failed to get a rustler indicted in Wyoming's Johnson County despite his evidence of several hides. (The "running iron" of the rustler could destroy the brand on the outside of the hide, but the original brand remained on the inside.) He doggedly trailed the rustler to Nebraska, caught him there in the act; he was then able to see that the thief was arrested and upon evidence submitted by the detective he was later convicted.

The Mining Camp Lawlessness

In the mining camps the law was the six-shooter strapped around a man's waist. A prospector had to battle

Seth Bullock, sheriff.

Calamity Jane (Martha Jane Canarray), notorious wild woman of the West.

Bill Carver, member of the Wild Bunch.

Cattle Annie and Little Breeches, outlaw girls with Bill Doolin's gang.

Cherokee Bill (Crawford Goldsby), outlaw chief of the Indian Territory.

George Cook, train robber.

claim-jumpers, robbers and homicidal drunkards. He was lucky to survive at all. When the news spread that "color" had been found, men of every description flocked to the gold diggings. There were honest men with dreams, but there were also parasites, gamblers, gunmen, thieves and saloon-keepers with jugs of colored alcohol.

Violence was commonplace as men fought to protect their miserable hovels and bags of gold dust. When the situation became intolerable for honest men, miners' committees were selected and vigilante committees formed. The "justice" administered by the vigilantes was swift, merciless, and ruthlessly efficient. There was usually an exodus of "sidewheelers" before dusk. Bodies were usually discovered at daybreak.

In Montana the hemp of the lynch law brought peace and, ironically, law and order. There, in the early sixties, the vigilantes, made up of honest, decent citizens, established a powerful organization. Under the leadership of X. Beidler, they broke up the vicious Plummer gang, one of the worst in the West, captured more than 20 outlaws, including the brutal Joe Slade within six weeks, and within a short period established an effective, informal government.

Crime in the Cattle Country

Rustling, horse-stealing and bushwhacking were major crimes in the cow country. It was bad enough for a killer to gun down a victim from ambush, but stealing a man's horse was almost as grave. This was his sole means of transportation on a vast, trackless plain. The unwritten law of the cattle country of the rider caring for his horse before himself underscores the great value placed on his mount by the Westerner.

Rustling was another major crime, but often its degree was measured by the time and place. Veteran cowmen knew that mavericks many times belonged to the "longest rope" and often arbitrated rather than resorting to gunfire. Even when a rustler was caught red-handed with a "running iron" smoking against a steer's hide, few ranchers took the step of seeking a stout branch from the nearest cottonwood for immediate retribution.

Jim Cook, U. S. Marshal, 1890.

Jim Courtright, marshal of Fort Worth.

Jim Cummings, member of the Jesse James gang.

George Curry, "Flat Nose George" of the Wild Bunch.

Bob Dalton, one of the outlaw "Dalton boys," cousins of Jesse James.

Emmett Dalton, a "Dalton boy."

There is little doubt that some rustlers kicked out their last moments of life, slowly strangling to death, but after studying many reports of stockmen and detectives, one is struck by the general fair-mindedness of the ranchers, who usually escorted the rustlers they caught to the nearest sheriff.

In some sections of the West, cowboy- and granger-filled grand juries often refused to recognize the crime of rustling by simply refusing to return a true bill. "If the big ranchers got their starts by roping other men's mavericks, how can they complain?" was a popular argument.

Rustling was big business. The gangs were well organized and perfected a relay system. The stolen steers would be bedded down for a night on a conveniently located ranch—not a rustler's—and would be moved the next day to another one. If a posse trailed them to the spot the rancher simply shrugged; he didn't know a thing about any stolen steers. . . .

Cattle "fences" and butchers were available. The gang usually had well-hidden ranches and, like the Wild Bunch, had a high-priced attorney on its payroll. Like the Middle Border gangs, they made use of the violent partisanship of the region and the era to their own advantage; few cowboys would turn informer against a former bunkmate.

The cattle barons, in turn, used despicable tactics to rid the range of the thieves. Gunmen like Tom Horn were employed to kill the rustlers and, like Horn, they shot mostly from ambush and, like shadows, melted away to strike again.

The barons were not above using their cowboys to bully sheriffs or to turn out a homesteader at gun-point. They were brazen in the use of their political power to gain their ends. One has only to study the shocking details of the "invasion" of Wyoming's Johnson County and its aftermath.

Violence and sudden death trailed the cattle drives into the early cowtowns, and it was to the credit of lawmen in such towns like Bill Tilghman, Bear River Smith, the Mastersons and others that they brooked no nonsense from the wild and unruly young punchers and did their best to maintain law and order in the rough streets and saloons.

Most of the lawmen would rather part a young cow-

Frank Dalton, one of the outlaw Daltons.

Wyatt Earp, U. S. Marshal.

Bob Ford, killer of Jesse James.

Pat Garrett, sheriff and killer of Billy the Kid.

Camilla Hanks, "Deaf Charley," one of the Wild Bunch.

John Wesley Hardin, killer, Texas, 1870's.

boy's hair with the barrel of a single-action .45 than kill him. In the dawn, head aching, eyes blurred, stomach rolling from the rotgut whiskey he had consumed the night before, a rambunctious young Texan usually dug deep for his last five dollars to pay his fine for disturbing the peace, then rode off to join his spread, ready to move homeward down the trail.

The Battle of the O. K. Corral

The Earp-Clanton feud on that dark and bloody ground of Arizona of 1881 has become legendary. Although there are half a dozen different versions, the blood-soaked facts are still available in court records and in the columns of that valiant frontier newspaper, the Tombstone *Epitaph*.

About 2:30 P.M., October 26, 1881, Ike (Isaac or Joseph) Clanton, his brother Billy Clanton, Frank and Tom McLaury, met Wyatt, Morgan and Virgil Earp and Doc Holliday in the Tombstone livery stable known as the O. K. Corral, an open lot about 30 feet wide. Facing it

was the two-story frame gallery of Camillus Fly, a frontier photographer.

There had been clashes between Ike and Holliday and the Earps. Therefore, when word spread that Ike and his "cowboys" were waiting for the Earps, Sheriff Johnny Behan, a pathetic figure in this encounter, went down to "disarm them." The Earps and Holliday brushed past him as he protested weakly.

According to later court testimony, Wyatt Earp shouted to the Clantons and McLaurys, "You s—s of b—s, you have been looking for a fight!" and then ordered them to throw up their hands. Who fired first is still argued, but when the gunsmoke drifted away, the McLaurys were dead or dying, Ike Clanton was running away, while his dying brother was trying to get off a last shot. But, as an eyewitness testified, he was stopped "by Mr. Fly, who took his revolver."

Frank McLaury was dead. His brother Tom, who may or may not have been armed, fell first, according to the testimony of R. F. Coleman, but raised himself and fired a last shot. Morgan Earp "was shot through," Virgil was

Pearl Hart, stagecoach robber, Arizona.

J. B. "Wild Bill" Hickok.

Doc Holliday, gambler and gunfighter, Tombstone.

Tom Horn, detective, peace officer, hired killer, Wyoming.

Frank James, in his youth.

Frank James, in his later days.

"shot in the leg, which staggered him some," while a ball glanced off Holliday's holster, bruising his leg. Wyatt Earp was not hit.

These are the facts. As in most cases of bloody gunfights on the frontier, little that is new concerning them has been uncovered down through the years. But recently Sylvester Vigilante, well-known western historian and member of the staff of the New York Historical Society, was given a package of "interesting material on the gun-fight in the O. K. Corral." The package contained letters written from Tombstone shortly after the burial of his brothers by the surviving McLaury brother to his relatives and to his law associate in Texas. Granted that the letters are one-sided and full of bitter hatred for the Earps and Holliday, they still, however, offer direct evidence of the aftermath of the fight. Certainly the picture painted by McLaury of Earp is far different from the idealized figure of contemporary television "westerns."

In the *Epitaph's* account of the long trial and in numerous books, the McLaury name has been consistently misspelled. The signature and the letterheads of these letters —published here for the first time—set the record straight after 78 years.

The Romantic Gunfighter

Unfortunately, in legend and story, standing shoulders high above the cowboy, the Plains tribesman, the prospector and the logger is the western gunman. In popular imagination he is a tall, slender, handsome man with an impassive face, cold black eyes, and a six-shooter tied to his thigh with rawhide. And of course he draws with the speed of a snake's tongue.

He towers over all the other personalities of the Great American West although the serious fact is that he and his counterpart, the western marshal or sheriff, are but a footnote to the majestic history of the West and that only because, as the French philosopher said, it takes not only saints but also sinners to make a frontier.

However, no one can deny that the Western gunfighters·

Jesse James, the youth.

Jesse James, the man.

Al Jennings, Oklahoma train robber who later ran for governor.

Sam Ketchum, brother of Tom Ketchum.

Tom "Black Jack" Ketchum of the Hole-in-the-Wall gang.

Ben Kilpatrick, "The Tall Texan" of the Wild Bunch.

[231]

have captured the imagination and won the hearts not only of most Americans but also of most Europeans. And their popularity was never greater than right now. What backyard or street in America doesn't have a make-believe O.K. Corral? What seven-year-old hasn't worn a pair of toy six-shooters on his hip as he snarls, "If you ain't yellow—draw!" The gesture is unmistakable.

Television has made the two figures—the desperado and the lawman—more durable than ever. Millions watch the glamorous figure of Wyatt Earp, that saccharine hero of the frontier, walk down a dusty street to his rendezvous with destiny. Of course his incredible draw and Buntline

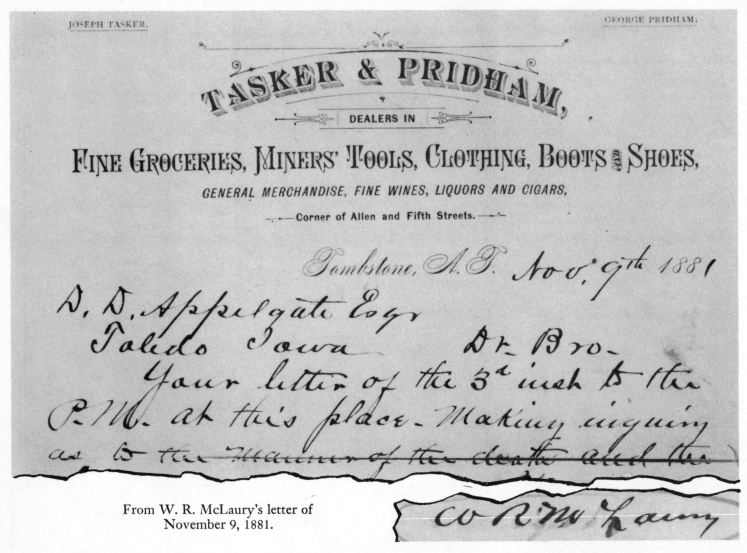

From W. R. McLaury's letter of November 9, 1881.

Tom McLaury. *Photo by Hassell.*

Frank McLaury. *Photo by Hassell.*

Ike Clanton. *Photo by Camillus S. Fly.*

From the Correspondence of W. R. McLaury

From letter to S. P. Greene, Esq., Fort Worth, Texas, dated Tombstone, A.T., Nov. 8, 1881:

Dear Capt.,

. . . I have sent you some papers that give the evidence of witnesses present at the time my brothers and the boy young Clanton were murdered. As to the perpetration of the crime, I can only say it was as cold-blooded and foul a murder as has been recorded. My brothers had no quarrel nor interest in any quarrel with these men. My brother Frank and young Clanton who was killed had been with other parties gathering stock for several weeks and had come to the town on business and had been here about fifteen minutes, had transacted their business and were ready to mount their horses to leave. Brother Tom and Isaac Clanton were going out in a wagon, the team being then ready—Brother Tom and I. Clanton had been in town from the morning of the day previous and were unarmed. Frank and William Clanton were armed but were completely surprised. After Frank was mortally wounded he shot Holliday, Morgan and Virgil Earp, wounding Morgan and Virgil severely.

When I arrived here on the 4th those who were able to be out were on the streets on bail and the people were many of them in dread of these men. They came into the court room heavily armed. The District Attorney was completely "cowed" and after promising me on the 4th to move the court to commit these men without bail he would not do it and after agreeing in the presence of all our attys. to do so would not do it and none of our attys. would do so and would not permit me to do so and said they did not want to see me killed. . . . I did not think they would make a move. The fact is I only hoped they would as I would be on my feet and have the first go and thought I could kill them both before they could get a start. . . . I made the motion. They were as quiet as lambs, only looked a little scared—it was granted after some discussion. They then got a writ of Habeas Corpus and we fought over that last night. The petition was dismissed. People were afraid to talk, our witnesses were running away. No one but the miners and ranchmen dared come forward to give any information unless brot into court by attachment. . . . We fear several of our witnesses will be killed by the friends of these brutes. There is two Earp brothers who were not engaged in the murder.

From letter dated Tombstone, A.T., Nov. 9th, 1881, to D. D. Appelgate, Esq., Toledo, Iowa:

Dr. Bro.

I find that with the exception of thirty or forty men here whose business is gambling and stealing, among whom are the Earp brothers and one J. H. Holliday, my brothers were universally esteemed as Honorable, Peaceable, and Brave citizens. . . . But these few desperate men had the town when I came here completely terrorized—I was advised frequently not to lodge at the Hotel. They were admitted to bail because of this feeling. I know they did threaten me. On their examination they sat in the courtroom heavily armed. I tried to have the Dist. Atty move the court to remand them without Bail. He would not do it. . . . Things went on this way nearly two days. These men on the streets and at large, seeing them free kept me on fire and witnesses were scared and some ran away. None with one exception would come to the Hotel or office—and I had mingled with the people and saw enough that if these men were locked up things would change at once. I went before the Court and was admitted. I then got associated as Counsel for the State in the case. I then stood where I could send a knife through their hearts if they made a move and made the motion and it was granted. They did not make a move—and it was perhaps good for me they did not—for I was anxious to have an opportunity to send them over the bay. The sheriff then took them into custody. This occurred about 3 P.M. . . . The Cause of the murder was this: Some time ago, Holliday, one of the murderers, attempted to rob the express of Wells Fargo Co., and in so doing shot and killed a stage driver and a passenger and the other parties engaged in the murder with him the Earp brothers were interested in the attempt at the exp. robbery and young Clanton, who was killed, a boy 18 years old, knew the facts about the attempted robbery and had told his brother, J. I. Clanton and Thos. and Robt. and they had got up facts intending to prosecute him Holliday and the Earp Bros. and Holliday had information of it—It is now known that two other men who knew of the murder in the attempted robbery have since then been killed in Mexico, the report was by "Greasers" but at the time they were killed, Holliday was out of town "said to be visiting in Georgia."

From McLaury's letter to his father from Fort Worth, Texas, April 13, 1884.

My experience out there has been very unfortunate as to my health and badly injured me as to money matters—and none of the results have been satisfactory. The only result is the death of Morgan and crippling of Virgil Earp and death of McMasters. Wyatt Earp was in this town about a month ago and stayed about six hours.

Special decide the issue. It has now reached the stage where TV "Western" actors seriously hold contests to see who is "fastest on the draw." One wonders how fast they would be if they were staring into the cold eyes of a Kid Curry or a Harry Tracy.

Curiously, a number of the western gunfighters and outlaws were handsome men. Lonny Logan, laid out in the morgue in Dodson, Missouri, after he had been killed by the Pinkertons in a wild gun battle, had the profile of a Hollywood actor. The Sundance Kid and the Tall Texan were both handsome men.

Few of the famous western outlaws reached the age of thirty-five. Most of them were dead at thirty. All were former cowhands except Jesse James and his Missouri bravos. There were few cowards among them. They revered friendship. To them, like all frontiersmen, a man's word was his bond.

Frank Dimaio, last of the great Pinkerton detectives who chased the outlaw bands for years, said in 1950, "I brought many of them in. If they refused to give me their word that they wouldn't make a break I'd hogtie them at

night, but if they gave me their word I'd respect it.

"'Spence' (Lowell Spence, the Pinkerton man who hunted Kid Curry for years) once told me how the Kid stared at him through the bars after they grabbed him down south and told Spence he'd be looking for him when he broke out. Spence said he felt a shiver go down his neck.

"He said he hadn't the slightest doubt that Kid Curry would seek him out and try to gun him before he died. After he broke out, Mr. Pinkerton (William) ordered Spence to go after the Kid. Spence said he knew that if he ever caught up with the Kid it would be either him or Curry. It was sort of decided that way."

Actually, the outlaw's prowess with a six-shooter is overrated. Jesse James, who rode with Quantrill's Raiders, called "the greatest revolver fighters in the world," missed a bank cashier with two bullets at close range. Doc Holliday, the menace of Dodge City and Tombstone, fired at a bartender in Texas, only to miss him six times. He was so mortified at his showing that he begged some of his friends who were eye-witnesses not to mention it.

The business of "fanning" a six-shooter is absurd. The

J. F. "Bud" Ledbetter, U. S. Marshal, Oklahoma, 1889.

Harvey Logan, the notorious "Kid Curry" of the Wild Bunch.

Dick Liddell of the Jesse James gang.

Bill Longley, gunfighter and killer, Texas, the 1870's.

Harvey Longbaugh, the "Sundance Kid" of the Wild Bunch.

Bat Masterson.

revolver itself weighed 3.2 pounds. Common sense tells us that it would be almost impossible for anyone to hit a target while slamming the trigger with the edge of his hand.

The late "Cimarron" George Bolds, frontiersman, deputy in Dodge City and leader of the Ingalls (Kansas) raiders into Cimarron, which touched off the savage county-seat wars, told this story about fanning:

"One of the characters in Dodge in those days was a young kid we called the 'Jersey Kid' simply because he came from New Jersey. He had come West after reading a lot of Buntline's trash. He wore a fancy vest, black sombrero and even grew a mustache to look mean.

"He was on the brag about how good he was with a gun, but no one paid any attention to him. One day in the Long Branch he started to pick on a young Texan who was drifting through—just a saddle tramp. The Texan didn't answer the Kid and moved away. Finally the Kid said something that you don't say unless you want to back it up with your hardware. They stepped out into the street and the Kid drew and started fanning. The bullets flew everywhere. The Texan drew also but just calmly aimed and fired.

"Someone sent the Kid's people a telegram and the local undertaker arranged for the body to be shipped back East. That was the only fanning I ever saw in my life."

After examining the whole outlaw era one is certain that although a particular crime or robbery may be forgotten the pageantry never fades. Nothing that the factual historian may say will tarnish the popular laurels of Jesse James and his Missouri bravos or Butch Cassidy and his Wild Bunch. One may not be able to name the bank or the train that was held up or where it took place, but who can forget the thrilling rides across the western plains with the posses far behind; the thunder of horses as Kid Curry leads his army of outlaws through the narrow slit of Hole-in-the-Wall to repulse the stockmen's army of mer-

Ed Masterson, peace officer and brother of Bat Masterson.

Captain Bill McDonald, Texas Ranger.

Frank McLean.

Clell Miller of the Jesse James gang.

Jim Murphy of the Sam Bass gang.

Tom O'Day, train robber, member of the Wild Bunch.

Butch Cassidy (George Parker), leader of the Wild Bunch.

Allan Pinkerton, founder of the Pinkerton Detective Agency.

Robert A. Pinkerton.

William A. Pinkerton.

Poker Alice, gambler.

William Clark Quantrill, guerrilla leader.

Bill Ryan (Tom Hill), train robber.

John Selman, who killed John Wesley Hardin.

Luke Short, Dodge City lawman, associate of Wyatt Earp.

"Green River" Tom Smith, the marshal who cleaned up Abilene.

Belle Starr, "Queen of the Bandits," associate of Cole Younger.

Henry Starr, bank robber and killer. Nephew of Belle Starr.

Fred E. Sutton, the "Crooked S. Kid."

Texas Jack Omohundro, scout and showman.

Bill Tilghman, U. S. Marshal.

Harry Tracy, killer, one of the Wild Bunch.

B. C. Bob Vandenberg, marshal of Dodge City, 1881.

Ben Thompson, Texas outlaw who surrendered to Wyatt Earp, 1873.

cenaries; the lonely watchers on the rims of the gang's hideout, silhouetted against the clear western sky; the blue-eyed boy whose name as recorded in the family Bible is Jesse Woodson James leading his howling guerrillas across the public squares of small towns, their Navy Colts blazing away at the street lamps, the wooden signs and the store windows; Frank James coming out of the unknown to unbuckle his gun belt and dramatically surrender to the Governor of Missouri. . . .

On the other hand, making allowances for the grand romantic pageantry and melodrama, we must, after an examination of their lives, come to the rather commonplace conclusion that crime, even on the frontier, did not pay.

It is difficult to find nobility or splendor in their lives. Despite all the legends of Jesse robbing the tax collector to get the widow's money and return it to her, he was a cold-blooded thief and killer. The plea "They (the Yankees) drove us to it," never took into account that a large number of Quantrill's and Bloody Bill Anderson's riders later became decent citizens, even lawmen.

Nonetheless, we do come to admit, however grudgingly, the vitality, self-confidence, recklessness and gusto of these men, particularly Butch Cassidy. Harry Tracy, the Tiger of the Wild Bunch, was a fast-drawing killer, a fighting machine without a bit of human dignity. Kid Curry was the same—deadly, merciless. He, on the record, killed 16 men with as much regret as if he had killed 16 animals. But like Jesse, they had an unrivaled evil charm that fascinated large numbers of people who shielded them and made it difficult to capture them.

Ironically, these men did do the West some good. Although such a statement might be compared to saying that a better race of deer was bred because of a vicious cougar that was in their midst, the outlaws of the West did help to develop the same forces that finally destroyed them. Certainly the outlawry and the violence did point up the corruption of some and the cowardice of others and finally awakened the citizens of the frontier communities to appoint better men to protect them.

Bill Thompson, Ben's brother, also surrendered to Wyatt Earp.

Big Foot Wallace, Texas Ranger.

Dick Ware, Texas Ranger who killed Sam Bass.

Zip Wyatt (Dick Yeager), Oklahoma train robber.

Bob Younger of the James-Younger gang.

Cole Younger of the James-Younger gang.

They Told the Story

THE excitement, drama, humor and glamour of the West was excellent material for writers. The public clamored for accounts, stories and shows about the fabulous West, and they got it. Desperadoes, marshals, Indian chiefs, generals, scouts, stage-drivers, cowboys and even horses were portrayed as heroes capable of fantastic achievements. Also desperadoes, Indian chiefs, rustlers and cowboys were portrayed as vicious villains, capable of the cruelest of crimes.

Probably widest circulated of this immensely popular and quite inaccurate school of writers was Ned Buntline (Col. E. C. Judson), whose name is virtually synonymous with Western dime thrillers. He is reputed to have written over a thousand novels, but that is undoubtedly an exaggeration. It is true, however, that thousands of such stories about the West were published and they helped to create the popular image of the West that persists even until now.

But there were serious writers also whose reports, essays, stories and books did present a faithful view of the Western scene. Most notable among these were Mark Twain and Bret Harte, whose writings about the West achieved fame and great circulation not only all over the country, but almost all over the world. Mark Twain's *Roughing It* is full of excellent descriptions of prospecting, mining camp life, ranch life, the Pony Express and other important elements of the West. His "Celebrated Jumping Frog of Calaveras County and Other Sketches," published in 1867, is a classic of western humor.

Mark Twain (Virginia City years). *Photo by Charles Watkins.*

"Ned Buntline," Colonel E. Z. C. Judson.

Bret Harte. *Photo by Sarony.*

Bret Harte wrote stories about the gold camps for the *Overland Monthly* which were published in 1870 as *The Luck of Roaring Camp and Other Sketches.* That and his famous ballad about the "Heathen Chinee" called "Plain Language for Truthful Jones" are also among the still widely-read great classics of the West. The writings of Theodore Roosevelt, previously mentioned, also achieved wide publication and had considerable influence.

Wild West shows and exhibitions like Buffalo Bill's were enormously popular in the East and the West and vied with regular theatrical fare for the public's attention. Although famous actors, actresses and various stock companies toured the West in successful plays, the Wild West melodramas and shows were almost always sure-fire attractions.

And, as previously mentioned, the photographers and artists such as Catlin, Bodmer, Schreyvogel, Moran and Remington, and many others supplied illustrative material for lectures as well as for magazines and books.

All these portrayed the West. The amount of truth in what they told varied and some of it assayed very low, but they helped to build the colorful legend of the Great American West.

California Theatre showbill. Note that Bret Harte was in the cast.

Be good + you will be lonesome.

Mark Twain

Mark Twain, in his later years.

William F. "Buffalo Bill," Cody, in his younger years.

Annie Oakley, famous markswoman, star of Buffalo Bill's show.

Lily Langtry, the "Jersey Lily," the actress most popular with western audiences in the late 1870's and 80's.

A Wild West show poster.

THE BIG INDIAN CHIEF
FIGHTING ELK!

Warrior of the Sioux Nation and Hero of the late Crazy Horse Fight.

TRIBE

WARM SPRING INDIANS!

SUPPORTED BY

GEO. C. DAVENPORT,

The Great Irish Comedian, and a

Full and Powerful Dramatic Company,

In the entirely New and Original Border Drama, in 4 Acts, written expressly for Texas Jack, entitled

SCOUTS of the PLAINS

WITH THE FOLLOWING CAST:

TEXAS JACK, ... **J. B. OMOHUNDRO**

PALE DOVE, ... **M'LLE MORLACCHI**

Capt. Bill.................................H. Mainhall
Nick Blunder, with Song ....Geo. C. Davenport
Jim Daws, a first-class Renegade and Horse
Thief ....S. Denmead
Uncle Henry Carter, a friend of the Scouts... S. H. Thompson
Ebenezer Longlank, Government Peace
Commissioner ....Harry Irving
Tom Dogget, in cahoots with Daws ....Frank Williams
Tall Oak, but on the square ....Dan Duboise
Big Thunder, Comanche Brave ....Fighting Elk
Black Wolf, Comanche Brave ....Joe Bruce
Running Turkey..............................R. Bourn
Aunt Annie Carter, wife of Uncle Henry........Bessie Clifton

Lulu ....⎫ Their ⎧...Miss Frankie E. Murrey
Ella ....⎭ Children, ⎩......... Miss Jessie Howard
Kotolka..Ono-Wiska
Winnie..Pete-o-Put
Bear Claw, Comanche Brave.......................Sic-o-fo-la
Raven Feather.........⎫
Little Elk ....⎪
White Arrow...........⎬ Warm Spring ⎫ TRIBE FROM THE
Little Panther..........⎪ Indians, ⎬ PLAINS.
Chip-o-Munwa........⎪ ⎭
O-tam-e-to ....⎭
Omakowasho, Sintagilisco, Chackasshopoggy, Powderface,
Little Thunder, Big Mouth, Red.Cloud, Spotted Tail.

An 1876 show poster.

Pawnee Bill (G. W. Lillie).

Stanley J. Morrow, photographer.

Frank Leslie, publisher of *Leslie's Weekly. Photo by I. W. Taber.*

John K. Hillers, photographer, in the field, 1871.

Tim O'Sullivan, photographer.

Twilight of the Indian Gods

DURING the long struggle of the red man against the white man in the West, there were always some peaceful tribes, herders and farmers who accepted what fate and the Great White Father gave them. But the warrior tribes kept fighting bitterly, and it took many years of tragedy and disaster to make the Indian chiefs accept the inevitable.

The first notable acceptance of the white men's way was that of Washakie of the Shoshones of Montana. He had been a fierce fighter, leading his tribe nobly against the neighboring tribes. But he made friends with the white men and when, as early as the 1840's he saw the hordes of emigrants coming over the Oregon Trail, he persuaded his tribe, and later others, to submit to the white men's rule. "We can make a bow and arrows," he said, "but the white man's mind is strong and light!"

Quanah Parker, chief of the Kwahadi Comanches, led a powerful alliance of Comanches, Kiowas and Cheyennes in the bloody battle of the Adobe Walls in the Panhandle Country in 1874. Quanah was the half-breed son of Peter-Nakomi and Cynthia Ann Parker of Baker Fort, Navasota County, Texas. As chief of the Kwahadi, he resolved to get all the Indians of the plains together to fight off the invading white men.

A great council was called and the united braves decided to attack, one by one, the various white men's camps in the Panhandle.

The trading post at Adobe Walls was the first target.

Washakie. Photo taken about 1882. *Photo by Baker and Johnston.*

Big Tree, a Kiowa sub-chief, 1871.

White Horse, famous Kiowa warrior.

Long Wolf's son, 1872.

Now the white man's "strong and light mind" was working too fast. Quanah Parker's defeat was the first note of eventual submission for the tribes. Chief Joseph of the Nez Percés had an even more dramatic encounter with the new arms, the new god of the white man.

Quanah Parker.

Asa-tu-at, a Comanche chief.

Kiowa braves, 1876. *Photo by W. P. Bliss.*

There were just 30 buffalo-hunters there, but they were alerted in time to the impending charge of Quanah Parker's 700 Indians. They barricaded themselves behind their stockade and were ready for a siege. And they had powerful new long-range weapons which the Indians did not expect and could not match. Charge followed charge and the fight lasted three days. Quanah was wounded, many of his men were killed or wounded, and the Indians knew that reinforcements would come for the white men.

Quanah knew there was no point in fighting any more. The red men could not beat the white men, and the only thing left to do was to join them. "I can learn the ways of the white men," he said. And he did. He became a successful businessman and won full citizenship for himself and the members of his tribe.

Chief Joseph and the Nez Percés

In 1876 a commission set up by Washington decided that the Nez Percés had to leave their beloved Wallowa Valley in Oregon and return to a reservation. In May of the following year Major General O. O. Howard, commanding the Military Department, was ordered by Washington to carry out the order.

Several councils were held at Fort Lapawi, Idaho. Chief Joseph, accompanied by a younger brother, Ollicut, White Bird and Looking Glass, attended the council.

Hoping to keep peace, Joseph agreed reluctantly to go on the reservation. While he was gathering his people and their pony herds, a band of young warriors murdered some settlers and raped their women. Also, a party of whites fleeing to Mount Idaho was massacred.

The young bucks rode into the camp of White Bird, waving their bloody scalps and calling upon Too-hul-hul-suit, the powerful head of the warriors' organization called the Dreamers, to demand war. His fierce oratory soon had the tribesmen united in a desire for battle. When Joseph

General O. O. Howard, 1881. *Photo by Rieman & Co.*

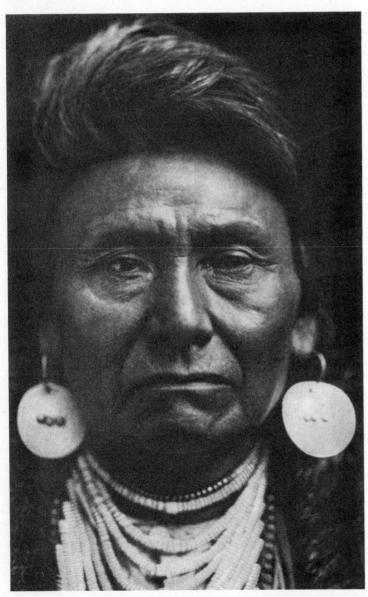

Chief Joseph, leader of the Nez Percés. *Photo by C. J. Curtis.*

Chief Joseph, in his younger days.

[246]

arrived he found his people calling for him to lead them. Reluctantly he obeyed.

The whole countryside was in a panic. Settlers were fleeing their ranches and hurrying to the larger settlements. Messengers were sent from Mount Idaho to Fort Lapawi with the news of the massacres. Howard, one-armed hero of the Civil War, sent part of his skeleton First Cavalry under Captains Perry and Trimble and Lieutenant Teller of the Twenty-First Infantry to protect the settlers.

Perry made a forced march covering 80 miles in 30 hours over terrible terrain. On the 17th of June he was joined by a handful of civilian volunteers.

Once the gauntlet was dropped, Chief Joseph plunged into organizing his small tribe into a mobile fighting unit. He joined White Bird's band on the Salmon River and pitched his camp with his back to the river and his front toward White Bird Canyon.

At dawn when the first soldiers appeared confident that the Nez Percés would not fight, Joseph ordered his women, children and spare horses across the river. Then he prepared an ambush at the mouth of the canyon.

Lieutenant Teller, leading a point of eight soldiers, moved cautiously into the canyon. The fours came up behind at 50 yards. The canyon was quiet until suddenly a body of hard-riding redskins charged out of the ravine toward the cavalrymen. A devastating cross-fire knocked the blue-coated soldiers out of their saddles. When Captain Perry arrived he ordered his force up a small hill. The soldiers traded shot for shot, although they were almost surrounded by Joseph on one side and White Bird on the other.

NEZ PERCÉ RESERVATION, IDAHO, WHERE THE NEZ PERCÉ WAR BEGAN

SKETCH BY CAPT. R.H.FLETCHER, U.S.A.

Looking Glass, 1871. *Photo by W. H. Jackson.*

The cavalrymen managed to retreat in good order though they had to abandon a small force which was wiped out to the man. A rear guard was slaughtered by the Nez Percés, and Teller and his whole command of 36 men were killed. It was only Captain Perry's cool leadership that saved the entire force from being destroyed. Joseph had demonstrated that he was a brilliant strategist.

General Howard quickly organized the largest force he could manage—300 soldiers—and marched to the Salmon River. When Joseph's lookouts caught the advancing troops in their glasses they galloped into camp and gave him the news. By late afternoon, Joseph had established his lines across the river in the mountains. If the soldiers wanted to fight, it was going to be on the battlefield of his choice.

Howard sent a troop under Major Whipple to Cottonwood Creek, where White Bird's camp was located, then moved in on Joseph. The Nez Percés' chief vanished, leaving the general entangled in the mountain vastness while the Indians struck Whipple's force and then almost destroyed a large civilian force coming to Whipple's defense.

When Howard finally made his way out of the mountains and hurried to help the besieged Major Whipple, Joseph, who had excellent scouts, retreated, to be joined by Looking Glass. His force now numbered about 250 warriors and 400 women and children.

Chief Joseph's movements were superb. Accompanied by the tribe's women, children, ponies, and livestock, he had swung his army in and out of the mountains cutting down Howard's force while he led the general on a chase like a bouncing jackrabbit luring on a tenderfoot.

Chief Joseph next moved to the Clearwater, a rushing mountain stream, with steep banks rising to level plateaus cut by ravines. When Howard appeared, Joseph attacked, and the fighting continued with charges and counterattacks for several days.

When Joseph saw Howard trying to turn his right flank he sent word he wanted to parley. Howard halted his advance while he listened to the ramblings of the sub-chief Joseph had sent in order to gain time while he prepared to flee away; he had finally decided to leave his beloved Idaho, cross the mountains to Montana and then join Sitting Bull in British Columbia.

With his women, children, stock and pony herds he struck north, then eastward along the famous Lo-lo Trail, which wound through ragged ravines and deep forests. It began raining and the muddy, slippery trail became almost impassable.

Howard, aware of Joseph's objective, was in pursuit. Some distance behind came the weary infantrymen and the cavalry troops. The singing wire, however, was Howard's ally and Joseph's enemy. Orders were flashing over the wire to commands in Montana. The Seventh Infantry under Gibbon made a forced march from Helena to Fort Missoula. In the meantime a detachment had left the fort to try to stop Joseph at Lo-lo Pass in the Coeur d'Alenes. But Joseph and the warriors fought so fiercely that the civilian volunteers vanished, leaving the troops no alternative but to move back to Missoula.

After a 75-day journey in which he kept two and three days ahead of Howard, Joseph made camp in a meadow on the south side of Big Hole River, without knowing that Gibbon was moving in on him from Fort Missoula.

On August 8, Gibbon attacked. For once Joseph's scouts had failed him. The attack was a complete surprise. However, Joseph, White Bird and Looking Glass rallied their men who put up such a fierce counter-attack that Gibbon soon realized he was fighting for his own life.

The fighting went on all day. The Indians drove Gibbon's force back across the river and even attacked his strongly fortified position. When they couldn't dislodge him Joseph set fire to the tall dried grass; only a freakish wind saved the soldiers from cremation. That night Joseph and his people vanished behind the screen of smoke.

Gibbon had sent messages to Howard, urging him to put on a forced march to save his command and so on the day after the battle Howard led an advance party of 50 weary men into Gibbon's camp. After one look at the number of wounded, Howard ordered Gibbon to return to Missoula while he continued with a number of volunteers from Gibbon's force.

On August 7, 1879, Howard led "150 rifles," as he called them, on Joseph's trail. This tenacity was rewarded when he found Joseph's camp in Big Hole. He attacked at dawn and another fierce fight took place. The Indians captured Howard's howitzer but were forced to leave 85

General David Perry.

dead on the field, many small children and women, and Joseph's best field commander, Looking Glass.

Once again Joseph led his people on a long, weary pilgrimage, a tortuous journey of many hundreds of miles, back and forth over much of the West—Idaho, across the Yellowstone, Wyoming, Montana. And Howard was always behind him, relentless in pursuit.

The famous Seventh was detailed to assist Howard, but Joseph outwitted them and escaped. Finally General Miles joined Howard. At Cow Island on the Missouri, Joseph attacked a large freight depot, then repulsed another force of the Seventh which had come down the river by steamboat from Fort Benton. Joseph finally halted on Snake Creek on the north slope of the Bear Paw Mountains. He could have easily escaped into Canada, but he would not desert his wounded and his women and children.

On October 3, Miles, armed with howitzers and Gatling guns, attacked the camp. After a bloody fight in which the soldiers suffered heavy losses, Miles decided to starve out the Indians. Only White Bird and a small force of warriors escaped to join Sitting Bull.

The artillery began a methodical shelling of the camp with devastating results. Meanwhile, Howard came up to join Miles and his troopers. The thermometer dropped and troopers and Indians alike suffered from the numbing cold. But although the shells were bursting among his people and the Gatling guns cutting them down, Joseph's marks-

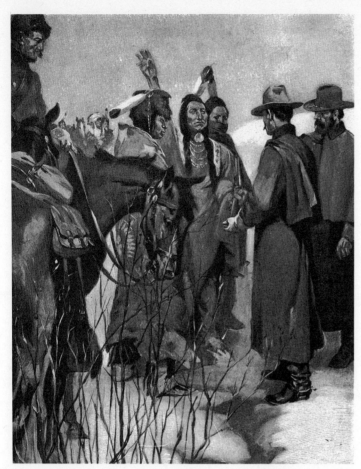

Chief Joseph's surrender to General Miles. *Painted by J. N. Marchand.*

Chief Joseph's Message

When he surrendered to General Miles, Chief Joseph asked that this message be delivered:

Tell General Howard that I knew his heart. What he told me before I have in my heart. I am tired of fighting. Our chiefs are killed. Looking Glass is dead. Too-hul-sul-suit is dead. The old men are all dead. It is now the young men who say "yes" or "no" (vote in council). He who led the young men (Ollicut, Joseph's brother) is dead. It is cold and we have no blankets. The little children are freezing to death. My people—some of them have run away to the hills, and have no blankets, no food. I want to have time to look for my children and see how many of them I can find; maybe I shall find them among the dead. Hear me, my chiefs, my heart is sick and sad. From where the sun now stands I will fight no more forever.

men made the troopers pay; one company lost 35 per cent of its numbers.

But the Nez Percés could not keep up the uneven fight; it was now rifles against howitzers and Gatling guns. On October 3 Joseph sent word he was surrendering. When the dead were counted, Miles had lost 20 per cent of his entire command; Joseph only 17 killed. With him were 87 warriors, 40 of whom were wounded, 184 squaws and 147 children.

The great Nez Percé rode into camp escorted by a delegation of five warriors. His scalp lock was tied with otter fur. The rest of his hair hung in thick plaits on each side of his head. He wore buckskin leggings and a gray woolen shawl through which could be seen the marks of four or five bullet-holes received in the last fight. His head and wrist were also scratched by bullets. He gave his rifle to Miles, then smiled as he shook hands with Howard.

All in all, Joseph's journey was remarkable. With a force never numbering more than 300, at different times he had engaged more than 2,000 soldiers. Of these his warriors had killed 176 and had wounded 140. He himself had lost 151 killed and 89 wounded. He had fought 11 engagements, five of which were forced, bloody pitched battles. He won three, drew one and lost one. He had marched more than 2,000 miles across the roughest terrain in the West.

Howard rightly called him one of the great chiefs of Indian history.

Nez Percé warriors.

The Surrender of Sitting Bull and the Sioux

On the morning of July 10, 1881, leading 187 men, women and children, Sitting Bull left Grandmother Land, as the Sioux called Canada, to return to the United States. Their journey to Fort Buford, North Dakota, was a sad one as the creaking carts rolled across the plains and past the skull and bones of the buffalo herds that littered the grass. Ten days later they entered Buford and the settlers along the borders of Montana and the Dakotas breathed more freely.

On July 29, Sitting Bull and his people were placed aboard the steamer *General* and the boat headed into the muddy Missouri for the three-day trip to Fort Yates and Standing Rock Agency. After a short stay at the agency, the Sioux were again moved, this time to Fort Randall as "prisoners of war."

There, Sitting Bull held court for visiting Sioux from all over the West who came to seek his advice; he told each one to lay down his rifle and move behind the plow. The white man was just too strong and now, with the buffalo gone, it was suicide to continue the wars. According to his biographer, Stanley Vestal, the old Sioux chief also received "fan mail" from all points of the globe.

On May 10, 1883, Sitting Bull was returned to Standing Rock Agency, where he lived out the rest of his years.

A view of the Sioux camp at Fort Randall. This and the other pictures of the Sioux camp shown on this and the following page and a half are from a series a number of which are believed to have been taken by Bailey, Dix and Meade.

Sitting Bull and his favorite wife, his eighth. At this time she was thirty years old and had borne six children.

One Bull, nephew of Sitting Bull.

Steps, a Nez Percé Indian, who joined the Sioux. His right hand and his feet had been frozen in a blizzard.

[250]

Winter quarters.

Eat Dog and family.

Battalion drill of the 25th Infantry, garrisoning Fort Randall and guarding the Sioux.

One Bull and Black Prairie Chicken examining a hide, while an officer's wife and child observe.

Standing Rock and the other Indian agencies, forts and military posts in the North—from Wisconsin and Minnesota to Oregon and Washington—played an important part in Indian affairs for many years.

Fort Snelling was the most notable of these, a bulwark throughout all the Indian wars, the base from which early Dragoons and later cavalrymen and infantrymen went out to engage the Sioux, the Mandans, Pawnees, Flatheads and numerous others. The early fur-trappers also knew its stout stone walls, which never failed to impress the nomadic Plains tribes.

Snelling was built on a triangle between the Minnesota and Missouri Rivers. Across the Minnesota, at what is now Mendota, was the headquarters of the famous American Fur Company. The site was established in 1820 on the orders of President Monroe. First named Fort Saint Anthony, it was later changed to Snelling.

Like most western forts and military installations, Snelling was located on a bluff, the site of an ancient Indian village. A magnificent panoramic view of the surrounding area could be seen from the palisades, while the steep bank of the bluff made attack almost impossible. The fort's famous long wooden stairway, which led from the Snelling Ferry to the post, was noted by many early Indian agents, missionaries and scouts in their letters and memoirs.

Another important fort built on the site of an old Indian village was Fort Abraham Lincoln, one of the most colorful and important posts on the western frontier.

Engineers originally sent out from Fort Rice, Dakota Territory, in 1872 to establish a military fortification which would protect the surveyors, engineers, and workmen building the Northern Pacific, wisely selected the site of an old Mandan village on the bank of the Missouri and near the mouth of the Heart River.

Like Snelling, the Mandan site on the bluff commanded

Sitting Bull with two wives, his twins and youngest child.

the ancient barren plain below it, while a steep bank protected one side. Stout cottonwood trees were dragged up from the river's bank for the palisade, and blockhouses and lumber was hauled in wagons from nearby Bismarck for construction of the officers' quarters and other structures.

The fort was first named McKeen after Colonel Henry Boyd McKeen of the First Pennsylvania Volunteers, but on November 19, 1872, the installation was renamed Fort Abraham Lincoln in honor of the martyred president.

The finished fort was one of the most impressive on the frontier. It was situated in a triangle area with blockhouses at each corner, palisade walls connecting them on two sides, and the steep bank protecting the third side. There were officers' quarters, barracks, a hospital, laundry and stables.

Through the gates of Fort Lincoln rode some of the most colorful figures in western History. Heading the list is General Custer and his Seventh Cavalry. When they rode into Lincoln in 1873, the installation became a nine-company cavalry and infantry post.

For the troopers of the famed Seventh, life at the fort, between expeditions and skirmishes with the Plains tribes, was dull and monotonous. In the summer they were plagued by hordes of mosquitoes that descended on men and horses like great buzzing blankets. In the winter, bone-numbing cold seeped through their thick buffalo robes.

Their only relief was an occasional visit to the "Point," a small settlement of saloons and gambling halls on the bank across the Heart. There was no bridge, and only a small ferry connected the point and the fort. In the winter the troopers walked across the ice. In the spring the thaw made it impossible to cross the torrent.

The fort's most momentous night was the stifling one in July, 1876, when the steamer *Far West*, loaded with wounded from Reno's command at the Little Big Horn, brought the news of the annihilation of Custer's command. The captain had made the 700-mile run in 54 epic hours, to inform 26 wives at the fort that they had become widows.

Inseparable with Fort Abraham Lincoln in the shaping of the Western frontier is the Standing Rock Agency, South Dakota. The great war captains of the Sioux, the

Seated, left to right: Sitting Bull, Swift Bear, Spotted Tail. *Standing,* Julius Meyer, an Indian interpreter, and Red Cloud. *Photo by Frank Currier.*

medicine men, warriors and the families moved in and out of this famed agency during the Indian Wars from 1866 to Wounded Knee in 1890.

Here, Sitting Bull was buried under the slender granite shaft in the corner of the Roman Catholic Cemetery. Most men have forgotten how soldiers kept walking, one at a time, into the carpenter's shop where the Old Bull's coffin was kept, and then seized the opportunity to "drive a nail in the chief's coffin." His big body was finally crammed into the crude box, and a husky soldier "sat on the lid to close it." The hole was dug and the chief's last remains were interred in quicklime, like those of a common felon.

Standing Rock, so closely related to the history of the Sioux, was named after the stone (Inyan Woslata) sacred to the Arikaras. The stone first placed on Proposal Hill was supposed to be the figure of a small shawled woman holding a child. Dakota legend tells how a young woman became jealous of her husband's second wife and refused to leave when the camp moved on. She was left standing before the fire with her child on her back. Later, when she

The Standing Rock that gave the Agency its name. *All the photos on this page and the next four pages are by General John T. Pitman, except as otherwise stated.*

A blockhouse at a corner of Fort McKeen, later Fort Abraham Lincoln. *Photo by General Pitman.*

Sioux chiefs and braves with soldiers at the Standing Rock Agency.

[253]

Sioux warriors, 1880's.

Sioux squaws, Standing Rock Agency, 1880's.

did not appear at the new camp, her husband sent his relatives to find out what happened. His in-laws returned to the old camp to find the woman and the child transformed into stone.

From that time on, the rock was carried with the tribe and occupied a position of honor in the center of each camp. The rock is one of two revered by the Sioux. The second (Inyan Bosdata-Erect Rock) is on the Cheyenne River.

Closely connected with Fort Lincoln and Standing Rock Agency was Bismarck, the small bustling town whose rooftops could be seen from the blockhouses of Fort Lincoln by the troopers of the Seventh, counting the days until their next pass.

Fort Abraham Lincoln.

A group in front of "Custer's house" at Fort Abraham Lincoln, 1889. *Left to right, seated:* Mrs. L. Powell, General Crook, Major Powell's wife; *Standing:* Governor Fasler, Major Powell, Major Warner, Major Randall. *Photo by D. F. Barry.*

Parade grounds at Fort Abraham Lincoln.

A group at Fort Abraham Lincoln, 1889.

The famous Rosebud Indian Agency of the Dakota Territory as it appeared in
1889. *Photo by J. A. Anderson.*

Fort Snelling, 1862. *Photo by J. E. Whitney.*

A view of Fort Snelling, 1880's. *Photo by General Pitman.*

A view of the long stairway up to Fort Snelling, 1880's. *Photo by General Pitman.*

Crow prisoners at the Crow Agency, Montana, 1887.

The Crow Reservation, Montana, 1890.

Geronimo

By 1882 the strength of the Plains tribes had been broken. There would be only a few last flare-ups before the fire died out. But in Arizona Territory the sullen, embittered Apaches were restless and ready to take to the warpath.

In the spring of 1882 the situation had so deteriorated that General Crook ("Three Stars" to the Plains tribes, "Gray Fox" to the Apaches) was reassigned to the Territory. Crook returned at once to Prescott and set out to get a first-hand account of what had happened. He learned that there had been some skirmishes with the Apaches, that the Apaches had heard talk that they were to be driven out of their reservation, that the Indian agent at San Carlos was crooked and involved in a swindle with Army contractors.

Crook arranged a meeting with the Apache leaders. Alchise, the leader of the 26 warriors, told Crook in detail of the grievances against the Indian agent at San Carlos, who had refused them food and had in fact ordered them to give up their farms and move to the malaria-breeding San Carlos Agency. Alchise plaintively asked the same question that had echoed across the plains for years: why does the white man break his promises?

The Indians had been making progress, were nearly self-supporting. But there was a close ring of crooked contractors in Tucson, determined that the Apaches would not be self-supporting, for if they did what would become of their lucrative business? To disturb the Indians' progress all they had to do was telegraph Washington that

Geronimo, 1884. *Photo by A. F. Randall.*

The San Carlos Agency, 1880.

[259]

the Indians were "restless" and jittery. The Indian Bureau would demand that the War Department send troops at once. Then, the contractors knew, there were always the rebels on the reservations who would incite the bucks and create the trouble that had been reported.

Also, coal had been discovered on the reservation and crooked Indian agents were trying to acquire that part of the land for speculation. They hoped to interest the Southern Pacific Railroad Company. There were rumors—unconfirmed—that silver also had been discovered, and every possible means was used to trick the Apache.

Crook investigated Alchise's charges and found that the rations issued by a man named Tiffany had shrunk to a shocking degree. A shoulder of beef was supposed to feed 20 persons; a cup of flour was issued every seventh day. The Indians told Crook they were forced to eat every part of the animal, from intestines to hoofs.

Before the arrival of Crook, Alchise, determined to get proof, had sent scouts to trail the wagons from the agency. The redskins found the wagons loaded with rations intended for tribesmen going to Globe or other towns where the supplies were sold.

One of the Apaches who spoke Spanish and English was delegated by the tribe to protest to the Indian agent. The warrior-spokesman found himself sentenced to six months' imprisonment without a trial and his cattle were confiscated. After his release he tried in vain to find out what his crime had been.

Captain Emmet Crawford, although firm with the warriors when he caught them drinking tizwin, was the one Army officer treated with respect by the Apaches at the post, but they regarded the agents with contempt. At San Carlos Crook talked to some of the chiefs who had returned and found that a number had been forced to leave their cool lands near the Cibicu for the searing flats of San Carlos. Before they left they had seen their fields of corn deliberately trampled. Crook reorganized the military affairs at San Carlos and put Captain Crawford, one of the finest officers in the Territory, in charge. Crawford ordered a spring planting and the Agency was prepared for the arrival of the Chiricahua Apaches.

The Chiricahuas had been on the warpath for years after they had fled into the Sierra Madre Mountains. Crook was now prepared to force them to come in and hold a council.

In March 1883 the Chiricahuas under Chief Cato broke out of their mountain strongholds and left a trail of fire and blood along the frontier. One of the band, Panayotishn, better known to frontier history as "Peaches," deserted Cato and came to San Carlos, offering to betray the Chiricahuas' hiding place. Crook organized a force of 193 Indian scouts and a company of the Sixth Cavalry and personally led it into the mountains. Among the scouts under the frontiersman Al Seiber was ugly Mickey Free, who had been captured as a boy and raised by the Apaches and Alchise.

Geronimo and his staff meet with General Crook and his staff, 1886. Geronimo is seen left center; General Crook is second from the right. *Photo by Camillus Fly.*

The attack was successful. Peaches led them to the stronghold camp and it was captured after a brief battle. Most of the warriors were absent raiding the Mexicans, and when they returned with their squaws they were put under arrest and sent back to San Carlos.

In July 1883, by the terms of a conference entered into between the Secretary of War, the Secretary of the Interior and Crook, it was agreed that the entire policing of the Apaches should be turned over to the War Department. Five hundred and twelve Chiricahuas were then sent to a spot on the White River, where they started to farm. In one year after Crook's reassignment Captain Crawford reported that the Indians were producing large barley crops and had cut with knives 400 tons of hay and 300 cords of wood, "for which they have been paid a liberal price."

However, Crook was infuriated about one matter—the selling of whiskey to the Indians. "It is a dead matter," he wrote bitterly to the Secretary of the Indian Rights Association in Philadelphia. "Indians who so desire can obtain from unprincipled whites and others all the vile whiskey for which they can pay cash. . . ."

On January 20, 1885, Crook requested to be relieved of the responsibility of policing the Indians and asked that such duties revert to the Department of the Interior. Major General John Pope, commenting that "General Crook's management of these Indians had been marked by unusual and surprising successes," told the Army's adjutant general that instead of relieving Crook he would recommend that "the entire control of the Indians be turned over to him."

Two months later, Secretary of War William C. Endicott, following Pope's recommendation, suggested to the Department of the Interior that the "entire control of the Indians in the Territory be placed under the charge of General Crook."

But before the Washington brass could make up its mind the Chiricahuas broke out after a dispute over the blasting of an irrigation ditch. The Army under Captain Crawford had told them to go ahead; the Indian agent had refused to give them permission.

If there was such discord between the white men, the Apaches said in council, why stay? Under Geronimo and

Captain Emmet Crawford.

Nachez and Geronimo, 1885.

Apaches on guard. *Photo by Camillus Fly.*

Nachez 124 took to their mountain strongholds. However, Cato and the others stayed behind.

In the months which followed, Geronimo, a wily old scoundrel who loved to get drunk on tizwin, led his bucks on many raids. Thirty-nine white men in New Mexico and 34 in Arizona were burned or tortured to death, together with a number of friendly White Mountain Apaches.

It was the battle of the lava beds all over again, and it was almost impossible to run down the Apaches.

In January, 1886, Crook's most valuable officer, Captain Crawford, was killed near Sonora, Mexico, in a skirmish with Mexican troops. It was after his death that Geronimo sent in word he wanted to talk in the Cañon de los Embudos, in the northeast corner of Sonora on the Arizona line. Crook, Alchise, the mayor of Tucson and Camillus Fly, the Arizona photographer, attended the meeting.

Geronimo's talk was long and rambling. Crook took him to task for lying and told him, "Think it over tonight and let me know in the morning."

The next day, March 27, Geronimo came down with word that he was "thinking better" and would surrender his people. After a speech about how the sun was at last looking down at him and the earth was listening, he shook hands and gave in. The other war chief, Mangus, was still at large with 13 Chiricahuas.

The Apaches were due to move out the next morning,

"Peaches," General Crook's guide.

Noncommissioned officers of the First U. S. Infantry, Turkey Springs, New Mexico, in the 1885-86 Apache campaign.

Geronimo's wife and child.
Photo by A. F. Randall.

[262]

Geronimo and his warriors after their surrender in the Sierra Madre Mountains,
New Mexico. Geronimo is at the right of the horse. Chief Nana is mounted.

the 28th. But at dawn Crook was awakened with the news that a Mexican trader had sold the Indians a load of mescal and the Indians were drunk.

Geronimo and Nachez escaped with a number of their braves and the fight had to be fought all over again. But before the search for the Apache remnants could be renewed friction with Washington caused Crook to resign and General Nelson Miles took charge.

With the aid of cavalry Miles pursued the Apaches relentlessly and finally Geronimo and Nachez agreed to a peace. The war with the Apaches was over. Eventually, the Apaches were settled and found a permanent home in the Indian Territory, Oklahoma.

Chief Nana. *Photo by A. F. Randall.*

Geronimo just before leaving Arizona for Fort Sill, Oklahoma.

The Ghost Dancers and the Massacre
at Wounded Knee

As the last decade of the nineteenth century approached there was little doubt that the Wild West was now tamed. The buffalo were gone, the great war chiefs dead, the old ways were ended. The Plains tribes confined on the reservations were beaten, spiritless, sick at heart. But there was one final eruption before the Indian Wars could be considered at an end.

About 1888 a Paiute Indian named Wovoka claimed he had a vision in which he was named the Messiah, and the defeated red men believed that he was the Christ of the Second Coming.

This time, because the Messiah had been crucified by the white men, He was returning to earth as an Indian. With him would be legions of dead Indians and vast herds of buffalo that would once again darken the great western plains. A new earth would appear in which there would be no white men. To the starving, beaten Sioux this tale of a new religion promised the restoration of all they had lost.

Wovoka promised that those who danced his sacred dance would be spared. It was a simple dance of holding hands and moving toward the left. The dancers had a special shirt which the Messiah claimed could stop the bullets of the white men.

The new movement was peaceful. "Do not harm anyone. Do right always. Do not tell lies. Do not fight. When your friends die you must not cry."

In all the agencies there was a tremendous religious revival. Dances were held daily. The more experienced Indian agents just shrugged and said that the cold weather would stop the dancing and it would be best to let them blow off their head of steam.

But in 1889 the Democrats swept the Republicans out of office. Indian agents were dismissed and green hands took their place. At Pine Ridge Dr. T. V. Gillicuddy had kept Red Cloud and his savage Ogalalas in hand for years without calling on the troops. But now the new agent, Royer, got panicky and called for troops.

General John R. Brooke, who wasn't familiar with Indians, arrived at Pine Ridge November 19, 1890, and the Ghost Dancers fled to the Badlands. The only damage the Indians did was to burn their own houses and haystacks, but the reporters who accompanied the so-called "Ghost Dance Expedition" sent back hair-raising stories of a new Indian outbreak.

At Standing Rock Agency the Army saw an opportunity to step into Indian affairs. An order was sent for the arrest of the Sioux. Early on the morning of December 15, 1890, Lieutenant Bullhead led his members of Indian police force into Sitting Bull's log cabin and dragged him from his bed.

Before they could start the policemen were surrounded

Wovoka.

Red Tomahawk, who killed Sitting Bull.

by a crowd of angry Sioux. Catch-the-Bear, leader of Sitting Bull's bodyguard, who hated Bullhead, shot his old enemy. As Bullhead fell he fired into Sitting Bull's body. At the same moment Red Tomahawk shot the chief in the head, killing him instantly.

Then a fierce battle of Sioux against Sioux broke out. Within minutes 12 were dead and three others gravely wounded. Only the arrival of troops saved the policemen.

The killing of Sitting Bull swept across the plains like an evil wind. Sioux families left their homes, seeking shelter in the camps of their relatives along the Cheyenne River Reservation. One small band reached the camp of Big Foot.

On Christmas Day the Cheyennes' government scouts clashed with Kicking Bear's Sioux on Battle Creek north of the Badlands. When an order came for Big Foot's arrest he started toward the bleak badlands with 356 men, women and small children. Three days later they surrendered to troops and were taken to Wounded Knee Creek, 20 miles northeast of the Pine Ridge Agency. Altogether there were eight troops of Seventh Cavalry armed with four Hotchkiss guns in addition to a company of scouts, the entire command totaling 470 fighting men.

The soldiers surrounded the camp, and the next morning the Indians were ordered to come out. The four Hotchkiss guns mounted on a small rise had the camp in their sights. The Indians were plainly frightened; it was only a few weeks after the killing of Sitting Bull at Fort Yates. There had been rumors that they were going to be sent down to the swamps of Florida in chains and their horses butchered.

In searching the Indians for weapons—the most foolhardy thing for a white man to do was to lay his hands on a half-savage Plains Indian—"a scuffle occurred between one warrior who had a rifle in his hand and two soldiers. The rifle was discharged."

What took place was one of the most dreadful massacres in our plains history. Within minutes, more than 200 Indian warriors, their wives and children were dead along with 60 troopers. The remnants of the band ran frantically down a dry ravine pursued by soldiers with their blood lust up; it was now "Remember the Little Big Horn. . . ."

The few straggling survivors staggered into Pine Ridge

Mass burial of Indians who died at Wounded Knee.

Agency and lit the fuse. Two Strike and his Brulé warriors swarmed in to attack the agency while a handful of outraged Sioux drove off the soldiers at the Wounded Knee camp. On the 30th a Sioux band attacked the Ninth "Buffalo Soldiers" and later forced Forsyth's Seventh to call for reinforcements. Now it was the Sioux remembering Wounded Knee, and so savagely did they bring the fight to Forsyth that it was only the arrival of the Ninth which saved the whole command.

For 32 days the pitched battles lasted; then suddenly they broke off and the Ghost Dance War was finished.

In Mason Valley, Nevada, in a small wickiup, Wovoka, the false prophet, covered his head with a blanket after he had told a visitor that the Sioux had "twisted things" so

badly that everybody had better "drop the whole business."

Now it seemed that all hope was gone for the red man. Even the Messiah, with all his great dreams, had failed; there was only one thing to do. . . .

The wrinkled old warrior, his blanket wrapped toga-fashion about his shoulders, walked about the Cheyenne camp and harangued his people: "Hoo-oo! My children, my children. In days behind many times I called you to travel the hunting trail or to follow the war trail. Now those trails are choked with sand; they are covered with grass, the young men cannot find them. My children, today I call upon you to travel a new trail, the only trail now open—the White Man's Road. . . ."

Viewing the hostile Indian camp, Pine Ridge, January, 1891. *Left to right:* Buffalo Bill, General Miles, Captain F. Baldwin, Captain M. P. Marco. *Photo by Grabill.*

Lieutenant Pratt's Indian School

THE government's Indian education policy began in 1819, but little progress was made for more than half a century in teaching the Indians the white man's way. The efforts to educate them came from outside; the teachers were white men and therefore the Indians were suspicious of them, resisted and opposed them. But a young Army lieutenant turned the tide. He was Lieutenant Richard H. Pratt of the 10th Cavalry and beyond any doubts, he is one of the true heroes of the West, much more important than the manufactured heroes —the Jameses, Billy the Kid and the assorted gunfighters who have been presented as authentic "greats" of our last frontier.

Pratt, like many great men, was not a legend in his own lifetime. Even today he is known only to the scholars and the specialists. Shy, unassuming, a gentle man, he wanted nothing for himself, only for the children of the red men against whom he had fought for so many years.

He fought in the Civil War with the Ninth Indiana Infantry, then with the Indiana Cavalry in which he achieved the rank of captain, a grade he still held when he left the service after Appomattox. In 1867 when the War Department was reorganizing the Regular Army to fight the Plains tribes, he re-enlisted as a lieutenant and was sent to join the famous 10th, or the "Buffalo Soldiers."

Pratt made his first contact with the red men in the Cheyenne, Kiowa and Comanche war, 1868-69, and again in 1875 when he was a commander of the Indian scouts.

In 1875 Sheridan ordered Pratt to make an investigation of crimes committed by the Kiowa and Comanche prisoners at Fort Sill. The interrogation of the prisoners and their families gave Pratt a deep insight into the savage mind. In 1875 as a result of his findings, 75 of the chiefs and warriors were ordered to Leavenworth, then to St. Augustine. It was a dangerous journey. Pratt was well aware that his wild charges, despite their arm and leg chains, would kill him and his small guard at the first opportunity. At Nashville Lean Bear, a chief, killed himself after stabbing a corporal to death and slashing another. Another time Graybeard, a Cheyenne chief, leaped from the car window and was killed by the guards.

So depressed were the Indians that many had to be removed by litter on arrival at St. Augustine. The young officer, although firm in his dealing with the prisoners, could not help feeling a great compassion for the once-free rovers of the plains who were now chained like animals. It was Pratt who unchained them and let them roam the yard under surveillance.

Gradually the redskins began to ask Pratt to teach them the "way of the white men . . . we first want our wives and our children . . . then we will go anywhere you say and learn to support ourselves as the white men do . . . we want to learn how to make corn and work the ground. . . ."

In 1875 Pratt wrote a letter to Washington outlining his plan to educate the Indians. "The duty of the govern-

 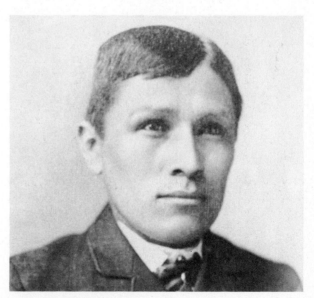

Tom Torlino, a Navajo (*left*) as he arrived at Carlisle and Tom Torlino (*right*) three years later. *This and all other Carlisle photos are studio photos taken by Choate in the 1880's, unless otherwise stated.*

ment to these Indians seems to me to be the teaching of
something that will be of permanent use to them. Teaching them to work is one thing, but St. Augustine offers
practically nothing to them in this line. They have be-
sought me repeatedly to try to get Washington to give
them the opportunity to work. They say they want to
learn to build a house, to make boots and shoes, to do
blacksmith work, to farm, etc. . . ."

Pratt, with his wife, then enlisted the help of Florida
curio dealers, who gave him sea beans for necklaces. Soon
the Indians were making souvenirs, arrows, bows, mocca-
sins. Local ladies' societies, who once were afraid to even
look at the proud, hawk-faced men who stared at them
with such impassiveness, organized classes to teach them
to read and write. When they learned English, Pratt organized religious services. Pratt begged, borrowed and
bought out of his small salary equipment for the crude
classrooms.

A few months after their imprisonment, Pratt gave them
guns and told them to guard themselves. For more than
two years there was not one violation recorded.

By this time the idea of an Indian school was branded
in Pratt's heart. He sent scores of letters, pleading to be
allowed to form such a school. He paid his own way to
Washington to plead his cause. For years he was tolerated
as an Indian-loving pest. By this time the people of St.
Augustine had employed all the red men; they were oper-

Ernest, son of White Thunder, who died at the school, 1880.

American Horse, Jr., on a visit to Carlisle in the early 1880's
to see his son, Robert.

Spotted Tail and Iron Wing.

Yellow Bear and daughter, Minnie.

ating sawmills, blacksmith shops. In fact, they became so skilled that local workers petitioned Washington to get them out of Florida; they were making it hard for white men to get a job!

In 1878 General Hancock was sent to Fort Marion to see what "Pratt's Indian business is all about." Hancock was astounded at what he saw and wrote a glowing report endorsing Pratt's suggestion that 22 of the young men be allowed to remain in the East for further study and development.

Pratt now had his foot in the door. He was not too proud to beg, and beg he did. He soon had a following of wealthy, influential men who were willing to subsidize his experiment. Next Pratt had to find a building. He reluctantly agreed to house his charges at the Hampton Negro Institute. Now the government was weakening and ordered him to corral 50 more wild youngsters from Chief Joseph's recently defeated Nez Percés, imprisoned at Leavenworth.

That same year the Army ordered him, through an amendment to the Army Appropriation Bill in 1878, to a permanent post "with reference to the Indian education."

Pratt was not satisfied with Hampton. He felt the problems of both races were not the same, so he went to Secretary of the Interior Carl Schurz and presented a plan to educate the Indians as Indians at the old Army barracks in Carlisle, Pennsylvania. Schurz was cool to the plan until Pratt—probably with his heart in his mouth—pointed out that it was only the great freedom of democracy that had enabled Schurz himself to gain such an important post in his adopted country.

Schurz saw the light and approved Pratt's plan. But there was a great deal of red tape to overcome. A special bill had to be drawn and passed by Congress; the Military Committees of both houses had to be soothed and pampered to agree to this rather radical experiment. Pratt was tireless. He lobbied strenuously day and night, but the bill was too late to be introduced. Then Pratt went to the Secretary of War, who was impressed by his enthusiasm and more importantly by the results he had achieved. He got Sherman to declare the barracks unfit for the Army. General Hancock, whose department took in Carlisle, went along with Sherman, and the barracks and old buildings were tentatively assigned to the Department of the Interior for the school.

"What do you plan to do?" Schurz asked.

"Feed the Indians to America. America will do the assimilating and annihilate the Indian problem," was the reply.

The Last Indian Raid

While the Battle of Wounded Knee marked the end of Indian tribal resistance to the white man's way, there were occasional minor local outbreaks. The last raid occurred in 1911 in Humboldt County, Nevada. It was led by Shoshone Mike who, with a band of his tribesmen, attacked a group of stockmen near Getchell's mine, killing several people. The outraged citizens of the area, led by the local sheriff, organized a posse to hunt down the Indian raiders. When the posse found Shoshone Mike and his raiders, a bitter gunfight took place. His ammunition exhausted, Shoshone Mike led his people, now armed with bows and arrows, in a suicidal charge. There were only three Shoshone survivors, a young squaw, a boy and a girl. They are shown here with Sheriff Ferell.

The war bonnet shown is the one Shoshone Mike was wearing when he was killed.

Pratt now began roaming the West looking for children to come to Carlisle. He sat in countless councils, argued, pleaded, cajoled and listened with patience to the long-winded oratory of the Indian speakers. In Rose Bud and Pine Ridge he corraled 72 boys and girls, many the sons and daughters of principal chiefs. Spotted Tail sent five of his own clan, which Pratt considered a major victory.

On October 6, 1879, the first contingent of copper-skinned children arrived at Carlisle. Crowds packed the depot and stared in silence as the stern-faced boys in blankets and wearing claw necklaces and feathers marched up the street. On November 1, 1879, the school formally opened with an enrollment of 147 pupils, 27 more than the Army had authorized. Pratt just did not have the heart to say no.

Two months later he happily reported to Congressman Pound in Washington that the children "were responding to discipline" and showed "eagerness to learn." So rapid had been the advancement of the school, he said, that they were including agriculture and mechanics.

That year, when the glowing letters began to arrive at the agencies, the western chiefs began bombarding Pratt with demands that he take more of their children. They also sent delegations to Washington begging that the school be enlarged. So strong was the movement that Congress passed a bill ordering several abandoned posts to be turned into Indian schools patterned after Carlisle. Re-tiring Army officers also volunteered to act as superintendents. However, the course was not followed immediately for budgetary reasons and Carlisle remained the sole Indian school until the Haskell Institute in Lawrence, Kansas, was opened.

Pratt not only wore himself out physically, but by the winter of 1880 was wrecked financially. It took an eight-year uphill fight before Pratt was able to force Congress to foot some of the bills. In the interim it was Pratt's energetic campaign with his wealthy benefactors and the Society of Friends which kept the school going. More than $125,000 was donated in three years.

Using Indian boy labor, Pratt turned the old stables into shops. Soon classes in tinsmithing, cabinet-making, shoe repairing, tailoring and many other crafts were being taught. When the school began to burst at the seams the Indians, under Pratt's supervision, built another building. Here the girls were taught dressmaking, nursing, laundry work and child care. Nothing was overlooked by the zealous officer; the girls even made their own dresses.

By now he had implanted in their minds that "God helps those who help themselves." Within five years the school was one of the most efficient in the country. Hundreds of savage "blanket Indians" were transformed into efficient workmen and their sisters into nurses, dressmakers, and teachers. And now all these could lead their brothers and sisters to the white man's way.

The Carlisle Indian School Track Team, about 1908. No. 1 is Jim Thorpe; No. 2 is Louis Tewanima, Hopi runner from Arizona who scored for the United States in the 1908 and 1912 Olympics; No. 4 is Glenn L. "Pop" Warner; No. 3 is unidentified.

The Last Frontier—The Cherokee Strip

ON the morning of April 19, 1889, a detachment of U. S. Army troops led thousands of settlers across the Cherokee Outlet, commonly called "The Strip," to the edge of the Oklahoma border, 62 miles to the south. There they would wait until high noon, April 22, when at the sound of a signal gun they would ride on horseback, in wagons, buggies—or even run—to plant their stakes and claim 160 acres each of America's last frontier.

There were more than 10,000 men, women and children in that strange column that morning; there were sodbusters who were weary of seeing their corn wither under the blazing Kansas sun; there were settlers from Nebraska with only a few dollars more than the $15 filing fee that was required; there were tinhorn gamblers from Dodge City, Santa Fe and Creede, Colorado, all riding sleek racehorses; there were soft-looking tenderfeet self-consciously wearing side-arms and a brand-new Winchester but who readily confessed they had never fired a shot in anger; there were the "boomers," whose raids into Oklahoma had drawn national attention to the unspoiled lands, creating the boom that gave the raiders their name and the land rush its greatest push.

There were farmers with many children who owned little more than a rickety prairie schooner, with a trail-worn cow bringing up the rear, a few treasured dollars and hearts full of golden dreams.

There were also hard-eyed men "on the dodge," as they called it in those days, wanted in a hundred towns and cities across the West, wondering how soon they could hold up the gambling tent.

Farmer, doctor, adventurer, tenderfoot and gunman—they all had one goal: to make the Run on the 22nd and stake their claim in the land that even the President had called "The Promised Land."

They had moved out that morning from Arkansas City, Kansas, the outlet to the Strip. It lay directly north from the land to be opened. It had the only railroad which went into that otherwise empty land. It had bridges over the Arkansas River which must be crossed by those coming from east and north. It was the last place to buy supplies; it had the last post office.

Almost overnight Arkansas City had been turned into a roaring boom town. The Central Hotel was crowded twice over; men slept three and four in a bed, on the floor, in the corridors, in the lobby chairs, in the cellar, for weeks at a time. In the last three weeks before the

Moving up to the starting line, April 22, 1889.

The long caravan of prairie schooners on the way to Oklahoma, April, 1889. *This and all other Land Rush pictures are by W. S. Prettyman unless otherwise specified.*

High noon, April 22, 1889, as the line of 10,000 men, women and children surged forward.

In Oklahoma City the day of the 1889 run. This settler arrived too late to plant a stake.

Oklahoma City two months after the run, June 18, 1889. *Photo by D. A. Miller.*

Army would guide the settlers across the Strip to the Border of Oklahoma, men wrapped in blankets, their Winchesters within easy reach, slept in the streets.

Stretched along the banks of the river were hundreds of boomers and settlers from all over Kansas and Missouri. Some had been camped on the river banks for more than a year.

The land they all were so eager to occupy had been set aside by the terms of the treaty of 1866 between the United States and the Indians of the Five Civilized Tribes —Cherokee, Choctaw, Chickasaw, Creek and Seminole— that part of the Indian Territory that was not assigned to any tribe. This tract had been called Oklahoma and was officially designated as the "Unassigned Lands."

The rush for the free lands officially began on March 27, 1889, when President Benjamin Harrison issued his proclamation opening Oklahoma for settlement. To give every settler an equal chance, the proclamation provided that "any person who should enter upon and occupy any of such lands before the hour of 12 noon on April 22 shall thereby forfeit his right to claim land," and soldiers from Fort Sill and Fort Reno constantly patrolled the area to keep out lawbreakers.

On the 19th, all settlers were permitted to cross the Kansas border and enter the Cherokee Outlet—popularly known as The Strip—to make the journey to the border of Oklahoma, where the Run was to begin. It was a two- or three-day ride, across a beautiful but empty land.

From the first, there had been that hunger for land in America, that desire to put down roots. The original set-

tlers from Europe had been drawn by the vast continental expanse across the ocean—land enough for anybody, and to spare. Later, as the coastal lands became more and more heavily populated, a man could always find room by moving westward. Plains that for centuries had known only Indians now sprouted farms. Farms that a few years before had marked the outward limits of civilization suddenly found themselves way stations on the road to a still farther West.

The advance picked up great momentum after Appomattox, spurred by the Homestead Act of 1862. More families moved along the rutted trails, more wagons. Log cabins appeared, then villages, then cities. All the land a man could ever want . . . free. . . .

Then, unexpectedly—to some men it seemed to happen overnight—the frontier had vanished.

The great herds of buffalo that once had roamed the prairies were now gone. In their places were cattle and sheep. The Plains tribes had been subdued, and the Indian Wars were virtually a thing of the past. The West of the explorers and the pioneers was already a legend; the men who had helped to tame it had begun their memoirs.

That was when men started to look covetously at the last remaining unsettled farm land: the Unassigned Lands of the Five Civilized Tribes, which had been promised to the Indians for as long as the waters should run . . . in other words, forever.

By sad, bitter experience the people of the Five Civilized Tribes knew perhaps better than any other Indian nation exactly what the white man's promise was worth.

Map of the Land Rush area.

Once these related tribes, so named because they had adopted many of the white man's ways, had hunted and camped across almost the whole of the American South: the Seminole in Florida, the Cherokee in northern Georgia and the western Carolinas, the Creek in Alabama and southwest Georgia, the Choctaw in central and southern Mississippi and Louisiana, the Chickasaw in Arkansas.

Little by little, as the white man pushed out from the seacoast, these Indians had been pushed back—by smooth talk, by force of arms, by gifts of hard drink, by trickery and even, surprisingly, by occasional legal sales of land. Each backward step was usually accompanied by a new treaty; virtually every treaty was ultimately broken.

The white man made his first move to cross the borders

of the Oklahoma Indian Lands in 1879. That year a man named C. C. Carpenter gathered some 20 families along the southern border of Kansas and announced they were going to enter the Unassigned Lands and claim farms. They were quickly discouraged from trying by the presence of federal troops. But an interested observer was Captain David Payne, a Union cavalry veteran, and a member of the Kansas legislature. After Carpenter's failure, Payne took over leadership of the boomers. He made eight unsuccessful attempts to establish Oklahoma settlements.

After Payne died in 1884, William L. Couch took over leadership of the boomers and established a camp near the present city of Stillwater. But troops under Colonel Ed-

In Guthrie, April 27, 1889. *Photographer unknown.*

ward Hatch evicted Couch and his boomer trespassers.

The invasions of Carpenter, Payne and Couch had failed, but they did bring the attention of the public to the Unassigned Lands. Then, while Washington argued the question of opening the lands to settlement, the harassed leaders of the Five Civilized Tribes themselves resolved the issue.

In January, 1889, a delegation of chiefs traveled to Washington with an offer to sell their lands. An agreement was soon reached with the Secretary of the Interior. The Creeks sold 1,392,704 acres of their land for $1.25 an acre, and additional acreage in the Cheyenne and Arapaho Reservations for $1.05 an acre. The United States paid $280,000 in cash, while the sum of $2,000,000 was held in trust with five per cent interest paid to the tribes. The Seminoles got $1,912,942 for 1,669,080 acres in the Cheyenne-Arapaho reservation and 500,000 acres in the Unassigned Lands.

On March 2, 1889, a homestead measure was rushed through Congress. The Unassigned Lands were opened by Presidential proclamation, with 1,887,796 acres ready for settlement. East to West the area extended about 30 miles, north and south about 50 miles.

The white man once again had begun his relentless march. The canvas-topped wagons rolled across the virgin land.

April 19. The dusty streets of Arkansas City were emptied now of the lines of wagons that had toiled through during the past months; now the wagons were deep in the Cherokee Outlet, heading for the Oklahoma border, where the Run would begin in three days. People were still arriving by rail; Arkansas City was the dividing

point; here trains making the Run were to be made up.

In Arkansas City beds and lodging were no longer available. The Gladstone House, as stylish as any Kansas City hotel, was filled to capacity. Settlers slept in back yards, behind sheds, wherever they could find room. Hundreds rolled themselves up in their blankets on the sidewalks in a three-block area about the Santa Fe station— and waited for the train.

During the morning 15 Santa Fe trains of ten cars each left Arkansas City for the Oklahoma border. Six came northward from Purcell. In Arkansas City thousands crowded the area about the station, fighting for seats or

Street scene in Guthrie. *Photographer unknown.*

standing room on the cars. The trains were filled before they could grind to a stop. Men hung from the windows or clung to the raised section of the roofs. When they reached the Oklahoma border the trains stood in one long line, waiting for noon of the 22nd. It was a long wait, but the people in the cars and even those on the roofs refused to give up their places. They munched their sandwiches, smoked their pipes, passed jugs of water and waited.

April 20. Captain Hays of Troop F, Fifth Cavalry, was up long before dawn, readying his patrols and defenses against sooners, those desperate men who hid out in the gullies and brush, hoping to beat the gun, get to the "Promised Land" sooner and file choice tracts of land.

Captain Hays and his troopers fanned out in a straight line to sweep their section of the Unassigned Lands clean of sooners. It was twilight by the time they returned to camp, reasonably sure that no man, no matter how cunningly hidden, could have escaped their sharp eyes.

Yet some men did, such as Frank Hilton Greer, a brilliant young Kansas newspaperman. Just 21, Frank had an idea he wanted to publish the first newspaper in Oklahoma. He named it the *State Capital*, had it printed in Wichita and mailed the issues to Guthrie—a town not yet in existence—addressed to himself. With what remained of his savings he bought a printing press and instructed his friends to take it apart and ship it to him in Guthrie so he could start printing immediately after the Run.

He had $39 left after buying the press. He gave his wife $10 and set out for Arkansas City on the Santa Fe with two friends. Within an hour after their arrival in Arkansas City, Greer knew that their chances of getting a choice town lot were indeed slim. It seemed there were ten men for every acre in Oklahoma. If they wanted land they had to become sooners.

On their way in, Frank had seen piles of telegraph poles on flatcars lined up in the railroad yards of Arkansas City. He recalled that someone had said you had to be a telegraph pole to get past the soldiers. At eleven o'clock that night the three young men crept up to a flatcar loaded that afternoon with poles. Each man slipped through a large crack arranged conveniently by a friendly trainman to whom Frank had slipped a dollar. One of his friends, a

Crossing on a railroad bridge.

Boomers on the Kansas state line ready for the Strip Run of 1893.

huge man, had some difficulty; it took a lot of grunting and shoving to wriggle into their hideout.

They also discovered they weren't alone. When Greer slid down into the space under the piled poles a deep voice floated up from under his feet: "Step on me, sonny —but not on my face." There were at least two others hidden among the poles.

They shivered through the night. Just about dawn the train jerked to a start. As the men held their breath it inched its way along the sidings and onto the main line.

The train sped across the Cherokee Outlet and slowed as it came to the Oklahoma line. They caught glimpses of troopers on both sides of the tracks, but the train did not stop.

At last they were in Oklahoma. The train chugged rapidly across the wilderness. Two miles outside Guthrie a trainman came back to the flatcar and told them to get off. Greer peered at the landscape racing past.

"We'll be killed jumping now!" he said. "Slow her down."

A hand reached in. Greer wearily took another dollar and gave it to the hand. It vanished. Minutes later the train began to slow down. At ten miles an hour they scrambled from under the poles and leaped, one by one. Greer and his two friends ran to the woods and camped in a small, beautiful ravine with a pool of clear water, using their coats for makeshift tents.

April 21. At twilight a strange quiet descended all along the Oklahoma line. Men were breaking up their camps, caring for their stock, greasing their wagon wheels; the women, helped by the children, packed the last of the food, the few clothes and the household goods. Tomorrow at noon the Run would begin. There was no singing, no shouting, no firing of six-shooters. In this wood-scarce prairie there were few camp fires.

In the cavalry's main camp at Taylor's Spring northeast of Guthrie, General McDuff, after reviewing reports from his men in the field, estimated to reporters there were more than 10,000 persons before nightfall, and thousands more were waiting at other jump-off points.

The trains backed up at the line, ready to chug across the Unassigned Lands, were crowded to suffocation. Men hung from every platform and lay like cordwood on the roofs. There was one press car, and the authorities back in Arkansas City had already disclosed that many top-hatted gentlemen had tried to force their way into the car with forged credentials. It took the *Tribune* man all morning to fight his way to his car.

All trains were required to run not more than 15 miles an hour—which was regarded as about equal to the speed of other means of transportation—so all would have a fair chance. Although some passengers would drop off and stake a claim near the railroad, the majority preferred town lots in Guthrie and Oklahoma City.

Tension mounted during the morning. Captain Hays, who had set his watch by railroad time, had his troopers spread out in a thin blue file across the prairie, a few hundred yards inside the line. The agreed signal was to be the bugle call reveille.

Long before dawn, sooners had slipped in from the south and from the Pottawatomie Indian country in the east, and from the wild lands in the west—sections not patrolled by the few troops.

At five minutes of twelve, on the northern line, thousands of eyes were glued on the right hand of Captain Hays as it slowly rose. At Purcell the settlers shaded their eyes from the sunlight dancing on the sandy Canadian to study Lieutenant Fraser on his white horse.

To those watching Captain Hays the signal brought the sound of thunder. The blue-clad arm fell, the high bugle notes had just sounded when the long line of farm wagons, horses, spring wagons and carriages leaped forward. The rumbling of the wheels shook the earth. There were shouts, curses, shrieks and prayers. The sound of guns mingled with the crack of whips.

Within two minutes the line was all strung out, horsemen in the lead, buggies and wagons coming up in the rear. A carriage hit a rock and overturned. Men fell out, cut their horses free and rode off.

Captain Hays, suddenly weary, gathered his men together and rode off to camp. Their big job was done.

Seconds after twelve o'clock, sooners popped out of their hiding places and staked their claims. Back in his ravine by the bubbling waterfall, Frank Greer timed his walk to reach Guthrie and stake a choice lot where he would begin publishing his Oklahoma *State Capital*. Shortly after he arrived baggage and mail were dumped off to one side of the Santa Fe tracks and Greer found his precious bundles. Tents were going up when he sold the first copies of the newspaper he had printed in Kansas.

Back in Arkansas City, train after train pulled out of the Sante Fe station. As the *Tribune* correspondent wrote,

"All along the land after we had passed the Oklahoma line, we could see wagons and riders racing like mad across the prairie. Some wagons were abandoned and more than one horse was riderless."

Not all men who won their land rode to it. Some ran on foot. The *Harper's* correspondent saw one man carrying on his back a tent, blanket, dishes and an axe, with food enough for two days, run down the Santa Fe tracks for six miles. He made it in 60 minutes. Then he staked his claim, crawled under a large tree and lay for some time unable to speak.

That first afternoon thousands of persons milled around in Guthrie. The only water came from the muddy Cottonwood. Enterprising settlers, after registering their lands, peddled water in buckets. Most of it was undrinkable. Red dust was everywhere. The streets were ankledeep. A thick film hung over everything and stuck to the sweaty, bearded faces.

In Guthrie and Oklahoma City trains kept dumping lumber and boxes alongside the Santa Fe tracks. The railroad representative put up a sign, "Pick up your stuff." It is to the settlers' credit that not one theft was reported. Food was scarce. Dusty ham sandwiches sold for a quarter, pork and a teaspoonful of beans for $2. One bitter Missourian estimated that if he wanted to eat normally it would cost him $7.50 a day—exactly what he spent in a week back home. He stayed one day.

Within 24 hours Oklahoma City, Guthrie, Norman and Kingfisher were established—with a singular lack of violence. The thousands of settlers who crowded these newborn cities were unknown to one another and had come from different parts of the country. Yet while the first tents were being raised they gathered together to demonstrate the American capacity for self-government. Barely 24 hours after the first wagons had leaped across the Oklahoma line, calls were issued for mass meetings to

Moving into line for the 1893 run into the Cherokee Strip.

Standing in line to register in El Reno.

Just before the first number was drawn at El Reno. The boxes in the foreground
held all the regulations for the lottery.

organize governments and establish law and order. Temporary regimes were set up which, with few changes, managed local affairs for a year, until legal government was provided by Congress. Ironically, one of the few men killed in Oklahoma City was Couch, the leader of the boomers, who had done so much to draw national attention to the need for settling the Unassigned Lands, and who became the elected mayor. He was shot to death in a dispute over a claim.

It had been a magnificent frontier melodrama. The Run of 1889 was the beginning. There would be several more. In 1893 the Cherokee Outlet itself was opened for settlement and more than 100,000 men, women and children would repeat, on a larger scale, what had taken place on that bright, crisp day of April 22, 1889.

There was a final run in 1911 when the last section of free land was opened for homesteading. But it was really during the 1889-93 land rushes that the last frontier was reached.

The dust had settled not only over Oklahoma, but essentially over all the West.

What had happened in the half-century since the first wagon trains of emigrants moved west over the Oregon Trail was, and is, unparalleled in history. In just about fifty years, a vast wilderness of some 2,000,000 square miles was made into a vast and flourishing empire. A virgin land, populated only by hostile tribes of savages, had been tamed by singularly independent men and women who were never satisfied until they had seen what lay beyond the rim of the next hill.

They had conquered this unknown land and its natural hazards with their hands and their hearts. They had broken trails where there had been seemingly impassable wilderness. They had delivered their mail by horse, pony, and stagecoach, at the cost of many lives. They had crisscrossed this land with railroad tracks and telegraph wires although lesser men said it could not be done. Their vigor and vitality had built towns and cities between dawn and sunset. They had dug fortunes from the earth that were greater than Solomon ever dreamed. Yet all of this had not been accomplished without some injustices, not without wounding the land they loved.

In their ruthless advance they had ended a way of life. They had not only wiped out the red man's culture by violence, broken promises, whiskey and bribery, but they had carelessly exterminated his buffalo. They had destroyed forests without thinking of the future. They had, without protest, allowed cattle barons to usurp enormous privileges and had granted almost tyrannical power and great land-holdings to railroad kings. In their rush to build an empire their indifference often bred corruption and lawlessness.

But they won the land. They had dug their mines, drilled their wells, plowed their fields, sown their seeds, thrust down their roots.

The troubles and tragedies of their early days were really only growing pains. Now the West had come of age; its people were ready to reap a rich harvest from a challenging land that had already demanded a full measure of sacrifice and iron courage.

First train leaving the line north of Orlando, bound for Perry, September 16, 1893.
The trains were ordered to travel at 15 miles per hour, the estimated speed of horses and wagons.

Bibliography

GENERAL REFERENCE WORKS

Aberly, Lloyd, *Pursuit of the Horizon: A Life of George Catlin.*

Baker, Ray Stannard, "The Great Southwest," *Century Magazine*, May–November, 1902.

Beadle, John H., *The Undeveloped West, or Five Years in the Territories*, Philadelphia, 1873.

Botkin, Benjamin Albert, *A Treasury of American Folklore*, Crown, N. Y., N. Y., 1944.

Davis, Clyde Brion, *The Arkansas*, N. Y. and Toronto, Ont., 1940.

Day, P. C., "The Winds of the U. S. and Their Economic Uses," *Yearbook of the U. S. Department of Agriculture*, Government Printing Office, 1911.

Dick, Everett, *The Story of the Frontier*, N. Y., N. Y., 1941.

Galloway, Tod B., "Private Letters of a Government Official in the Southwest," *Journal of American History*, 1909.

Gard, Wayne, *Frontier Justice*, University of Oklahoma Press, Norman, Okla.

Griswold, Don and Jean, *Colorado: A Century of Cities.*

Havighurst, Walter, *Upper Mississippi: A Wilderness Saga*, N. Y., N. Y., 1937.

Jones, Charles J., *Buffalo Jones' Forty Years of Adventure* compiled by Henry Inman, Topeka, Kans., 1899.

Journal of the Expedition under the Command of Col. Henry Dodge to the Rocky Mountains during the Summer of 1835, report of the Secretary of War, February 27, 1836.

King, *Memoirs of Clarence*, N. Y., N. Y., 1914.

McClintock, Walter, *The Old North Trail*, London, 1910.

Otero, Miguel Antonio, *My Life on the Frontier*, N. Y., 1935.

Smith, Henry Nash, *Virgin Land: The American West as Symbol and Myth*, Cambridge, Mass., 1950.

Taft, Mrs. Walter, "Across the Plains in the Early Sixties," *The Trail*, July, 1910.

Thwaites, Reuben Gold, ed., *Edwin James' Account of an Expedition to the Rocky Mountains Performed in the Years 1819–1820 under the Command of Maj. S. H. Long*, Cleveland, Ohio, 1904.

Turner, Frederick J., *The Frontier in American History*, N. Y., N. Y., 1920.

MANUSCRIPTS

The West (two bound books of clippings covering every subject from reports of stagecoach robberies to frontier political feuds), owned by the author.

Collection of personal and business letters (c. 1850–1860) from a frontier lawyer, owned by the author.

NEWSPAPERS

Bad Lands Cowboy, The (Little Missouri, Medora P. O., D. T.), February 7, 1884–April 9, 1885.

Bismarck *Tribune*, The (Bismarck, D. T.), July 11, 1873–December 27, 1876.

Black Hills Pioneer (Deadwood, D. T.), June 8, 1876, January 6, 1877–February 14, 1878.

Cheyenne County Rustler (Wano, Kans.), July 10, 1885–October 30, 1885.

Deadwood *Pioneer-Times* (Deadwood, D. T.), 1876–1877.

Dodge City *Times* (Dodge City, Kans.) October 14, 1876–October 6, 1877.

Hays City *Railway Advance* (Hays City, Kans.), June 23, 1868.

Kansas Cowboy (Dodge City, Kans.), June 28, 1884–December 27, 1884.

Mining Journal, The (Black Hawk, Colo.), November 30, 1863–January 2, 1864.

Missouri Intelligencer (Franklin, Mo.), March 1824–December 1826.

Montana Post (Virginia City, Mont.), August 27, 1864–April 15, 1865; November 3, 1866.

Nebraska News (Nebraska City, Neb.), January 17, 1857–May 8, 1858.

Omaha City *Times* (Omaha, Neb.), June 11, 1857–July, 1858.

Sioux City *Tribune* (Sioux City, Iowa), March 24, 1876–June 15, 1877.

THE SPANISH INFLUENCE

Abbott, John S., *History of Cortès*, N. Y., N. Y.

Acton, Arthur Scott, *Secret Visita against Viceroy Mendoza*, Los Angeles, Calif., 1932.

Bandelier, A. F., *The Gilded Man*, N. Y., N. Y., 1893.

Bandelier, Fanny, *The Journey of Alvar Nunez Cabeza de Vaca*, N. Y., N. Y., 1905.

Bawne, Edward Gaylor, ed., *Narratives of the Career of Hernando de Soto as Told by a Knight of Elvas*, N. Y., 1922.

Blackmar, Frank W., *Spanish Institutions of the Southwest*, Baltimore, Md., 1891.

Bolton, Herbert E., *Spanish Explorations in the Southwest*, N. Y., N. Y., 1916.

Butler, Mrs. C. E., pub. *The Coronado Magazine*, Coronado Quarto Centennial, N. M., 1940.

Catlin, George, *North American Indians*, Philadelphia, Pa., 1891.

Davenport, Herbert, and Wells, Joseph K., "The First European in Texas," *Southwestern Historical Quarterly*, Vol. XXII.

Dellenbaugh, Frederick S., *The True Route of Coronado's March*, American Geographical Society, Washington, D. C., 1897.

Donoghue, D., *Coronado and Quivira*, Chicago, Ill., 1936.

Dunn, William E., "The Apache Mission on the San Saba River," *Southwestern Historical Quarterly*, Texas State Historical Association, Austin, Tex., Vol. XVII, 1914.

Hackett, C. W., *Revolt of the Pueblo Indians*, Albuquerque, N. M., 1940.

Hammond, George, and Rey, ed., *Narratives of Coronado's Expedition 1540–1542*, Albuquerque, N. M., 1940.

Keating, Maurice, transl., Bernard Diaz del Castillo's *True History of the Conquest of New Mexico*, London, 1800.

Morris, J. Bayard, ed., *Hernando Cortès' Letter to Charles V*, N. Y., N. Y., 1929.

Pfefferkorn, Ignaz, *Sonora: A Description of the Province*, 1949.

Ruberica, Juan de Cubas, "Coronado's Muster Roll," *American Historical Review*, Richmond, Va., 1939.

Thomas, A. B., *The Plains Indians and New Mexico, 1751–1758.*

Winship, George Parker, *Coronado's Expedition, 1540–1542*, Washington, D. C., 1892.

Winship, George Parker, transla., Pedro de Casteñada's *Coronado's Journey to New Mexico and the Great Plains*, N. Y., N. Y., 1894.

Wissler, Clark, "The Influence of the Horse in the Development of Plains Culture," *American Anthropologist.*

NATIVE WILD LIFE

Dodge, Richard I., *The Hunting Ground of the Great West*, London, 1877.

Merriman, C. Hart, "The Prairie Dog of the Great Plains," *U. S. Department of Agriculture Yearbook*, Government Printing Office, 1902.

Nelson, E. W., "The Rabbits of the United States," U. S. Department of Agriculture, Bureau of Biological Survey, Government Printing Office, Washington, D. C., 1909.

Palmer, T. S., "The Jackrabbit of the United States, U. S. Department of Agriculture, Bureau of Biological Survey, *Bulletin No. 8*, Government Printing Office, Washington, D. C., 1897.

Santee, Ross, *Men and Horses*, N. Y., N. Y., 1926.

Stone, Witmer, and Cram, William E., *American Animals*, N. Y., N. Y., 1913.

LEWIS AND CLARK

Bakeless, John E., *Partners in Discovery*, N. Y., N. Y., 1947.

Brooks, Noah, *First Across the Continent*, N. Y., N. Y., 1922.

Burroughs, Raymond D., *Explorations Unlimited*, Detroit, Mich., 1953.

De Voto, Bernard, ed., *Journals of Lewis and Clark*, Boston, Mass., 1953.

Flandraus, Grace C., *Lewis and Clark Expedition*, St. Paul, Minn., 1927.

Fletcher, Robert Henry, *American Adventure*, American Pioneer Trails Association, N. Y., N. Y., 1954.

Gass, Patrick, *Journals of Lewis and Clark*, Philadelphia, Pa., 1812.

Guiness, Ralph B., "The Purpose of the Lewis and Clark Expedition," *Mississippi Valley Historical Review*, Cedar Rapids, Iowa, 1933.

Thwaites, Reuben, ed., *Lewis and Clark Journals*, N. Y., N. Y., 1904.

ZEBULON PIKE

Hafen, Leroy R., "Zebulon Pike," *Colorado Magazine*, Denver, Colo., 1931.

King, Nicholas, *An Account of Pike's Journey*, Washington, D. C., 1807.

Pike, Zebulon, *Journals*, Philadelphia, Pa.

Pritchard, Jesse L., "To Pike's Peak in Search of Gold in 1859," *The Trail*, September, October, 1911.

Quaile, Milo, ed., *Southwestern Expedition of Zebulon Pike*, Chicago, Ill., 1925.

THE FUR TRADE

Chittenden, Hiram Martin, *The American Fur Trade of the Far West*, N. Y., N. Y., 1902.

Gregg, Joseph R., *History of Oregon and the Santa Fe Trail*, Portland, Ore., 1935.

Inman, Henry, *The Old Santa Fe Trail*, Topeka, Kans., 1916.

Parsons, Eugene, "The Story of the Trapper," *The Trail*, July, 1911.

Vanderwalker, Victor, "Over the Santa Fe Trail in '64," *The Trail*, June, 1909.

Vandiveer, Clarence A., *The Fur Trade and Early Western Exploration*, Cleveland, Ohio, 1929.

EARLY TEXAS

Barker, Eugene C., *The Life of Stephen F. Austin, Founder of Texas, 1793–1836*, Nashville, Tenn., 1925.

Gillett, James Buchanan, *Six Years with the Texas Rangers, 1875–1881*, Austin, Tex., 1921.

Gray, A. C., ed., *Diary of Col. William F. Gray*, Houston, Tex., 1909.

James, Marquis, *The Raven*, Bobbs Merrill, N. Y., N. Y., 1929.

King, W. H., *The Texas Ranger Service and the History of the Rangers with Observation on Their Value as a Police Protection*, Dallas, Tex., 1898.

Reid, Samuel C., *The Scouting Expedition of McCulloch's Texas Rangers*, Philadelphia, Pa., 1848.

Webb, Walter Prescott, *The Texas Rangers*, Boston, Mass. and N. Y., N. Y., 1935.

THE OREGON TRAIL

Driggs, Howard, and Meeker, Ezra, *The Old Oregon Trail*, N. M., 1922.

Meeker, Ezra, *Old Oregon Trail*, Omaha, Neb., 1906.

Old Oregon Trail, The, compiled by the WPA., N. Y., N. Y., 1939.

Old Oregon Trail, The, hearing before Congress on roads, Washington, D. C., 1925.

Page, Elizabeth, *Wagons West*, N. Y., N. Y., 1930.

Parkman, Francis, Jr., *The Oregon Trail*, N. Y., N. Y., 1847.

Spaulding, Kenneth, ed., *On the Oregon Trail by Robert Stuart*, University of Oklahoma Press, Norman, Okla., 1953.

Wade, Mason, *The Oregon Trail*, from the notes of Francis Parkman, N. Y., N. Y., 1943.

JOHN CHARLES FRÉMONT

Bigelow, John, *Life of Frémont*, Cincinnati, Ohio, 1856.

Derby, G. H., *John Charles Frémont*, Buffalo, N. Y., 1849.

Frémont's Reports on Explorations to the Rocky Mountains, 1842, Washington, D. C., 1845.

Gudde, Erwin G. and Elizabeth K. (ed.), Charles Preuss' *Exploring with Frémont*, University of Oklahoma Press, Norman, Okla., 1958.

Harrington, Fred H., "Frémont and the North Americans," *American Historical Review*, Richmond, Va., 1939.

Nevins, Allan, *Frémont: The West's Greatest Adventurer*, N. Y., N. Y., 1928.

Nevins, Allan, *Frémont: Pathmarker of the West*, Appleton-Century, N. Y., N. Y., 1939.

Nevins, Allan, ed., *John Charles Frémont's Narratives of Exploration and Adventure*, N. Y., N. Y., 1956.

THE MORMONS

Driggs, Howard, *Mormon Trail*, Manchester, N. H., 1947.

"Hand Cart Brigade," *Huntsman's Echo*, Wood River, Neb., July 26, 1860.

THE GOLD RUSH

Allen, W. W., and Avery, R. B., *The California Gold Book*, N. Y., N. Y., 1893.

Delano, Alonzo, *Life on the Plains and Among the Diggings*, N. Y., N. Y., 1857.

Delano, Alonzo, *Pen Knife Sketches*, San Francisco, Calif., 1857.

Delavan, James, *Notes on California and the Placers*, N. Y., N. Y., 1850.

Hambleton, Chalkley J., *A Gold Hunter's Experiences*, Chicago, Ill., 1898.

Jackson, Joseph Henry, *Gold Rush Album*, N. Y., N. Y., 1949.

Johnson, W. C., *Experiences of a Forty-Niner*, N. Y., N. Y., 1892.

McIlvaine, William, Jr., *Sketches and Notes of Personal Adventures in California and Mexico*, N. Y., N. Y., 1850.

Pritchard, Jesse L., "To Pike's Peak in Search of Gold in 1859," *The Trail*, September, October, 1911.

Revere, J. W., *A Tour of Duty in California*, Chicago, Ill., 1849.

Stokes, George W., and Driggs, Howard R., *Deadwood Gold*, N. Y., N. Y., 1926.

Webster, Kimball, *The Gold Seekers of '49*, Manchester, N. H., 1917.

UNCLE SAM'S CAMELS

Bonsal, Stephen, *Edward Fitzgerald Beale*, N. Y., N. Y., 1912.

Hoffman, Velma Rudd, "Lt. Beale and the Camel Corps through Arizona," *Arizona Highways*, October, 1957.

Lesley, Lewis B., *Uncle Sam's Camels: The Journals of May Humphreys Stacey Supplemented by the Report of Edward Fitzgerald Beale (1857–1858)*, Harvard University Press, Cambridge, Mass., 1929.

"Report upon the Purchase, Importation and Use of Camels and Dromedaries to Be Employed for Military Purposes," *Senate Executive Document N 62*, 34th Congress, Government Printing Office, 1857.

THE PONY EXPRESS

Chapman, Arthur, *The Pony Express*, N. Y., N. Y. and London, 1932.

Driggs, Howard R., *The Pony Express Goes Through*, N. Y., N. Y., 1935.

Jones, Lloyd, "Pony Express," *Collier's*, September, 1910.

Pack, Mary, "The Romance of the Pony Express," *Union Pacific Magazine*, August, 1923.

Visscher, William Lightfoot, *A Thrilling and Truthful History of the Pony Express, or Blazing the Westward Way*, Chicago, Ill., 1908.

THE TELEGRAPH

Merriam, Lucius S., "The Telegraphs of the Bond-Aided Pacific Railroads," *Political Science Quarterly*, Vol. IX, No. 2.

Rush, David H., "Singing Wires in the Wilderness," *The Westerners' Brand Book*, Chicago, Ill., May, 1958.

STAGECOACHES

Beitleman, John L., "An Attack on the Stage Stations," *The Trail*, June, 1909.

Collins, William Oliver, drawings of the interiors and exteriors of early stage stations, Library, Colorado State Archives.

Davis, Theodore R., "A Stagecoach Ride to Colorado," *Harper's Monthly*, July, 867.

Greeley, Horace, *An Overland Journey*, N. Y., N. Y., 1860.

STEAMBOATS

Chittenden, Hiram Martin, *History of Early Steamboat Navigation on the Missouri River*, (2 vols.), N. Y., N. Y., 1903.

Hunter, Louis C., *Steamboats on the Western Rivers*, Cambridge, Mass., 1949.

Petersen, William J., *Steamboating on the Upper Mississippi*, Iowa, 1937.

RAILROADS

Buchanan, J. R., "The Great Railroad Migration in Northern Nebraska, *Proceedings of the Nebraska Historical Society*, Lincoln, Neb., Vol. XV, 1907.

Creighton, Edward, Biographical Sketch of," *Nebraska History Magazine*, Vol. XVII.

Cruise, J. D., "Early Days of the Union Pacific," Kansas State Historical Society, Topeka, Kans., Vol., XI, 1910.

Davis, John P., *The Union Pacific*, Chicago, Ill., 1894.

Dodge, Grenville M., "Wonderful Story of the Building of the Pacific Roads," Trans-Continental Railways, Omaha, Neb., 1889.

Eastwood, Colin S., "Construction Work on the Old U. P.," *The Trail*, June, 1910.

Galbraith, R. M., "He Railroaded in Wyoming in Days When Peril and Romance Were Merely a Matter of the Day's Work," *Union Pacific Magazine*, September, 1922.

Harlow, Alvin F., *Old Waybills: The Romance of the Express Companies*, N. Y., N. Y., 1934.

Hibbard, Benjamin H., *A History of the Public Land Policies*, N. Y., N. Y., 1924.

Paxson, Frederic L., "The Pacific Railroads and the Disappearance of the Frontier in America," *Annual Report of the American Historical Association*, Vol. I, 1907.

Settle, Mary Lund, and Raymond W., *Empire on Wheels*, Stanford, Calif., 1949.

Trottman, N., *History of the Union Pacific*, N. Y., N. Y., 1923.

Waters, L. L., *Steel Trails to Santa Fe*, Lawrence, Kans., 1950.

THE INDIAN WARS

Aken, David, *Pioneers of the Black Hills, or Gordon's Stockade Party of 1874*, Milwaukee, Wis., 1920.

Arnold, Lt. Col. Frazier, "Ghost Dance and Wounded Knee," *Cavalry Journal*, Vol. XLIII, May-June, 1934.

Bourke, John G., *An Apache Campaign in the Sierra Madre*, N. Y., N. Y., 1892.

Bourke, John G., *Mackenzie's Last Fight with the Cheyennes*, Governors Island, N. Y., 1890.

Bourke, John G., *On the Border with Crook*, Scribner's, N. Y., N. Y., 1891.

Bourke, John G., "General Crook in the Indian Country," *Century Magazine*, March, 1891.

Brininstool, Earl A., *Fighting Red Cloud's Warriors*, Columbus, Ohio, 1926.

Carrington, Frances C., *My Army Life and the Fort Phil Kearny Massacre*, Philadelphia, Pa., 1910.

Congressional hearing on the Chivington massacre, 1865. Report of the Joint Special Committee, Washington, D. C., March 3, 1867.

Connolly, Alonzo P., *The Sioux War and the Minnesota Massacre*, Chicago, Ill., 1896.

Crook, George, *Resumé of Operations against Apache Indians, 1882–1886*, Omaha, Neb., 1886.

De Land, Charles Edmund, "The Sioux Wars," South Dakota Historical Society, Pierre, S. D., Vol. XV, 1930.

Dixon, Joseph K., *The Vanishing Race*, Garden City, N. Y., 1913.

Donaldson, A. B., "The Black Hills Expedition," South Dakota Historical Society, Vol. VII, 1914.

Dorsey, George A., "The Sun Dance," Field Museum, Chicago, Ill., Anthropological Series, Publication 103, Vol. IX, No. 2, 1905.

Dunn, Jacob P., *Massacres of the Mountains: A History of the Indian Wars of the Far West*, N. Y., N. Y., 1886.

Fee, Chester A., *Chief Joseph: The Biography of a Great Indian*, N. Y., N. Y., 1936.

Finerty, John F., *Warpath and Bivouac, or The Conquest of the Sioux*, Chicago, Ill., 1890.

Gibbon, Col. John, "Hunting Sitting Bull," *American Catholic Quarterly Review*, October, 1877.

Gibbon, Col. John, "Last Summer's Expedition against the Sioux," *American Catholic Quarterly Review*, pp. 271-304, April, 1877.

Hieb, David I., "Fort Laramie," National Park Service, *Handbook No. 20*, 1954.

Hodge, Frederick Webb, ed. *Handbook of American Indians North of Mexico*, Bureau of American Ethnology, Government Printing Office, Washington, D. C., 1912.

Hughes, Col. Robert Patterson, "The Campaign against the Sioux," *Journal of the Military Service Institution of the United States*, January, 1896.

Hyde, George E., *Red Cloud's Folk: A History of the Oglala Sioux Indians*, Norman, Okla., 1937.

Keim, D. Randolph, *Sheridan's Troopers*, Philadelphia, Pa., 1885.

Libby, Orin Grant, ed., *The Arikara Narrative of the Campaign against the Hostile Dakotas, 1876*, North Dakota Historical Society, Bismarck, N. D., Vol. VI, 1920.

Lockwood, Frank C., *The Apache Indians*, N. Y., N. Y., 1938.

Lounsberry, C. A., "Account of Life at Fort Abraham Lincoln," *The Record*, Fargo N. D., June, 1898.

Malin, J. C., "Indian Policy and Westward Expansion," Kansas Humanistic Studies, Lawrence, Kans., Vol. II, No. 3, 1921.

Marcy, Randolph B., *Thirty Years of Army Life on the Border*, N. Y., N. Y., 1866.

Miles, Nelson A., *Personal Recollections and Observations*, Chicago, Ill., 1896.

Mills, Anson, *My Story*, Washington, D. C., 1918.

Mooney, James, "The Ghost Dance Religion and the Sioux Outbreak of 1890," 14th Annual Report, Part II, Bureau of American Ethnology, 1895.

Mumey, Nolie, "John Milton Chivington, The Misunderstood Man," The Denver Westerners' Monthly Roundup, November, 1956.

Myers, Pvt. Frank, *Soldiering in the Dakotas among the Indians*, Huron, Dakota, 1888.

Neill, Edward D., *Fort Snelling, Minnesota*, N. Y., N. Y., 1888.

Payne, Doris Palmer, *Captain Jack, Modoc Renegade*, Portland, Ore., 1938.

Riddle, Jeff C. D., *The Indian History of the Modoc War and the Causes That Led to It*, San Francisco, Calif., 1914.

Smith, Cornelius C., "The Fight at Cibicu," *Arizona Highways*, May, 1956.

Stuart, Granville, *Forty Years on the Frontier* (2 vols.), Paul C. Phillips, ed., Cleveland, Ohio, 1925.

Tallent, Annie D., *The Black Hills, or The Last Hunting Ground of the Dakotahs*, St. Louis, Mo., 1899.

Taylor, Joseph Henry, "Bloody Knife and Gall," *North Dakota Historical Quarterly*, July, 1947.

Tilghman, Zoe A., *Quanah, The Eagle of the Comanches*, Oklahoma City, Okla., 1938.

Vestal, Stanley, *Siting Bull*, Boston, Mass., 1932.

Vestal, Stanley, *Warpath*, Boston, Mass., 1934.

Vestal, Stanley, *Warpath and Council Fire: The Plains Indians' Struggle for Survival in War and in Diplomacy, 1851–1891*, Random House, N. Y., N. Y., 1948.

Vestal, Stanley, compiler, *New Sources of Indian History, 1850–1891, The Ghost Dance, The Prairie Sioux: A Miscellany*, Norman, Okla., 1934.

Wellman, Paul I., *Death on the Prairie*, N. Y., N. Y., 1934.

Wharton, Clarence, *Santana: The Great Chief of the Kiowas and His People*, Dallas, Tex., 1934.

Wissler, Clark, *North American Indians of the Plains*, American Museum of Natural History, N. Y., N. Y., 1927.

Manuscripts in the Manuscript Room, New York Public Library

Brown, Edwin M., trumpeter, B Company, letters.

Cresson, Lt. Charles Clement, 1st Cavalry, description of a punitive expedition, June 4–August 10, 1878.

Forsyth, James B., defense of his actions at the Battle of Wounded Knee.

McClellan, James, diary of the expedition against Dull Knife, 1876–1877.

Miers, Col., letters from Fort Leavenworth, Kans., 1876, 1877.

Struckman, William, bugler, 3rd Regiment, U. S. Cavalry, 1858–1862, letters.

CUSTER AND THE LITTLE BIG HORN MASSACRE

Adams, Jacob, "A Survivor's Story of the Custer Massacre on the American Frontier," *Journal of American History*, Vol. III, pp. 227–32, 1909.

Barry, David F., *Indian Notes on the Custer Battle*, ed. by Usher L. Burdick, Baltimore, Md., 1937.

Brackett, William S., "Custer's Last Battle on the Little Big Horn in Montana, June 25, 1876," contributed to the Historical Society of Montana, Vol. IV, 1903.

Brininstool, E. A., *The Custer Fight: Captain F. W. Benteen's Story of the Battle of the Little Big Horn*, Hollywood, Calif., 1940.

Brininstool, E. A., *Troopers with Custer: Historic Incidents of the Battle of the Little Big Horn*, Harrisburg, Pa., 1952.

Brinkerhoff, Henry, "Account of the Custer Battle," *Custer Scrapbooks*, Billings Public Library, Billings, Mont.

Britt, Albert, "Custer's Last Fight," *Pacific Historical Review*, Vol. XIII, 1944.

Byrne, Patrick E., "The Custer Myth," *North Dakota Historical Quarterly*, Vol. VI, April, 1932.

Coughlan, Col. T. M., "The Battle of the Little Big Horn," *Cavalry Journal*, January–February, 1934.

Custer, Elizabeth B., *Boots and Saddles*, N. Y., N. Y., 1885.

Dustin, Fred, *Echoes from the Little Big Horn Fight*, Saginaw, Mich., 1953.

Dustin, Fred, *The Custer Fight*, Hollywood, Calif., 1936.

Dustin, Fred, *The Custer Tragedy*, Ann Arbor, Mich., 1939.

Flying Hawk, *Flying Hawk's Tale: A True Story of Custer's Last Fight*, N. Y., N. Y., 1936.

Fougera, Katherine Gibson, *With Custer's Cavalry*, Caldwell, Idaho, 1940.

Garland, Hamlin, "General Custer's Last Fight as Seen by Two Moon," *McClure's*, September, 1898.

Ghent, William J., "Windolph, Benteen and Custer," *Cavalry Journal*, November–December, 1934.

Graham, Col. William A., *The Story of the Little Big Horn*, N. Y., N. Y., 1952.

Graham, Col. William A., *The Custer Myth: A Source Book of Custeriana*, Harrisburg, Pa., 1953.

Graham, Col. William A., *The Reno Court of Inquiry*, Harrisburg, Pa., 1954.

Hogner, Francis R., letters and articles relating to Custer and the Little Big Horn, Manuscript Room, New York Public Library.

Hunt, Frazier, *Custer, The Last of the Cavaliers*, N. Y., N. Y., 1928.

Hunt, Frazier and Robert, *I Fought with Custer: The Story of Sergeant Windolph*, N. Y., N. Y., 1947.

Kellogg, Mark, "Notes, May 17 to June 9, 1876, of the Little Big Horn Expedition," contributed to the Historical Society of Montana, Vol. IX, 1923.

King, Capt. Charles, "Custer's Last Battle," *Harper's Magazine*, August, 1890.

Luce, Edward S., *Keogh, Comanche and Custer*, St. Louis, Mo., 1939.

Luce, Edward S. and Evelyn S., "Custer Battlefield," National Park Service *Handbook Series 1*, Washington, D. C., 1955.

Roe, Charles F., *Custer's Last Battle*, N. Y., N. Y., 1927.

Stewart, Dr. Edgar I., "The Literature of the Custer Fight," *The Pacific Northwesterner*, Vol. I., winter, 1956–57.

WESTERN PHOTOGRAPHERS

Brown, Mark, H., and Felton, W. R., *The Frontier Years: L. A. Huffman, Photographer of the Plains*, Henry Holt and Company, N. Y., N. Y., 1955.

Carvalho, S. N., *Incidents of Travel and Adventure*, reissued N. Y., N. Y., 1959.

Cunningham, Robert E., ed., *Indian Territory: A Frontier Photographic Record by W. S. Prettyman*, University of Oklahoma Press, Norman, Okla., 1957.

Dellenbaugh, Frederick, *A Canyon Passage*, New Haven, Conn., 1926.

Dix, Ross John, *Amusing and Thrilling Adventures of a California Artist While Daguerreotyping a Continent*, Boston, 1854.

Farquhar, F. P., *Place Names of the High Sierra*.

Hurt, Wesley R., and Lass, William E., *Frontier Photographer: Stanley J. Morrow's Dakota Years*, University of Nebraska Press and University of South Dakota, 1956.

Jackson, W. H., and Driggs, W. R., *The Pioneer Photographer*, N. Y., N. Y., 1929.

Newhall, Beaumont, *The History of Photography*, N. Y., N. Y., 1949.

Root, Marcus A., *The Camera and the Pencil*, N. Y., N. Y., 1864.

Taft, Robert, *Photography and the American Scene: A Social History, 1839–1889*, The Macmillan Company, N. Y., N. Y., 1938.

Taft, Robert, *Artists and Illustrators of the Old West, 1850–1900*, Charles Scribner's Sons, New York and London, 1953.

Wheeler, George, *Preliminary Report of Explorations and Surveys in Nevada and Oregon in 1871*, Washington, D. C., 1872.

PIONEER PHOTOGRAPHIC TRADE JOURNALS

Anthony's Bulletin
Daguerrean Journal, The
Philadelphia Art Journal, The
Philadelphia Photographer, The
Photographic Art Journal, The

PAMPHLETS AND ARTICLES

Haynes House Bulletin, March, 1922.
Jackson, William H., *Descriptive Catalogue of Photographs of North American Indians*, Miscellaneous Publications, No. 9, U. S. Geological Survey, 1877. (The U. S. Geological Survey, Miscellaneous Publications, No. 5., 1875, also includes a catalogue of Jackson's negatives.)
Jackson, William H., an article on early western photographers in the *Kansas Historical Quarterly*, Vol. III, February, 1926.

Taft, Robert, an article on Alexander Gardner's stereoscopic views of frontier Kansas in the *Kansas Historical Quarterly*, Vol. III, No. 1, and Vol. VI., 1937.

CATTLE AND COWBOYS

Abbott, E. C., and Smith, H., *We Pointed Them North*, N. Y., N. Y., 1939.

Aldridge, Reginald, *Life on a Ranch: Ranch Notes in Kansas, Colorado, the Indian Territory and Northern Texas*, London, 1884.

Ambulo, John, "The Cattle on a Thousand Hills," *Overland Monthly*, March, 1887.

Applegate, Jesse, *A Day with a Cow Column*, Chicago, Ill., 1934.

Armour, Philip D., *The Present Condition of the Live Cattle and Beef Markets in the United States*, Chicago, Ill., 1889.

Ashton, John, "The Texas Cattle Trade in 1870," *Cattleman*, July, 1951.

Barnes, Will C., "The Chisholm Trail—For Whom Was It Named?" *Producer*, January, February, 1929.

Bronson, Edgar Beecher, *Cowboy Life on the Western Plains*, N. Y., N. Y., 1910.

Cook, James H., "The Texas Trail," E. S. Ricker, ed., *Nebraska Historical Magazine*, October, December, 1935.

Cox, James, *Historical and Biographical Record of the Cattle Industry and the Cattlemen of Texas and Adjacent Territory*, St. Louis, Mo., 1895.

Crawford, Samuel J., *Kansas in the Sixties*, Chicago, Ill., 1911.

Cross, Cora Melton, "Up the Trail with Nine Million Longhorns," *Texas Monthly*, February, 1930.

Cross, Fred J., *The Free Lands of Dakota*, Yankton, D. T., 1876.

Cushman, George L., "Abilene, First of the Kansas Cow Towns," *Kansas Historical Quarterly*, August, 1940.

Dick, Everett, "The Long Drive," Kansas State Historical Society, August, 1940.

Dobie, J. Frank, "The Chisholm Trail," *Country Gentleman*, February 28, 1925.

Dobie, J. Frank, *The Longhorns*, N. Y., N. Y., 1941.

Farnham, T. J., "Travels in the Great Western Prairies, 1839," *Early Western Travels*, Vol. XXVIII, R. G. Thwaites, ed., Cleveland, 1906.

Fink, Maurice, *Cow Country Cavalcade*, Denver, Colo., 1954.

Haley, J. Evetts, *Charles Goodnight, Cowman and Plainsman*, Boston, Mass., 1936.

Harger, Charles Moreau, "Cattle Trails of the Prairies," *Scribner's Magazine*, June, 1892.

Hastings, Frank S., "A Ranchman's Recollections," *The Breeders' Gazette*, Chicago, Ill., 1921.

Hebard, Grace Raymond, and Brininstool, E. A., *The Bozeman Trail* (2 vols.), Cleveland, Ohio, 1922.

Herrington, George Squires, "An Early Cattle Drive from Texas to Illinois," *Southwestern Historical Quarterly*, October, 1951.

Hershfield, John, "When War Broke Out on Wyoming Range," Omaha *Daily Journal-Stockman*, Omaha, Neb., June 19, 1928.

Hough, Emerson, *The Story of the Cowboy*, N. Y., N. Y., 1897.

Hunter, J. Marvin, ed., *The Trail Drivers of Texas*, Vol. I, 1920, Vol. II, 1923, Cokesbury Press, Nashville, Tenn.

Kohrs, Conrad, "A Veteran's Experience in the Western Cattle Trade," *Breeders' Gazette*, Chicago, Ill., December 18, 1912.

Love, Clara M., "Cattle Industry of the Southwest," *Southwestern Historical Quarterly*, Austin, Tex., April, 1916.

McCoy, Joseph G., *Historical Sketches of the Cattle Trade of the West and Southwest*, Kansas City, Mo., 1874.

Moody, Dave, "Tales of a Cow Camp," *The Trail*, February, 1910.

Nimmo, Joseph, "The Range and Ranch Cattle Traffic of the United States," *Report on the Internal Commerce of the United States*, Part III, Bureau of Statistics, Washington, D. C., 1886.

Nimmo, Joseph, "The American Cowboy," *Harper's Monthly*, November, 1886.

Osgood, Ernest, *The Day of the Cattleman*, Minnesota, 1929; N. Y., N. Y., 1954.

Paxson, Frederic L., "The Cow Country," *American Historical Review*, October, 1916.

Ponting, Tom Candy, *Life of Tom Candy Ponting*, Decatur, Ill., 1904; Ill., 1952.

Potter, Jack, *Cattle Trails of the Old West*, N. M., 1935.

Prose and Poetry of the Livestock Industry, the U. S. National Livestock Association, Kansas City, Mo., 1904.

Rollins, Philip Ashton, *The Cowboy*, N. Y., N. Y., 1921.

Rossel, John, "The Chisholm Trail," *Kansas Historical Quarterly*, February, 1936.

Siringo, Charles A., *A Lone Star Cowboy*, Santa Fe, N. M., 1919.

Siringo, Charles A., *Riata and Spurs*, Boston, Mass. and N. Y., N. Y., 1927.

Streeter, Floyd Benjamin, *Prairie Trails and Cow Towns*, Boston, Mass., 1936.

Stuart, Granville, *Montana As It is*, N. Y., N. Y., 1865.

Taylor, T. U., *The Chisholm Trail and Other Routes*, San Antonio, Tex., 1936.

Tenth Census of the United States, 1880, Vol. III, Government Printing Office, Washington, D. C., 1883.

Thoburn, Joseph B., "Jesse Chisholm, A Stalwart Figure in History," *Frontier Times*, April, 1936.

Vestal, Stanley, *Queen of the Cowtowns: Dodge City*, N. Y., N. Y., 1952.

"Vivid Story of Trail-Driving Days," Missoula *Missoulan*, August 20, 1922.

Von Richthofen, *Cattle Raising on the Plains of North America*, N. Y., N. Y., 1885.

Webb, W. P., "The American Revolution and the West," *Scribner's Magazine*, February, 1927.

Wellman, Paul I., *The Trampling Herd*, N. Y., N. Y., 1939.

"Wild Cattle-Hunting in Texas," *Leisure Hour* No. 632, February 6, 1864.

Wilkeson, Frank, "Cattle Raising on the Plains," *Harper's Monthly*, April, 1886.

THEODORE ROOSEVELT

Hagedorn, Hermann, *Roosevelt in the Bad Lands*, Boston, Mass., 1921.

Lang, Lincoln, *Ranching with Roosevelt*, Philadelphia, Pa., 1926.

Roosevelt, Theodore, "Sheriff's Work," *Century Magazine*, 1882.

Volweiler, A. T., "Roosevelt's Ranch Life in North Dakota," *Quarterly Journal of the University of North Dakota*, October, 1918.

BET-A-MILLION GATES, BARBED WIRE

Warshow, Robert Irving, *Bet-a-Million Gates*, N. Y., N. Y., 1932.

Wendt, G., and Kogan, Herman, *Bet-a-Million Gates: The Story of John Warne Gates*, N. Y., N. Y., 1948.

Clippings, articles, etc. from the American Iron and Steel Institute Library, N. Y., N. Y., and the United States Steel Corporation, N. Y., N. Y.

WINDMILLS

Barbour, E., "Wells and Windmills in Nebraska," *U. S. Geological Survey No. 29, House Document N 299*, 55th Congress, Government Printing Office, Washington, D. C., 1899.

Bates, Walter G., "Water Storage in the West," *Scribner's Magazine*, January, 1890.

Hayden, F. V., *Preliminary Report of the U. S. Geological Survey of Wyoming and Portions of Contiguous Territory*, Government Printing Office, Washington, D. C., 1872.

Letters of a windmill-maker, Nebraska, 1870, owned by the author.

Morris, R. C., "The Notion of the Great American Desert East of the Rockies," *Mississippi Valley Historical Review*, September, 1926.

Newell, F. H., "Irrigation on the Great Plains," *U. S. Department of Agriculture Yearbook*, Government Printing Office, Washington, D. C., 1896–1897.

Powell, J. W., "Institution for the Arid Lands," *Century*, May, 1890.

Shaw, Lucien, "The Development of the Law of Waters in the West," California Supreme Court *Report No. 189*, San Francisco, Calif., 1922.

Smythe, William E., *The Conquest of Arid America*, N. Y., N. Y., 1911.

Washburn, Charles G., *Industrial Worcester*, Worcester, Mass., 1917.

Wiel, Samuel C., *Water Right in the Western States*, San Francisco, Calif., 1911.

HOMESTEADS AND PUBLIC LANDS

Adams, R., "Public Range Lands—A New Policy Needed," *American Journal of Sociology*, November, 1916.

Dick, Everett, *The Sod-House Frontier*, N. Y., N. Y., 1937.

Hibbard, Ben H., *A History of the Public Land Policies*, N. Y., N. Y., 1924.

Munson, Judge Lyman E., "Pioneer Life on the American Frontier," *Connecticut Magazine*, Vol. XI, Montana State Historical Society library.

U. S. Land Office Report, 1875, Government Printing Office, Washington, D. C., 1876.

SHEEP

Chapman, Arthur, "The Sheep Herders of the West," *The Outlook*, June 24, 1905.

Gilfillan, Archer B., *Sheep*, Boston, Mass., 1929.

Harger, Charles Moreau, "Sheep and Shepherds of the West," *The Outlook*, November 22, 1902.

Randal, Henry S., *The Practical Shepherd*, N. Y., N. Y., 1875.

Wilcox, E. Vernon, "Sheep and the Forests," *The Forum*, Vol. XXXI.

BUFFALO

Allen, Joseph Asaph, "The American Bison, Living and Extinct," Publication of the

Museum of Comparative Zoology, Vol. IV, No. 10, Cambridge, Mass., 1876.

Davis, Theodore R., "The Buffalo Range," *Harper's Magazine*, Vol. XXXVIII.

Garretson, Martin S., *The American Bison*, N. Y., N. Y., 1938.

Holden, W. C., "The Buffalo of the Plains Area," *West Texas Historical Association Yearbook*, Vol. II, 1926.

Hornaday, William T., "The Extermination of the American Bison," *Smithsonian Institution Report*, Washington, D. C., 1887.

Jacobs, John Cloud, "The Last of the Buffalo," *The World's Work*, Vol. XVII.

LUMBERING

Bullen, C. A., "Lumbering in Chippewa Valley," The *Daily Telegram*, Eau Claire, Wis., April 12, 1916.

BAD MEN AND THE WILD WAYS

Adams, Ramon F., "Billy the Kid's Lost Years," *Texas Monthly*, Dallas, Tex., Vol. IV, September, 1929.

Aikman, Duncan, *Calamity Jane and the Lady Wildcats*, N. Y., N. Y., 1927.

Breckenridge, William M., *Helldorado*, Boston, Mass. and N. Y., N. Y., 1928.

Burns, Walter Noble, *The Saga of Billy the Kid*, Garden City, N. Y., 1926.

Burns, Walter Noble, *Tombstone, An Iliad of the Southwest*, Garden City, N. Y., 1929.

Clum, John P., "It All Happened in Tombstone," *Arizona Historical Review*, Phoenix, Ariz., October, 1929.

Coolidge, Dane, *Fighting Men of the West*, N. Y., N. Y., 1932.

Cunningham, Eugene, *Triggernometry*, N. Y., N. Y., 1934.

Dalton, Emmett, and Jungmeyer, Jack, *When The Daltons Rode*, Garden City, N. Y., 1931.

Dobie, James Frank, "Clay Allison of the Washita," San Antonio *Light*, reprinted in *Frontier Times*, February, 1943.

Forrest, Earle Robert, *Arizona's Dark and Bloody Ground*, Caldwell, Idaho, 1936.

Gard, Wayne, *Sam Bass*, Boston, Mass. and N. Y., N. Y., 1936.

Gard, Wayne, "Texas Robin Hood," *Southwest Review*, Dallas, Tex., autumn, 1935.

Garrett, Patrick Floyd, *The Authentic Life of Billy the Kid*, Santa Fe, N. M., 1882.

Haley, James Evetts, *Jeff Milton, A Good Man with a Gun*, University of Oklahoma Press, Norman, Okla., 1948.

Holbrook, Stewart H., "Robbing the Steam Cars," *American Mercury*, October, 1946.

Jennings, Alphonso J., *Beating Back*, N. Y., N. Y., 1914.

Lake, Stuart N., *Wyatt Earp: Frontier Marshal*, Boston, Mass. and N. Y., N. Y., 1931.

McNeal, Thomas Allen, *When Kansas Was Young*, N. Y., N. Y., 1922.

Mercer, Asa S., *The Banditti of the Plains*, Cheyenne, Wyo., 1894.

Myers, John, *The Last Chance*, N. Y., N. Y., 1950.

O'Connor, Richard, *Bat Masterson*, N. Y., N. Y., 1957.

O'Connor, Richard, *Wild Bill Hickok*, N. Y., N. Y., 1959.

"Picturesque Characters among Women of the Wild West," the Kansas City *Star*, January 20, 1932.

Raine, William MacLeod, *Famous Sheriffs and Western Outlaws*, Garden City, N. Y., 1929.

Raine, William MacLeod, "Taming the Frontier: The Apache Kid," *Outing*, N. Y., N. Y., August, 1905.

Rascoe, Burton, *Belle Starr, the Bandit Queen*, N. Y., N. Y., 1941.

Santee, Ross, "Tales the Cow Punchers Tell," *Travel*, N. Y., N. Y., August, 1932.

Sonnichsen, Charles Leland, *Roy Bean*, N. Y., N. Y., 1943.

"Story of Billy the Kid, A," extracts from the Laredo *Times*, July 13, 1881, August 10, 1881.

Sutton, Fred Ellsworth, *Hands Up!* Indianapolis, Ind., 1927.

Tilghman, Zoe Agnes, *Outlaw Days*, Oklahoma City, Okla., 1926.

Walrath, Ellen F., "Stagecoach Holdups in the San Luis Valley," *The Colorado Magazine*, Denver, Colo., January, 1937.

Walters, Lorenzo, D., *Tombstone's Yesterday*, Tucson, Ariz., 1928.

White, Owen Payne, "Come A-Smokin'," *Collier's*, August 28, 1926.

White, Owen Payne, *Lead and Likker*, N. Y., N. Y., 1932.

THE CARLISLE INDIAN SCHOOL

Scrapbooks, Hamilton Library, Carlisle, Pa.

Tousey, Lt. Col. Thomas, *Military History of Carlisle and Carlisle Barracks*, Richmond, Va., 1939.

OKLAHOMA—LAST FRONTIER

Nix, Evett Dumas, *Oklahombres*, St. Louis, Mo., 1929.

Rainey, George, *The Cherokee Strip*, Guthrie, Okla., 1933.

Tilghman, Zoe, *Oklahoma Stories*, Oklahoma City, Okla., 1956.

Picture Credits

t = top
b = bottom
c = center
l = left
r = right
American Museum of Natural History = AMNH
Arizona Pioneers' Historical Society = APHS
Bureau of American Ethnology = BAE
F. Bourges Collection = FBC
California State Library = CSL
State Historical Society of Colorado = SHSC
Culver Service = CS
Denver Public Library Western Collection = DPL
George Eastman House = GEH
Nick Eggenhofer = NE

Hamilton Library and Historical Association of Cumberland County, Pennsylvania = HL
Hispanic Society of America = HSA
Stewart Holbrook = SH
James D. Horan Western Americana Collection = JDH
Idaho Historical Society = IHS
A. C. Jancovic = ACJ
J. Leonard Jennewein, Mitchell, S. D. = JLJ
Church of Jesus Christ of Latter Day Saints = LDS
Library of Congress = LC
Mercaldo Archives = MA
Historical Society of Montana = HSM
Minnesota Historical Society = MHS
Fred and Jo Mazzulla Collection = FJM
National Archives = NA

National Park Service = NPS
Nevada Historical Society = NHS
New-York Historical Society = NYHS
New York Public Library = NYPL
Oklahoma Historical Society = OHS
Museum of the University of South Dakota = MUSD
Smithsonian Institution = SI
Library of the University of Texas = LUT
Collection of The Travelers Insurance Companies = TIC
Union Pacific Railroad = UPR
United States National Museum = USNM
United States Steel Corporation = USSC
Utah State Historical Society = USHS
State Historical Society of Wisconsin = SHSW
Coe Collection, Yale University Library = YUL

11-12. NYPL
13. t, Roswell Museum and Art Center, Roswell, N. M. b, NYPL
14. ACJ
15. l, c. Das Trachtenbuch des Christoph Weiditz Von Seinen Reisenbrach Spanien (1529) und Den Neiderlanden (1531-32) edited by Theodore Hampe, Berlin, 1927. HSA.
r, BAE, 14th Annual Report, Plate LV.
16-17. JDH.
18-19. HSA.
20-21. JDH.
22-23. Hoofs, Claws and Antlers of the Rocky Mountains, by the Camera, Frank S. Thayer, Publisher, Denver, Colo., 1894.
24. HSA.
25. LC.
26. CS.
27. tl, tc. CS. tr, USNM. b, JDH.
28. NA.
29. t. John C. Luttig's Journal of a Fur Trading Expedition on the Upper Missouri, 1812-13, edited by Stella Drumm. Courtesy Missouri Historical Society.
c, bl, br, from Across the Wide Missouri, Bernard De Voto. Courtesy of the Houghton Mifflin Company, Boston, Mass., 1947.
30. The Mounted Riflemen by James Parker, Banta Publishers, Menasha, Wis., 1916.
31. t, c. bl, br, courtesy SHSW.
32. l, LUT; r, courtesy H. Armour Smith.
33. TIC.
34-35. NA.
36. AMNH.
37-39. JDH.
40. Travels in the Interior of North America by Prince Maximilian of Prussia, edited by R. G. Thwaites, Cleveland, 1905. Copy in the possession of the Boston Athenaeum.
41. l, YUL; r, LUT.
42. t, YUL; b, NA.
43. ACJ.
44. Photo by T. Grady Gallant, Chattanooga Free Press.
45. USHS.
46. t, JDH; c, ACJ; b, BAE.
47. c, MA; b, LC.
48-49. NA.

50-51. t, LDS.
51. b, USHS.
52. NA.
53. t, GEH; b, courtesy Arizona Highways.
54. t, GEH; b, NYHS.
55. JDH.
56-57. NYHS.
58. APHS.
59. l, NYHS; r, MA.
60. t, CS; b, USHS.
61. bl, bcr, br, JDH; bcl, NA.
62. MHS.
63. t, bl, bcr, JDH; bcl, NA; br, MHS.
64. JDH.
65. l, DPL; r, OHS.
66. SHSC.
67. t, MUSD; c, bl, br, JDH.
68. t, NA; cl, HSM; cr, NE; b, LC.
69. tl, JDH; tr, NE; b, NYHS.
70. CSL.
71. tl, tr, cl, cr, JDH; b, UPR.
72. UPR.
73. t, courtesy of Charles Banks Wilson and Jackson Lake Lodge, Wyo.
b, TIC.
74. Copyright 1951 by the University of Oklahoma Press.
75. Courtesy of Cities Service Company.
76. Travels in the Interior of North America by Prince Maximilian of Prussia, edited by R. G. Thwaites, Cleveland, 1905. (Copy in the possession of the Boston Athenaeum.)
77. TIC.
78. From The Old West Speaks, Howard Driggs, Prentice-Hall, New York, 1956.
79. TIC.
80. FBC.
81. l, JDH; tr, Bettmann Archives; cr, UPR; br, IHS.
82. t, UPR; b, IHS.
83. tl, tr, cl, br, JDH; cr, bl, NE.
84. l, NA; r, LC.
85. NA.
86. l, LC; r, APHS.
87. NA.
88. t, c, BAE; b, HSM.
89. t, c, NA; cl, cr, br, HSM; bl, JDH.
90. HSM.
91. NA.

92. t, bl, NA; br, JDH.
93. t, bl, NA; br, JDH.
94-96. NA.
97. MA.
98. tr, bl, Indian Fights and Fighters, Cyrus Townsend Brady, Doubleday, Page & Company, N. Y., 1909; br, MA.
99. b, Indian Fights and Fighters, Cyrus Townsend Brady, Doubleday, Page & Company, N. Y., 1909.
t, NA.
100. NA.
101. MA.
102. t, JDH; c, Pioneers of the Black Hills, or Gordon Stockade Party of 1874, David Aken, Milwaukee, 1920. b, courtesy Way Museum, Custer, S. D.
103. NA.
104. l, JDH; r, courtesy Historical Division, U.S. Army.
105. t, NA; b, MUSD.
107. l, BAE; r, JDH.
108. tl, tr, br, Indian Fights and Fighters, Cyrus Townsend Brady, Doubleday, Page & Company, N. Y., 1909; bl, BAE.
109. tl, MA; tr, br, NA; bl, BAE.
110-11. NA.
112. t, BAE; b, NA.
113. Courtesy Charles Banks Wilson, from The Mustangs by J. Frank Dobie, Little, Brown & Company, Boston, Mass.
114-15. JDH.
116. Patrick Patterson, Woolaroc Museum, Bartlesville, Okla.
117-18. Report on Indians Taxed and Indians Not Taxed in the United States, Government Printing Office, Washington, D. C., 1894.
119. The Old West Speaks, Howard R. Driggs, Prentice-Hall, Inc., N. Y., 1956.
120. MA.
121-22. NA.
123-37. JDH.
138. GEH.
139-62. JDH.
163. tl, tr, JDH; b, HSM.
164. t, MUSD; b, FJM.
165. JDH.
166. t, NE; b, JDH.
167. NE.
168. JDH.

169. l, NE; r, LC.
170. LC.
171. MA.
172. tl, courtesy Melvin Nichols; tr, b, MA.
173. tr, MA; c, NE; b, JDH.
174. JDH.
175. HSM.
176. t, NA; b, MA.
177. t, MA; b, JDH.
178. JDH.
179-83. JDH.
184. The Iron Age, June 24, 1926.
185. Frederic Remington by Harold McCracken.
186. FBC.
187. t, Frederic Remington by Harold McCracken; b, FBC.
188. FBC.
189. From Steelways, published by American Iron and Steel Institute.
190-92. Courtesy Hammer Galleries and Homer H. Boelter Lithographers, Hollywood, California.
193-94. Courtesy USSC.
195. t, NE; b, courtesy M. T. Jensen, Vice President, Aermotor Company, Chicago, Ill.
196. Drawings by Evelyn Curro from The Look of the Old West by Foster-Harris, The Viking Press, N. Y., 1955.
197. LC.
198. JDH.
199. t, FJM; b, NA.
200. JDH.
201. NA.
202. SH.
203. t, LC; b, JDH.
204. Courtesy Pat McDonough.
205. c, NYHS; b, NE.
206. t, JDH; c, b, NE.
207. The American Bison by Martin S. Garretson, American Bison Society, N. Y., 1934.
208. t, MUSD; b, The American Bison by Martin S. Garretson, American Bison Society, N. Y., 1934.
209. NPS.
210. The American Bison by Martin S. Garretson, American Bison Society, N. Y., 1934.
211. t, NE; b, MA.
212. l, NYHS; cr, MA; br, MUSD.
213. t, NA; cr, NE; br, MUSD.
214. t, NA; b, MUSD.

215. t, NE; c, JDH; b, IHS.
216. JDH.
217. NE.
218. t, NE; b, SH.
219. JDH.
220-21. SH.
222-23. JDH.
224. SH.
225-31. JDH.
232. t, bc, br, NYHS; bl, JDH.
234-38. JDH.
239. t, bl, JDH; br, MA.
240. l, JDH; br, Courtesy Emily Driscoll.
241. tl, b, JDH; tc, tr, MA.
242. JDH.
243. tl, tr, JDH; tc, MUSD; bl, Photography and the American Scene by Robert Taft, The Macmillan Company, N. Y., 1938; br, courtesy Miss H. M. Baumhofer.
244. t, SI; b, NA.
245. tl, tr, NA; br, JDH.
246. t, NA; bl, JDH; br, IHS.
247. t, BAE; b, Northwestern Fights and Fighters, Cyrus Townsend Brady, Doubleday, Page & Company, N. Y., 1909.
248. Northwestern Fights and Fighters, Cyrus Townsend Brady, Doubleday, Page & Company, N. Y., 1909.
249. b, JDH; tr, Northwestern Fights and Fighters, Cyrus Townsend Brady, Doubleday, Page & Company, N. Y., 1909.
250-51. JLJ.
252. t, JLJ; b, JDH.
253. tl, JLJ; tr, b, JDH.
254-57. JDH.
258. NA.
259. t, JDH; b, NA.
260. NA.
261. t, APHS; bl, FJM; br, NA.
262. t, br, JDH; bl, NA.
263. t, b, NA; c, JDH.
264. t, BAE; b, FJM.
265. HSM.
266. NA.
267-68. HL.
269. t, HL; c, W. Cann, Reno, Nev.; r, NHS.
270. HL.
271-73. OHS.
274. Collier's, 1957.
275. JDH.
276-79. OHS.

Index